Creative Multilingualism

A Manifesto

Edited by
Katrin Kohl, Rajinder Dudrah, Andrew Gosler,
Suzanne Graham, Martin Maiden,
Wen-chin Ouyang and Matthew Reynolds

© Katrin Kohl, Rajinder Dudrah, Andrew Gosler, Suzanne Graham, Martin Maiden, Wen-chin Ouyang and Matthew Reynolds. Copyright of individual chapters is maintained by the chapters' authors.

This work is licensed under a Creative Commons Attribution 4.0 International license (CC BY 4.0). This license allows you to share, copy, distribute and transmit the work; to adapt the work and to make commercial use of the work providing attribution is made to the author (but not in any way that suggests that they endorse you or your use of the work). Some of the material in this book has been reproduced according to the fair use principle which allows use of copyrighted material for scholarly purposes.

Attribution should include the following information:

Katrin Kohl, Rajinder Dudrah, Andrew Gosler, Suzanne Graham, Martin Maiden, Wen-chin Ouyang and Matthew Reynolds (eds), *Creative Multilingualism: A Manifesto*. Cambridge, UK: Open Book Publishers, 2020. https://doi.org/10.11647/OBP.0206

In order to access detailed and updated information on the license, please visit https://doi.org/10.11647/OBP.0206#copyright

Further details about CC BY licenses are available at http://creativecommons.org/licenses/by/4.0/

All external links were active at the time of publication unless otherwise stated and have been archived via the Internet Archive Wayback Machine at https://archive.org/web

Any digital material and resources associated with this volume are available at https://doi.org/10.11647/OBP.0206#resources

Every effort has been made to identify and contact copyright holders and any omission or error will be corrected if notification is made to the publisher.

ISBN Paperback: 978-1-78374-929-4
ISBN Hardback: 978-1-78374-930-0
ISBN Digital (PDF): 978-1-78374-931-7
ISBN Digital ebook (epub): 978-1-78374-932-4
ISBN Digital ebook (mobi): 978-1-78374-933-1
ISBN Digital (XML): 978-1-78374-934-8
DOI: 10.11647/OBP.0206

Cover image: Cedoux Kadima, *Mappa Mundi* (2017), mixed media on canvas.
Cover design by Anna Gatti.

Contents

Creative Multilingualism — A Manifesto		ix
Introducing Creative Multilingualism *Katrin Kohl and Wen-chin Ouyang*		1
1.	The Creative Power of Metaphor *Katrin Kohl, Marianna Bolognesi and Ana Werkmann Horvat*	25
2.	Creating a Meaningful World: Nature in Name, Metaphor and Myth *Karen Park, Felice S. Wyndham, Andrew Gosler and John Fanshawe*	47
3.	Not as 'Foreign' as You Think: Creating Bridges of Understanding across Languages *Martin Maiden, Chiara Cappellaro and Aditi Lahiri*	69
4.	A Breath of Fresh Air… Ivan Vyrypaev's *Oxygen* (2002): From Moscow to Birmingham via Oxford *Rajinder Dudrah, Julie Curtis, Philip Ross Bullock and Noah Birksted-Breen*	87
5.	Multilingualism and Creativity in World Literature *Wen-chin Ouyang*	109
6.	Prismatic Translation *Matthew Reynolds, Sowon S. Park and Kate Clanchy*	131
7.	Getting Creative in the Languages Classroom *Suzanne Graham, Linda Fisher, Julia Hofweber and Heike Krüsemann*	151
8.	Inspiring Language Learners *Jane Hiddleston, Laura Lonsdale, Chiara Cappellaro and Daniel Tyler-McTighe*	177

9.	Languages at Work	203
	Katrin Kohl and Jonathan Black	
10.	Creating Languages	223
	Katrin Kohl	

Why Learn a Language?	249
Find Out More	255
Bibliography	271
List of Illustrations	291
Notes on the Authors and Contributors	299
Acknowledgements	309
Index	311

*We dedicate this manifesto to all young people
who are challenging the older generations
in many languages
to make our shared world sustainable*

Creative Multilingualism
A Manifesto

---

1. Language diversity nurtures diversity of identity, thought and expression

2. Language diversity protects biodiversity

3. We're more multilingual than we think

4. Language diversity inspires creativity in performance

5. Languages travel and migrate

6. Translation is inherently creative

7. Language learning opens your mind

8. Languages hold infinite potential for creativity

9. Languages create connections with people

10. We create language every day

Introducing Creative Multilingualism

Katrin Kohl and Wen-chin Ouyang

Creative Multilingualism is a manifesto. It signals that multilingualism is fundamental to the human condition and that we are all in some way multilingual — both in terms of talent and in terms of our daily 'language lives'. It also points to the key role languages play as a creative force in our thought and emotions, our expression and social interaction, and our activity in the world — languages are a creative force in how we live.

This volume presents fruits of collaborative research conducted over four years across disciplines ranging from the humanities through the social sciences to the natural sciences. It is designed to illuminate how multifariously language diversity intersects with creativity, though the book is not intended to offer a coherent, watertight theory or closed set of findings. Rather, it is framed in exploratory terms, inviting further research. And it is a manifesto calling for change on two fronts:

- *Language* needs to be understood as intrinsically diverse — as *languages*. The entitlement of individuals and cultural groups to express themselves in their distinctive language must be supported as a fundamental human right, and must be nurtured as vital to the sustainability of the natural and cultural world.

- *Creativity* needs to be understood as intrinsically bound up with our capacity for linguistically diverse thought, expression and action. Languages are far more than communicative 'tools': they are creative. Language diversity and creativity are mutually enriching.

Our ten manifesto statements highlight interactions between language diversity and creativity. Over four years, these interactions have stimulated our joint research on Creative Multilingualism, taking us into different disciplinary fields, prompting us to try out new methodologies, and fuelling productive debate about connections between languages and creativity. The research was conducted in seven strands, and their work forms the basis for Chapters 1 to 7, which were written by the respective research teams. Each of these chapters has a particular disciplinary focus and associated methodological principles, suggesting new ways of seeing languages through the lens of creativity. The multiplicity of perspectives and approaches is reflected in diverse styles and modes of presenting the research. This pluralism reflects our belief that all academic disciplines have something distinctive to offer research on languages, and that creativity must be given full rein in academic research across the arts and sciences if we are to understand complex human processes such as languages, and creativity itself.

Who is this book for? It is dedicated to young people. A key reason for this is that young people are often sold short on language learning, particularly if emphasis in education is placed primarily on maths, sciences and technology. Especially in societies where the first language is English, language learning may seem unnecessary, so the advantage of knowing what is currently the most widely spoken language in the world often goes hand in hand with too little opportunity to develop language-learning skills ambitiously early on. The chief reason for dedicating this book to young people is that they are the future of our multilingual world. We would like them to embrace human diversity through languages, and we hope that our research will enhance appreciation of the deep connections between language diversity and human creativity.

Our book is also intended for fellow researchers, teachers in schools, universities and the wider community, and more generally for anyone who is already interested in languages, or who would like to find out more about them. This includes parents, who will in any case be taking an interest in their children's linguistic development. We hope our research will encourage them to give their children every possible access to more than one language and, if the home is bilingual, to exploit that opportunity to the full.

This book is a manifesto promoting language diversity as a human advantage and human right. As such, it is addressed to policymakers, especially in the field of education, but also more broadly with respect to multilingualism in our societies. Diversity of languages needs to be supported as a rich source of creativity in the arts, and recognized for its vital importance in the sciences. Creative Multilingualism is an experiment in interdisciplinary research in which each project demonstrates the role of languages at the creative heart of human endeavour. By placing the focus on the connection between language diversity and creativity, we seek to demonstrate that beyond their communicative usefulness, languages also sustain and enrich thought, literacy, social cohesion, the creative arts and scientific engagement with sustainability.

We are passionately committed to promoting language diversity in research. It is therefore a severe shortcoming of our volume that it is currently available only in English — the language that threatens linguistic pluralism in our present world more than any other language. The rationale is contextual, strategic and practical.

The pertinent contextual factors are that English is the only shared language of the research team, the research was funded by a UK research council in response to a call focused on modern languages in the United Kingdom and primarily addressed in an Anglophone context, and our most immediate audience are Anglophone readers. We are therefore using English as the most wide-reaching lingua franca for our volume, while also addressing the specific roles of lingua francas in relation to other, often more local languages (see Chapter 10 in this volume).

The key strategic objective is to engage readers whose Anglophone context can make it difficult to see beyond an Anglo-centric view of the world, and establish the many benefits and pleasures of embracing language diversity, discovering one's own existing multilingualism, and learning languages. The medium is therefore English, but the examples we discuss are from a very wide range of languages, elucidating the riches beyond individual linguistic comfort zones.

The chief practical impediment to multilingual dissemination is our staff capacity and budget since translation into many languages would vastly overstretch our resources. However, in order to enable and encourage dissemination in other languages, we are making the content of this volume freely available under a Creative Commons licence (CC BY) that permits translation without special permission so long as the original authors are appropriately credited. We would be delighted if our collaborative project inspired many other researchers to take up our ideas and extend their communicative possibilities in their own linguistic environment.

Our research has been conducted in a variety of contexts that have taken us beyond universities, libraries and laboratories. We have been working with a wide range of partners across society who have helped us to identify fruitful research questions and fields of investigation, contributed to events for the wider public, and helped us to communicate our findings in ways that make sense not just to other researchers but also to people who may hitherto have had little occasion to think about what makes languages so fascinating. The concept of Creative Multilingualism has provided a matrix for experimentation with ideas, approaches and methods. We hope you will want to join us on our journey of discovery.

What is Multilingualism?

'Multilingualism' is usually defined in contrast to 'monolingualism' and refers to speech communities that use more than one language, as is typical of most parts of Africa and India, for example. An individual who is a member of such a speech community, or who has learned languages to a high level, is also 'multilingual', though in the case of their using two languages, they are usually referred to as 'bilingual'. A further term that has come into use is 'plurilingualism', which places less emphasis on a high level of linguistic attainment in the respective languages and is often taken to embrace intercultural competence (see e.g. Mehmedbegovic and Bak 2019 for a brief discussion of the terminology). There is fluidity in the use of these terms, which causes some controversy in the context of sociolinguistic research and at the interface between academic discussion and popular usage. However, it also points to a fluidity within language diversity that requires both acknowledgement and further investigation.

We have placed the term 'multilingualism' at the centre of our research on the grounds that it reflects the fluid interplay between language varieties which is intrinsic to human communication. Our understanding of the term is rather more open than the above definition would suggest, and it is not our concern to establish firm terminological boundaries separating it from 'monolingualism', 'bilingualism' or 'plurilingualism'. The purpose of this project is to explore the multilingual potential we all activate to a greater or lesser extent in the course of our lives even if we live in a 'monolingual' environment and see ourselves as using only one language.

In order to appreciate this, it is worth taking a step back to consider what we mean by 'language'. This abstracts a generic phenomenon from the multitude of languages people actually speak. We can only access it via theories about it — no one knows or speaks 'language'. When we think of ourselves as using 'language', we are in fact always sharing the communicative practices of a particular community. What we experience, learn and use in our lives is a particular language — or more than one — which is culturally specific, and part of the very lifeblood of the community or communities we grow up in. It is one of many languages, and diversity is built into it.

We can see this in the fact that languages typically have many dialects (such as Scouse in England or Bavarian in Germany) and many registers (such as formal and informal, 'high' and 'low'). And if you dig deeper, you find that every professional group develops its own jargon, and perhaps even its own grammatical shortcuts. Languages evolve through time, absorbing and responding to changing material and cultural conditions that shape our lives, so different generations speak differently. Young people or other particular groups may wish to establish their identity as distinct by using a distinct vocabulary and/or pronunciation and special grammatical features that other groups may consider 'incorrect'. New technologies such as artificial intelligence (AI) or games such as *Dungeons & Dragons* may swiftly generate communities that develop words and ways of speaking which are partially incomprehensible to other people.

What this tells us is that we're all equipped to learn new languages, and happy to do so if the social need or personal incentive arises. And if we observe how we use language(s) in our daily lives, we find that the way we speak or write is highly flexible and changes depending on who we are talking to — Gran, friend Dave, toddler Rosie, the rather formal boss, the dog, the laptop that has just crashed. Emails and social media give us written evidence of the phenomenal speed with which we adapt our language to new contexts and communication practices, and the extent to which we vary our usage according to who we're communicating with. When emojis became standard on mobile phones in 2010, a type of pictogram invented in Japan in 1997 — *e* (絵, 'picture') + *moji* (文字, 'character') — suddenly became a globally utilized feature of communication that few of us would now want to do without.

> Creative Multilingualism is a provocation to think of language not as typically homogeneous, monolithic and unified, but as intrinsically diverse — languages.

Language Lives

We all have complex 'language lives' that evolve out of our heritage and life experience. If we go far enough back, our family will have migrated to where it now lives. Few families live in one place without at some point embracing people from other regions, countries or continents, for example by marriage. Many families speak a different language at home to the language that is spoken where they live, study or work. At school we may learn one or more languages, even if only to a very modest level, and we may have classmates who are from different parts of the world. At work, or when we go shopping, or visit a hospital, we generally encounter people who speak different languages — though they may do so only at home and in their communities. When we travel, we experience different linguistic worlds. Each encounter with someone speaking a different dialect or language subtly contributes to our 'language life' — be it because we're fascinated by it, manage to learn even just the odd word, become interested in the cultural context it gives us access to, or suddenly realize what it feels like to be in an alien environment.

In this chapter and some of the others in the volume (see Chapters 5, 6, 7 and 9), we have included 'Language Lives' — reflections by individual people on what role languages play in their own personal lives, on biographical circumstances that have shaped their knowledge

Language Lives
A Place for Languages

Mohandas Karamchand Gandhi

Today I cannot but think with gratitude of Krishnashankar Pandya. For if I had not acquired the little Samskrit that I learnt then [age twelve], I should have found it difficult to take any interest in our sacred books. In fact I deeply regret that I was not able to acquire a more thorough knowledge of the language, because I have since realized that every Hindu boy and girl should possess sound Samskrit learning.

It is now my opinion that in all Indian curricula of higher education there should be a place for Hindi, Samskrit, Persian, Arabic and English, besides of course the vernacular. This big list need not frighten anyone. If our education were more systematic, and the boys free from the burden of having to learn their subjects through a foreign medium [English], I am sure learning all these languages would not be an irksome task, but a perfect pleasure. A scientific knowledge of one language makes a knowledge of other languages comparatively easy.

Mohandas K. Gandhi, *An Autobiography or The Story of My Experiments with Truth* [1927–1929], trans. from Gujarati by Mahadev Desai (2007: 32).

Fig. 1 Mohandas K. Gandhi in South Africa (1906). Wikimedia Commons, Public Domain, https://commons.wikimedia.org/wiki/File:Gandhi_London_1906.jpg#/media/File:Gandhi_London_1906.jpg

and use of languages, and on their attitude towards languages. In the present chapter we have also included the 'Language Lives' of a London bus, and food. These language stories are intended to exemplify the highly individual nature of language and the many ways knowledge and use of languages intersect with the experiences, circumstances and situations that make up our lives. This individual dimension matters. It can be easy to assume — especially in an environment which views monolingualism as the norm — that the language(s) we have a command of are simply a function of the community or country we grow up in. But the Language Lives make clear that languages are much more alive and individual than this would suggest. It is worth reflecting on one's own language life, the linguistic diversity within it, and the value of the distinctive linguistic richness that has come about through biographical circumstances, personal interests — and serendipity.

Attending to the linguistic diversity that is at work in our daily lives and encounters, and valuing that diversity, is especially important in countries where the national language is English, since its dominance as theme global lingua franca is otherwise liable to become a means of repressing others, and impacting negatively also on cultural diversity. It can also significantly impoverish English speakers, who are increasingly in a very different position from those growing up in other countries. Whereas people living in other countries have an increasingly strong incentive to learn at least English, and thereby the skill of learning a foreign language, it's difficult for speakers of English as a first language who live in an Anglophone context to muster the energy, time and sheer hard work required to learn another language, especially since it isn't self-evident which one might be most useful, and a mobile device can conjure up a translation in seconds. For policymakers in English-speaking countries, investing in language education will tend to seem less of a priority than it is in countries where the need to learn at least English is obvious. This in turn generally leads to under-investment in language learning.

What are the effects of monolingualism for the creativity of speakers of English as their only language? How does it affect their language lives? Will they lose out on mental and cultural flexibility by comparison with their more multilingually and multiculturally trained competitors? And what about future-proofing — do we know that the

Language Lives
Sharing Languages in India

Sheela Mahadevan

My parents moved to the UK from India in 1979 and I grew up in Kent. After a BA in French and German and a masters in German, I trained as a teacher and lived for three years in India teaching French and German at an international school. This gave me the opportunity to regularly visit my elderly grandparents, and allowed me to witness their multilingualism, and how it affected their lives.

My grandmother begins her day chanting Sanskrit prayers for worship, after which the local maidservant will arrive to clean the flat. The maidservant speaks the regional language, Kannada, spoken in Karnataka, though this is not our mother tongue. Within seconds of completing her prayers, my grandmother is conversing as well as she can with the maidservant in Kannada, which she actually learnt from her. She then talks to my grandfather in Tamil, before switching on the TV to watch a film in Malayalam, to reconnect with the language of Kerala, where she lived during her youth.

Then there'll be a knock on the door from the neighbours, who are North Indians, and my grandmother starts chatting to them in Hindi. Then she'll chat to me in English, or in Tamil, or a fusion. Sometimes she wants to watch a TV programme which is in another South Indian language, Telegu, and she tries to learn this by watching the programme. My grandfather operates on a similar basis, and added to this is his knowledge of French, as he used to live in Pondicherry, a former French colony. Not a day goes by without my grandparents operating multilingually; it is part and parcel of their lives, and is common for many Indians.

Sheela Mahadevan is Head of French at a school in Greater London.

Fig. 2 Sheela Mahadevan with her grandparents, Ganga Narayanan and Guruvayur Krishna Narayanan. Reproduced with their kind permission. Photograph by Subramaniam Mahadevan (2020).

world will *always* prefer global English to other lingua francas? The story of Latin suggests perhaps not; Latin gained massive influence as the Roman Empire extended its reach, became the lingua franca of the Catholic Church and the Western learned world right through to the seventeenth century, but then lost out to the vernacular languages. French then took over, becoming the language of diplomacy and polite society, and a key colonial language that is still enormously influential, for example in Africa. English only just outcompeted German to become the main language of the United States, and the basis for its now global influence was laid by British colonialism. But as Asia has asserted itself economically and politically, non-European languages have been coming to the fore. In 2013, Prime Minister David Cameron urged the British to 'look beyond the traditional focus on French and German and get many more children learning Mandarin', and in 2018, Chinese A-Level entries overtook German ones in the British school system (Stacey and Warrell 2013; Allen-Kinross 2018). In fact, it's likely that many of those entrants have come from China, or grew up with Chinese as their first language. Chinese speakers have become increasingly enterprising about learning at least English and often other languages as well. They are therefore likely to be getting better equipped multilingually, and more competent multiculturally, than speakers of English as their first language. And while Chinese may not be prominent on the Internet seen in Europe and the US, the Internet available to Chinese people is increasingly powerful. So it's not just fanciful to think that as power relations change, English might one day — potentially within our lifetime — lose its status as the (only) global lingua franca.

Lingua francas are, in any case, only one side of the language story. They are convenient for exchanging practical information across language groups and local contexts, and they fulfil a vital role in international communication in all fields and for all purposes. But there has never been a time when everyone has shared a single lingua franca. And when used as a lingua franca, a language is often divested of its local colour, idiomatic quirks and creative richness in order to be more broadly comprehensible. Moreover, languages are not just about conveying practical information, and their value is not just defined by communicative convenience and international power. If that were all, the Welsh, Scots and Irish would happily have abandoned their languages long ago and confined themselves to English as the lingua franca that has long prevailed across the British Isles. The reason they haven't done so is because their distinctive languages are a fundamental part of their specific cultural identities and sense of themselves as cultural groups, and their individual sense of identity. Languages evolve with the groups and individuals that speak them, and passing them on to the next generation is crucial for sustaining collective knowledge and understanding of the group's heritage. Sharing a language sustains community building and audibly distinguishes the speech community from other groups — a principle that underpins the creation and standardization of national languages as much as it can motivate twins or friends to invent a private language that no one else understands.

Each one of us has their very individual 'language life'. It's made up of who we talk to at home, at school and at work; where we grew up and where we live; what language community we belong to; who we love, live with and meet; our educational opportunities and experiences; where we travel and how much we want to open ourselves to other language communities; and, not least, our own language choices. Each of these aspects holds creative potential which we can activate.

We tend to think of this only in terms of the language qualifications we have — or more likely those we don't have, the skills we failed to develop and the knowledge we've forgotten. But this is to ignore that our languages are part of us, ready to play a tiny role or a big one, highly complex when they're the language we have grown up with and the one we use every day, and restricted if we have not learned them to a high level and don't have much opportunity to practise them. They shape and express our emotions, our ways of conceptualizing the world and our relationships with other people. Through the language we grow up with, we will already have become familiar with a multitude of other languages that have contributed words at different points in the history of that language — rich potential that is waiting to be explored. And we will have learned to select different words, structures and often even pronunciations depending on the situation we are in and who we are talking to. Our individual language life began when we were in the womb, and it developed with phenomenal speed as we grew up and became active in the world. And it is part of us now, waiting to be enriched.

Language Lives
The Language Life of Bus 29

Wen-chin Ouyang

I rarely hear Queen's English on Bus 29. Everybody speaks Global English peppered with diverse accents, words and grammatical constructions they bring to it from the other languages they know. Most of the passengers Bus 29 picks up and discharges as it winds its way through London from Trafalgar Square to Wood Green through the West End, Camden Town, Finsbury Park and Haringey speak more than one language.

They switch with ease from one language to another depending on their audience. A Turkish young professional argues with a French colleague in English between Warren Street and Camden Town. The bus picks up his friends at Manor House. He speaks to them in Kurdish. A mixed English-French couple have it out with each other now in English and then in French all the way from Holloway Prison to Seven Sisters Road. Algerian men, Syrian women, Iraqi families and Saudi youths talk to each other on the bus, or to friends on their mobiles, in different varieties of spoken Arabic on their way to the popular Turkish and Kurdish kebab restaurants on Green Lanes' Grand Parade, to eat there or pick up a takeaway for their families. A young Polish mother gets on at Manor House. She coos to her baby daughter in Polish. Her mobile rings. She answers. She speaks English to the phone.

Life on Bus 29 is an adventure in multilingualism, a microcosm of the Global City of London. London is a meeting place for people, their ideas, stories and languages from around the world. The city is multilingual, and so are many of the people who live there or come for a visit. Multilingualism is integral to the fabric of London's soundscape, and to the patterns of communication and thinking among Londoners and their guests. Languages coexist and do their work as a means of communication side by side, and together.

Fig. 3 London Bus 29. Photograph by mattbuck (2012). Wikimedia Commons, CC BY-SA 3.0, https://en.wikipedia.org/wiki/London_Buses_route_29#/media/File:Camden_Road_railway_station_MMB_05.jpg

> If you talk to a man in a language he understands, that goes to his head. If you talk to him in his language, that goes to his heart.
>
> Attributed to Nelson Mandela, explaining why he learned Afrikaans, the language of his prison guards in South Africa (Garamendi 1996: vi).

The Creative Potential of Multilingualism

We might say that creating something is to make something that wasn't there before. The creative act may be associated with an individual urge to make an original artefact that leaves a unique footprint. But creativity may also be more experimental and playful than this suggests, and connect the individual with others more fluidly — performance is a case in point. If we consider the interplay between languages and creativity, it becomes clear that the creative potential and creative forces at work in, with, and through languages are complex and infinite, and they affect every aspect of an individual's or group's interaction with the world.

Creativity is above all about process, and a spirit of change and transformation. These are dimensions that tend to get lost in definitions. To take just one example, the editors of the useful essay compendium entitled *The Cambridge Handbook of Creativity* (Kaufman and Sternberg 2010) contend that 'the first step to understanding creativity is to define it', and their starting point is that 'a creative response is novel, good, and relevant' (p. xiii). The problem with this definition is that it kills creativity stone dead. And is it even true? Immediately, examples of creativity spring to mind that fail to meet at least part of the definition. Moreover, it seems focused above all on a product.

Creativity doesn't lend itself naturally to definition — unsurprisingly, perhaps, since definitions are concerned with establishing stable features, setting identifiable boundaries and taking the object of investigation out of the flux of time. Creative Multilingualism therefore takes a different starting point. It seeks to keep the process in play in the course of exploring tangible, concrete works. Moreover, it celebrates the impetus for expression and communication that connects individuals with the community, forges a sense of common purpose in joint enterprises and events, and generates creative energy in different types of performance.

We speak many languages with each other, and when we think and feel, these languages interact. Dialogue is at the heart of linguistic creativity. The ideas, meanings and performances that come into being during linguistic creativity are as alive as their creators, and they are continually in flux, both generative and transformational. Each of the research projects discussed in this volume has evolved its own understanding of what Creative Multilingualism generates, what it means and what effects it has. Each will therefore investigate the nexus between creativity and languages on its own terms and with its own particular approach and methodology, contributing distinctive facets to our collective understanding of how Creative Multilingualism works.

One might object that this doesn't allow Creative Multilingualism to be tested, measured, verified or falsified. An answer might be that the proof of the creatively multilingual pudding lies in the eating. The purpose of Creative Multilingualism is above all to provoke questions, stimulate discussion and allow the value and excitement of languages to be experienced live.

Language Lives
The Multilingual Life of Food

Wen-chin Ouyang

Languages evolve through time in specific cultural contexts. They are personal and communal, regional and/or national, local and/or global. They connect with identities and arouse passionate feelings of cultural allegiance. We can see all these processes at work in the language of food and 'cuisine' — a word introduced into English in the late eighteenth century that reflects the admiration of sophisticated French cooking among the upper classes. Different languages have their own names for foodstuffs such as flour, rice, bread or eggs, and many dishes stay local. But some travel across cultures together with their names.

Yorkshire pudding started life as 'dripping pudding' before it became associated with a particular region and then advanced to the status of a British national dish while retaining the regional name. Unlike *rosbif*, though, it hasn't travelled much beyond the British Isles — perhaps because of its local name. In fact a controversy erupted in 2018 over a *New York Times* recipe for a 'Dutch baby' — supposedly of German origin but actually a Pennsylvania Dutch creation from around 1900. Brits claimed it as 'their' Yorkshire pudding — though it was recommended for 'breakfast, brunch, lunch and dessert' (Morrissy-Swan 2018).

Dishes migrate with their eaters and their names, and globalization has increased the range especially in cities. It would not make sense to translate couscous, falafel, hummus, kebab, ramen or spaghetti into English. Each of these words denotes not only a food item but also a dish prepared with a particular recipe and traditionally consumed within a specific cultural context that comes with occasions and conventions for serving, and that may be associated with particular table manners, religious beliefs and even politics.

Couscous refers to small grains of crushed durum wheat semolina as well as the North African party dish served with a meat stew. The recipe may vary from region to region but it is habitually served at social gatherings such as family reunions when members of the family and their guests sit around the elaborately presented dish and enjoy it together. Falafel (fried chickpea and parsley balls or patties) and hummus (a dip made from chickpeas, sesame paste and lemon juice garnished with parsley and olive oil) are two Eastern Mediterranean side dishes that have become a popular stuffing and spread for sandwiches everywhere in Britain, Europe and North America. Their already diverse Mediterranean recipes have picked up even more flavours and colours along their global travels.

In Israel/Palestine these dishes are today subject to competing claims. They are Palestinian dishes, Palestinians would say. No, Israelis will retort, they're staples of Israeli cuisine. Kebab, the familiar grilled meat, originates in the Middle East, where it is only eaten in restaurants. It marks the special occasion of a family outing. Ramen and spaghetti are both noodle dishes but Japanese ramen is served in a clear soup while Italian spaghetti is eaten with a variety of cream or tomato-based sauce. Their names in the language of the people who first invented them evoke our experience of the dishes as both food (how they look, taste and smell) and culture (when, where and how they are prepared, served and consumed). Translations can rarely convey the fullness of our experience.

Fig. 4 Ramen with soft boiled egg, shrimp and snow peas. Photograph by Michele Blackwell (2019) on Unsplash, https://unsplash.com/photos/rAyCBQTH7ws

The following points give an insight into some of the ideas that have generated fruitful discussion in the course of our research.

- Every language is interconnected with the thought patterns, perceptual habits and environment of its speech community, creating a window onto the world that differs subtly from that opened up by any other language, and providing a medium for creating understanding of that point of view.

- Each speech community develops the vocabulary it needs to describe and create the world around it, giving linguistic prominence to the things it is most concerned with. Moving between languages and translating between them opens our minds to different ways of seeing the world, and creates new meanings.

- Languages evolve in creative interaction with their natural environment, and in this process they become an essential part of that environment's preservation. A language that identifies local species, and gives each one a distinctive place in its vocabulary, myths and religious beliefs, becomes a living resource for curatorial expertise and provides an invaluable basis of experience in creative husbandry.

- A language has distinctive morphological, phonetic, syntactic, semantic and pragmatic parameters, but it is also always in flux and without intrinsic boundaries. This gives speech communities immense scope for drawing on other languages in creative ways by borrowing, translating and adapting. And they can be equally creative in evolving new forms, positing difference from a linguistic neighbour, and defining standards that resist the processes of change. An analogy that springs to mind is that of each language being like a garden, offering the potential for trellises, fences, and a burgeoning wealth of weeds and herbs, vegetables and flowers, shrubs and trees.

- Languages can take many forms. Spoken words, written texts, sign language, picture language, facial expression, gesture and voice can play an important part in conveying meaning. Diverse cultures develop different genres and media, with each one opening up new creative possibilities, as is evident in graffiti, literature, theatre, film, social media.

- We are aware of language death — this normally comes about because the members of the speech community have sadly died out. What is less obvious is when a new language comes into being. In the contexts of conquest, colonialism and global migration, mixing of peoples also brings mixing between languages. 'Hybrids' such as Hinglish may seem like impure, inferior forms that have no distinctive status. Yet all our languages have emerged as people have migrated — and the 'fusions' of today may be the languages of tomorrow. 'English' as we know it wouldn't exist if Anglo-Saxon hadn't gradually mingled with Norman French. Hybridity offers considerable creative potential because people can manipulate and exploit the wider range of linguistic possibilities that become available.

- We learn languages in interaction with learning to think, articulate our feelings, and do things with others. We are continually processing language we have never heard before in quite that constellation, and learning the new words that are coming into our language every day. Language learning is therefore part of what we do throughout our lives, whether or not we think of ourselves as language learners. Some people enjoy experimenting with artistic forms of creative learning while others prefer to keep their eye on practical goals. But creativity is always part of it, whether you're a linguistic trapeze artist, linguistic football player or linguistic cook.

- Each language has evolved with a distinctive toolkit for innovation in its processes of word formation, its sound system, handling of gender, number and tense, its syntactic structures, conventions of oral use and — in literate communities — its conventions of writing. Each speech community therefore has distinctive options for responding creatively to the world. We can conclude from this that no language is intrinsically more important than any other — each contributes distinctive creative potential and offers our joint planet distinctive creative solutions.

Researching Creative Multilingualism

Creative Multilingualism is the concept that connects and shapes the research presented in the following chapters. It highlights the interconnection between language diversity and creativity, and provides an experimental space for investigating the creative processes that make languages what they are, inspire their speakers to generate new expressive forms, and contribute to learning languages. Creative Multilingualism is designed to explore how creativity works across the whole spectrum of language production, expression and learning, focusing on specific questions from the perspectives of different disciplines. These disciplines traditionally approach languages with different presuppositions, methods and toolkits. The research presented here has been developed in a process of collaboration, discussion, debate and exchange of ideas between the researchers and with partners beyond academia. And it has involved working closely with people from many countries, age groups and walks of life. For Creative Multilingualism is above all about people talking to each other across cultural groups — communicating ideas, sharing what matters, and evolving new ways of thinking and doing things.

Ten Manifesto Statements form the start of the book, and each one is picked up as a key theme in one of the subsequent ten chapters.

The Creative Power of Metaphor (Chapter 1) looks at processes of figurative language in the interplay between thought and language from the vantage point of cognitive linguistics, exploring how different languages give their speakers different perspectives on the world through the ways metaphors shape even the most fundamental concepts, such as time.

Creating a Meaningful World: Nature in Name, Metaphor and Myth (Chapter 2) uses the linguistic and cultural resources of the Ethno-ornithology World Atlas (EWA) and draws on comparative and historical linguistics, anthropology and biology to investigate the creative processes at work as linguistically diverse communities respond to the natural world through naming, metaphor and myth.

Not as 'Foreign' as You Think: Creating Bridges of Understanding across Languages (Chapter 3) deploys methods from historical and experimental linguistics to examine how speakers of one language manage to understand people speaking another (related) language, identifying strategies they use to create meaning in response to the 'other language' — and strategies with which they create barriers to understanding in order to preserve a distinctive identity.

A Breath of Fresh Air... Ivan Vyrypaev's *Oxygen* (2002): From Moscow to Birmingham via Oxford (Chapter 4) investigates interaction between languages in the performing arts — theatre, stand-up comedy, grime, rap, hip-hop — and the types of creativity this generates in response to cultural contexts and audiences, drawing on media and performance studies, and working with artists ranging from Russian dramatists to Black British and British Asian musicians from Birmingham and Leicester.

Multilingualism and Creativity in World Literature (Chapter 5) explores multilingual literatures to critique current theories of world literature, and investigates how drawing on more than one language in writing and reading generates new ways of seeing and understanding.

Prismatic Translation (Chapter 6) develops an innovative theory of translation that captures its creative dimension. The metaphor of the 'prism' enables translation to be seen not in terms of functional equivalence but as a release of multiple signifying possibilities. This idea is put into practice through literary critical research into the many translations of Charlotte Brontë's *Jane Eyre*, and into the importance of different scripts (e.g. Chinese, Arabic, alphabetic) as a factor in translation; we also use the approach to inspire creative writing in schools.

Getting Creative in the Languages Classroom (Chapter 7) draws on empirically based methodologies in the field of Second Language Education to consider creative alternatives to the prevalent emphasis on language learning for functional purposes, investigating the extent to which they may enhance foreign-language acquisition in schools and beyond.

Inspiring Language Learners (Chapter 8) showcases work with schools in creative writing workshops and the Multilingual Performance Project (MPP), exploring the energy languages can bring to classroom work when they provide a context in which it's OK just to have fun with languages, encourage experimentation with new expressive resources, and build confidence with linguistic diversity.

Languages at Work (Chapter 9) looks at the role languages play in working contexts. It examines how increasing your linguistic flexibility and learning languages extend your communicative and cultural range in ways you can deploy for career purposes; and how glimpses of careers in which people use foreign languages tell us something about what makes languages valuable personally, culturally, professionally and financially — sometimes all at once.

Creating Languages (Chapter 10) sets out on a journey of discovery, homing in on some key questions concerning the interplay between creativity and languages, and finding out what motivates language inventors to create an artificial language such as Esperanto and equip mythical folk such as Elves and the Dothraki with distinctive languages. It further considers the extraordinary linguistic inventiveness that allows us to create and appreciate language play, such as puns.

Works Cited are given at the end of each chapter and listed also at the end of the book in a comprehensive bibliography. The end of each chapter additionally offers suggestions for further reading in **Find Out More**, with all the suggestions also appearing at the end of the book. More information and resources can be found at our Creative Multilingualism website.

Why Learn a Language? forms the conclusion of the book. Building on the ten Manifesto Statements, this section offers some concrete reasons why it's worth spending time and effort learning a language.

Works Cited

Allen-Kinross, Pippa. 2018. 'A-level Results 2018: Chinese A-level Overtakes German for First Time', *Schools Week*, 16 August, https://schoolsweek.co.uk/a-level-results-2018-chinese-a-level-overtakes-german-for-first-time/

Creative Multilingualism. 2020. https://www.creativeml.ox.ac.uk

Gandhi, Mohandas K. 2007. *An Autobiography or The Story of my Experiments with Truth*, trans. from Gujarati by M. Desai (Harmondsworth: Penguin).

Garamendi, Patricia W. 1996. 'Peace Corps… More Than You Can Imagine', in *At Home in the World: The Peace Corps Story*, ed. by Mark D. Gearan et al. ([n.p.]: Peace Corps), pp. v–vii, https://babel.hathitrust.org/cgi/pt?id=umn.31951d012241914;view=1up;seq=6

Mehmedbegovic, Dina, and Thomas H. Bak. 2019. 'Bilingualism, Multilingualism and Plurilingualism: Living in two or more languages', 27 March 2019, *Healthy Linguistic Diet*, http://healthylinguisticdiet.com/bilingualism-multilingualism-and-plurilingualism-living-in-two-or-more-languages/

Morrissy-Swan, Tomé. 2018. 'Have Americans re-invented the Yorkshire pudding as the 'Dutch Baby?', *The Telegraph*, 14 May, https://www.telegraph.co.uk/food-and-drink/news/have-americans-re-invented-yorkshire-pudding-dutch-baby/

Stacey, Kiran, and Helen Warrell. 2013. 'David Cameron urges UK schools to teach Mandarin', *Financial Times*, 4 December, https://www.ft.com/content/056eb1da-5ccd-11e3-81bd-00144feabdc0

Find Out More

Bilingualism Matters. 2020. http://www.bilingualism-matters.ppls.ed.ac.uk

Founded by Antonella Sorace, Bilingualism Matters is a research and information centre on bilingualism based at the University of Edinburgh. The initiative has spread across the world, and its mission is to work with a wide range of partners to research, support and promote bilingualism.

Creative Multilingualism. 2020. https://www.creativeml.ox.ac.uk

This website represents the research that underpins the content of this volume. The research was conducted by the authors between 2016 and 2020 and funded by the Arts and Humanities Research Council (AHRC, part of UK Research and Innovation) in the context of its Open World Research Initiative (OWRI). The website includes the projects conducted by the seven research strands (see Chapters 1 to 7) and further sections with blogs, resources and reports on conferences and public engagement work, some of which is presented in Chapters 8 and 9.

Creative Multilingualism. 2020a. LinguaMania: The Podcast, https://podcasts.ox.ac.uk/series/linguamania

This series of eight podcasts was made by the Creative Multilingualism team. It explores connections between languages and creativity, and opens up a wide range of perspectives on language learning.

Crystal, David. 2010. *The Cambridge Encyclopedia of Language*, 3rd edn (Cambridge: Cambridge University Press).

David Crystal's depth of insight into everything to do with language and languages is unsurpassed, as is his talent for making complex research accessible. This book offers an invaluable point of entry on fundamental questions concerning languages.

Jones, Rodney H. (ed.). 2016. *The Routledge Handbook of Language and Creativity* **(Abingdon: Routledge), https://doi.org/10.4324/9781315694566**

A volume that presents current research on the relationship between language and creativity in various disciplines, including sections on literary creativity, multimodal and multimedia creativity, and creativity in language teaching and learning.

Kharkhurin, Anatoliy V. 2012. *Multilingualism and Creativity* **(Bristol: Multilingual Matters).**

This valuable study examines theoretical approaches to the connection between multilingualism and creativity, offering useful discussions of relevant research on both areas as a basis for presenting empirical evidence and educational applications.

Maher, John C. 2017. *Multilingualism: A Very Short Introduction* **(Oxford: Oxford University Press), https://doi.org/10.1093/actrade/9780198724995.001.0001**

An excellent overview of the topic with a wealth of interesting facts and thought-provoking comments on multilingualism as a feature of the human condition. The final section on revitalization concludes with the view that 'indigenous is the new cool'.

Marsh, David, and Richard Hill. 2009. *Study on the Contribution of Multilingualism to Creativity: Final Report,* **Public Services Contract no EACEA/2007/3995/2, http://www.dylan-project.org/Dylan_en/news/assets/StudyMultilingualism_report_en.pdf**

A European Commission study which sets out to establish the scientific basis for the claim that multilingualism — understood as the ability to engage with more than one language in everyday life — contributes to individual and collective creativity.

Martin-Jones, Marylin, Adrian Blackledge and Angela Creese (eds). 2012. *The Routledge Handbook of Multilingualism* (Abingdon: Routledge), https://doi.org/10.4324/9780203154427

This collection of essays provides a stimulating insight into a complex field of research, taking account of social, cultural and political angles and contexts. It is aimed at postgraduates and many of the essays are specialized in focus, but it also offers good scope for browsing.

Mehmedbegovic-Smith, Dina, and Thomas H. Bak. 2020. *Healthy Linguistic Diet*, http://healthylinguisticdiet.com/

An engaging project based on an analogy between physical and mental health, showcasing evidence that using two or more languages has lifelong benefits for cognitive development and well-being.

Project MEITS, Heather Martin and Wendy Ayres-Bennett (eds). 2019. *How Languages Changed My Life* ([n.p.]: Archway).

Stories that illuminate how languages have shaped the careers of individuals from many walks of life, including writers and musicians, politicians and activists, teachers and students, scientists and sportspeople.

Singleton, David, and Larissa Aronin (eds.). 2018. *Twelve Lectures on Multilingualism* (Bristol: Multilingual Matters), https://doi.org/10.21832/9781788922074

A collection of thought-provoking essays on key topics currently being pursued in research on multilingualism, aimed at undergraduates and postgraduates.

Credits

Permission to include their contribution was kindly granted by the following:

Sheela Mahadevan for the Language Life 'Sharing Languages in India' and the photograph of herself (Fig. 2).

Ganga Narayanan for the photograph of herself (Fig. 2).

Guruvayur Krishna Narayanan for the photograph of himself (Fig. 2).

1. The Creative Power of Metaphor

Katrin Kohl, Marianna Bolognesi and Ana Werkmann Horvat

> Language diversity nurtures diversity of identity, thought and expression

The following principles are central to the work of Creative Multilingualism's research strand 'The Creative Power of Metaphor':

Our innate talent for metaphor connects our thought, language and action in a fluid process.

Our metaphorical thinking is influenced by the language(s) we know and the culture(s) we inhabit.

Metaphor opens up an infinite range of pathways to creativity.

'"Space-time" is simply the physical universe inside which we and everything else exists. And yet, even after millennia living in it, we still don't know what space-time actually is' (Carroll 2019: 34). This statement sums up current scientific knowledge about the interplay between three-dimensional space and one-dimensional time. Yet we all cope with the practical challenges of our daily routines, which involve knowing — roughly or precisely, depending on context and need — which specific location we are in, and what time of day, month or year it is. So how do we manage to get a mental grip on space and time, and how they connect? The answer is: we use our extraordinary talent for thinking and communicating through metaphor.

Take the concept of 'progress'. This assumes that we move forward through time much as we progress along a path or road. Or the more obviously metaphorical saying 'time flies', which gives expression to an everyday sense of time passing faster than expected or faster than seems natural to a human being (see Fig. 1). The metaphor makes the abstract, intangible and shapeless concept of 'time' imaginable as a physical, animate body that moves swiftly through space, by analogy with the familiar phenomenon of a bird. Shared among speakers of English, the proverb goes back to Virgil's poem *Georgics* — though his Latin metaphor is in fact 'tempus fugit' (line 284) — 'time flees'. We may speculate what prompted the change of action as the metaphor became established in English. Did the vowel correspondence between 'time' and 'fly' make the phrase more memorable? Certainly, a shift in the English semantic system played a part, in that 'fly' used to encompass 'flee' as a (metaphorical) meaning, but this part of the associative range of the word became obsolete. Meanwhile German never adopted the classical quotation as a proverb despite an equally strong classical heritage — 'die Zeit fliegt' is less common than 'die Zeit vergeht', equivalent to the pedestrian statement that 'time passes'.

Fig. 1 Even well-worn metaphors are not 'dead'. They can gain new force when they are highlighted as meaningful, for example by elaboration. *Peanuts* © 1976 Peanuts Worldwide LLC. Dist. by Andrews McMeel Syndication. Reprinted with permission. All rights reserved.

We here gain a glimpse of the dynamic interplay between cognition, culture and language, and the creative potential generated by that process. This becomes evident in extensions and adaptations of the metaphor, as in the gently humorous Peanuts cartoon, or a message attributed to business leadership coach Michael Altshuler, which relies on his audience's familiarity with modern methods of travel: 'The bad news is: time flies. The good news is: you're the pilot.'

When we use one type of thing — in this case the bird or flying object — to give shape to another — here the abstract concept of time — we're training our ability to think creatively. We do so from the moment we start listening to the language(s) around us. And it's not too far-fetched to assume that the human ability to create analogies between concepts, transfer concepts from one conceptual 'domain' to another, and adapt established metaphors to new contexts, is akin to the engineer's creative adaptation of the flying mechanisms of feathered birds to create a flying machine. In recent decades, our talent for metaphorical invention has enabled us to extrapolate from physical webs, nets and networks to create the 'World Wide Web', the 'Internet' and 'networking'. Neural 'networks' are now being appropriated for robots that emulate human beings. Metaphorical creativity has generated new words and new meanings for existing words, and these in turn have facilitated collaborative development of innovative technologies. These are quite literally changing the world and the way we live with each other and the world around us.

> **Metaphor in Science**
>
> The different views of a particular problem arise from the prevailing metaphors held by each discipline. Sharing different metaphorical representations of a problem appears to open up possibilities for creative thinking. [...]
>
> Metaphor plays a central role in the development of a scientific subject, from its very beginnings through to its full development as a mature body of knowledge and understanding. It figures in the scientist's initial creative impulses, in interpretations of experimental data, in formulations of scientific explanations, and in communication between scientists and between scientists and the rest of the world.
>
> Theodore L. Brown, *Making Truth. Metaphor in Science* (2003: x).

We can see here how metaphor operates dynamically at the interface between cognition, culture and language, establishing a shared frame of reference in a particular temporal and situational context. What can disappear from view is that these processes happen within a particular language, using the linguistic material available to the speakers of that language together with its cognitive and cultural inflections, in the time and space the speaker and their audience inhabit. 'Time flies' is not identical to 'tempus fugit'; and a new technology has opened up the potential for conceptualizing 'time flies' not in terms of an animate bird but in terms of an inanimate aeroplane that is subject to human control.

The purpose of this chapter is to look more closely at the dynamics of metaphorical creativity and what approaches can help to understand them, taking account of cognition, language and culture as interactive participants in a complex process of creating meaning that thrives on diversity.

Metaphorical Diversity

Conceptualizations of time illuminate the diverse ways in which human beings imagine abstract phenomena and make their concepts communicable through language. Like Latin 'tempus fugit', the English metaphor 'time flies' imagines time as a being that moves linearly from A to B, facing in the direction of motion. Implicit is the idea that the speaker is moving with it. By contrast, if we say 'winter is approaching', we envisage its coming towards us. Time may also be conceptualized in English as the observer moving across a landscape, as in the verb and noun 'progress', or the sentence 'She's approaching her thirtieth birthday'. The future is conceptualized as being in front of the observer while the past is behind: 'I'm looking forward to my holiday'; 'It's good to have that ordeal behind me'. These conventional time metaphors are acquired at such an early age by English speakers that they seem simply to reflect a natural reality, especially since they form part of a coherent system of conceptualizing time: in all the above examples, the movement is linear and happens on a horizontal plane. Yet comparisons with other languages demonstrate that these metaphors are grounded in culturally specific patterns of thought.

Over recent years, research has revealed an enormous variety of ways in which time is conceptualized. Studies in the field of psychology conducted by Lera Boroditsky and others, and summarized in her essay 'How Languages Construct Time' (2011), give a sense of how fundamental the differences are. For example, a study comparing English and Mandarin speakers showed that the latter were more inclined to use vertical metaphors for time than English speakers, and that this correlated with a greater tendency to think about time in vertical terms (pp. 334–35). The direction of travel associated with time also varies from culture to culture: speakers of the South American language Aymara refer to the past as being in front of the observer while the future is behind (p. 336). And speakers of the Australian aboriginal language Kuuk Thaayorre, who use cardinal direction terms like 'east' or 'west' rather than relative terms such as 'right' or left', organize their time references on the basis of their spatial orientation — i.e. they are so aware of which direction they are facing in at any given point that they use this as the basis for referring to time (pp. 337–38; see also Boroditsky and Gaby 2010).

Moreover, in literate cultures the configuration of time is affected by the writing system: while speakers of languages that use Latin script order temporal events from left to right, speakers of Arabic and Hebrew, who read text from right to left, were found correspondingly to order events from right to left (p. 336). Further factors shown to influence conceptualizations of time are the metaphors that are being used in the specific discourse context, and, in the case of bilingual speakers, the language they are operating in (pp. 335–36, 339). Moreover, research including learners demonstrated that increased experience of talking about time vertically led to more vertical representations of time (p. 335).

These differences indicate that our linguistically articulated conceptualization of abstract domains involves an immensely complex interaction between the following:

- our cognition, including our emotions and imagination,
- our bodies in their spatial environment,
- our cultural heritage and cultural context,
- our language(s) in its/their oral and written manifestations,
- our linguistic and situational context.

The implications of this complex interdependence go to the heart of one of the great philosophical questions concerning language: to what extent language affects thought. Platonic philosophy is predicated on the absence of such a connection: the realm of ideas is considered to be independent of language, and consequently not affected by linguistic diversity. Yet the evidence concerning the cultural *and* linguistic diversity of concepts of time points to a fundamental interdependence of language and thought: how we think about time depends on the language we speak. Daniel Casasanto puts it like this: 'It may be universal that people conceptualize time according to spatial metaphors, but because these metaphors vary across languages, members of different language communities develop distinctive conceptual repertoires' (2008: 75).

> **Does Language Shape How We Think? The Issue of Linguistic Relativity**
>
> People who speak different languages appear to conceive of the world somewhat differently and diversity of thought, perspective, and innovation seem intuitively linked to naturally occurring language diversity. Why is it, then, that many scholars in science, linguistics, and philosophy (perhaps in those fields more than elsewhere) are sceptical, if not overly critical, of the idea that languages may go hand in hand with different ways of conceiving and paying attention to the world, but also literally holding different perceptions?
>
> Guillaume Thierry, 'Neurolinguistic Relativity: How Language Flexes Human Perception and Cognition' (2016: 691–92).

This linguistically inflected diversity of conceptualizations holds immense potential for individual and collective creativity. Throughout our lives, we learn to work creatively with the linguistic and conceptual repertoire we acquire as members of our cultural community, and our scope for creativity is structured and constrained by that repertoire. But we are not locked into a metaphorical straitjacket. This is evident in our ability to adapt conventional metaphors within a language and create new ones, and the ability of individuals to modify their conceptualizations if they are exposed to alternative metaphors, for example by learning another language.

Researching Metaphor — The Perils of Ignoring Language Diversity

A central tenet of cognitive theories of metaphor is that metaphorical expressions reveal metaphorical conceptual systems, that these systems are primary by comparison with the expressions, and that the concepts can be separated from the language in which they are expressed. A convenient consequence of these assumptions is that the language of the examples used in the research is not critical.

This has important implications for how we conduct research on metaphor. The tendency in cognitive linguistics and psycholinguistics has been to use English examples, often without acknowledgement of the limitations this may entail. For example, Gilles Fauconnier and Mark Turner focus exclusively on English examples when discussing the metaphor TIME AS SPACE in their essay 'Rethinking Metaphor' in *The Cambridge Handbook of Metaphor and Thought* (2008). Their purpose is to investigate the 'complexity of integrations that lie behind observable metaphorical conceptual systems' (p. 65) but the question whether examples in one language are sufficient is not posed. The implicit premise is that the language in which a metaphor is articulated has no significant bearing on metaphorical thought. Yet we have already seen that to even begin to understand the complex diversity of ways in which human beings create concepts of time, we need to look not only beyond English, but beyond western languages.

The need to take account of language difference when researching metaphor is also evident if we look at the conventions for conceptualizing metaphor established by George Lakoff and Mark Johnson in their seminal volume *Metaphors We Live By*, first published in 1980. They focus on the metaphor pattern 'A is B', which identifies the target domain and source domain of the metaphor, e.g. 'life is a journey' or 'argument is war'. The conceptual metaphor is distinguished by capital letters from its varied metaphorical expressions, as in the following example:

> ARGUMENT IS WAR
> Your claims are *indefensible*.
> He *attacked every weak point* in my argument.
> I *demolished* his argument. (2003: 4)

The statement in capital letters equates a linguistic activity (argument) with a physical armed conflict (war), and the expressions underneath exemplify — as a few examples among many — how the metaphor manifests itself in ordinary language (see also Fig. 2). The capital letters signify the purely conceptual nature of 'argument is war', with the implication that this statement is pre-linguistic or supra-linguistic.

Fig. 2 This cartoon about examinations of doctoral theses exemplifies the conceptual metaphor that 'ARGUMENT IS WAR'. 'Thesis Defense' (2014), xkcd.com, CC BY-NC 2.5, https://imgs.xkcd.com/comics/thesis_defense.png

Unlike the symbols used in Logic, however, words are always part of a specific natural language. We need go only as far as the German translation of *Metaphors We Live By* to find that the word 'argument' depends for its range of meanings on the English language, where 'argument' typically denotes a heated or angry exchange of diverging views. The translation 'ARGUMENTIEREN IST KRIEG' (Lakoff and Johnson 2018: 12) diverges from the English statement because the verbal noun 'Argumentieren' suggests a rational process of presenting reasons for or against a position without the association of anger. Although there is a shared Latin origin, the meaning has diverged within the respective language systems — the words are 'false friends'. In fact, German has no single word with the same set of associations as the English noun 'argument'. This is not an isolated difficulty but one that arises systematically from the fact that the meaning(s) and associations of a word are defined by its place in the semantic system of the relevant language. Any idea expressed in words is therefore to some extent dependent on the language in which it is expressed — and the idea will subtly change when it gains expression in another language. Translation opens up creative options — see Chapter 6, on 'Prismatic Translation'. When researching conceptual metaphors, the need to attend to language diversity is therefore imperative. Every cultural group that develops a language creates its own ways of making its world meaningful through metaphor. To ignore that diversity is to ignore the creative power that comes with our talent for metaphor.

Traversing Metaphorical Pathways

When we use a language, we are continually treading established pathways of metaphorical association, training our metaphorical muscles and extending our metaphorical repertoire. In conceptualizing abstract entities, we often draw on universal aspects of human life, such as our bodies or kinship. Yet even closely related languages which draw on the same aspect will tend to differ in their selection from the range of possibilities. We can see this process at work in the lexical field of company structures in English, German and French (see the following page).

Each language is taking us along a slightly different route, creating different connections and suggesting new associative opportunities that have evolved over time and in interaction with the cultural context of its speakers — creating diachronic and synchronic relationships and connections which can only be captured imperfectly in schematic form. These may draw on words provided by other languages (in the examples given, German and French draw both on Latin and on each other), and they may interact with non-lexical features of the language. For example, the selection of 'mother company' in German (*die Muttergesellschaft*) and French (*la société mère*) from the possible kinship options accords with the feminine gender of *Gesellschaft* and *société*.

Leafing through a dictionary of a language quickly shows how important metaphor is in supplying us with words for abstract concepts. For example, the meanings listed for any common verb denoting a physical action will include metaphorical ones. Take the verb 'to run': it conveys a

TARGET DOMAIN	SOURCE DOMAIN		ENGLISH	GERMAN	FRENCH
COMPANY	general hierarchical structure		subsidiary		
	human body	body part at the top of the body	head office	Hauptsitz (*'head' / main 'seat'*)	
		piece of furniture used by the body to seat itself		Hauptsitz (*'main seat'*) Niederlassung (*branch, cf. 'sich niederlassen' 'to sit down'*)	siège (*'seat', place where something is located*)
	kinship relations	parent	parent company		
		mother		Muttergesellschaft (*'mother' company*)	société mère (*'mother' company*)
		father			
		child [of parent]		Filiale ([*from Latin filialis:*] *branch*)	filiale ([*from Latin filialis via German:*] *'child' company, subsidiary*)
		daughter		Tochtergesellschaft (*'daughter' company, subsidiary*)	
		son			
	non-human life form	tree	branch	Zweigniederlassung (*branch*)	
INDUSTRIAL SECTOR				Branche ([*from French:*] *industry, sector*)	branche (*industry, sector*)

physical movement as in 'run to the bus' or 'run a marathon', and it is also used metaphorically as in 'run into trouble' or 'run a company'. We learn these conventionalized metaphorical meanings from a young age and use them as a standard part of the semantic system of the language we speak. The relationship between the literal and metaphorical meanings is part of our 'living' semantic system, which we draw on to comprehend and create new uses of words and new words.

In order to understand better how we cognitively process metaphorical meanings of words that also have non-metaphorical meanings, our research group conducted two related experiments, one with native speakers of English (Werkmann Horvat, Bolognesi et al.(a)), and one with two groups of Croatian learners of English who had intermediate and advanced competence respectively (Werkmann Horvat, Bolognesi et al. (b)). What we wanted to find out was firstly, whether native speakers of a language (in this case English) access metaphorical meanings with the same ease as non-metaphorical meanings of a given word, and secondly, how this compares with the processing of metaphorical meanings by learners of the same language (in this case Croatian learners of English).

Both psycholinguistic experiments deployed the same set of stimuli, consisting of a series of verbs used with a direct object that might yield a literal or metaphorical meaning, e.g. 'expose'+'skin' versus 'expose'+'truth'. The study with native speakers of English revealed no significant processing differences between literal and metaphorical meanings of the verb. This addressed the question of whether native speakers access a metaphorical meaning via the same word's literal meaning or directly. Our experiment confirmed what has largely become the consensus, namely that native speakers access metaphorical meanings directly and effortlessly rather than via a literal meaning. In effect, they treat such verbs as polysemous words, i.e. words with multiple meanings, irrespective of whether these are literal or metaphorical.

The second experiment, involving two groups of non-native speakers with differing degrees of proficiency, revealed significantly slower processing of all the meanings, which was to be expected for learners. Beyond that, however, the results were much less homogeneous both within and across the two groups than for native speakers and permitted no straightforward conclusions about how the learners were processing metaphorical meanings by comparison with literal meanings. The results indicated, however, that learners were generally less familiar with the metaphorical than the literal meanings. This has important implications for teaching vocabulary to learners, suggesting that in a foreign language, metaphorical meanings need to be actively taught without relying on learners inferring those meanings from literal meanings. It also suggests that learners should be given practice in understanding the semantic system of the language as consisting of literal and related metaphorical meanings. This finding accords with research on vocabulary learning conducted in the field of education by the Creative Multilingualism research strand on 'Linguistic Creativity in Language Learning' in this volume (see Chapter 7), which suggests that giving learners opportunities to engage with metaphorical language in poetry may produce better vocabulary learning outcomes than an exclusive focus on more information-focused text types. Further research is however needed in this area.

The difference we found between native and non-native speakers accords with the findings of a study investigating the role of the right hemisphere (RH) of the brain in processing meaning: 'the unique role of the RH in activating and maintaining a larger range of word meaning and semantic features may be limited to native language, and does not fully extend to later acquired non-native languages' (Faust, Ben-Artzi et al. 2012: 230). From what we know about metaphor, we may surmise that our effortless understanding of a word's range of literal and metaphorical meanings is deeply embedded in early learning processes where language learning is integrally connected with learning to use our bodies, move around in space, and interacting with a living human community and natural environment.

A key area requiring more research is the extent to which metaphorical meanings are 'stored' in our lexical system in the same way as non-metaphorical words, with lexicalization potentially eliminating awareness of connections with literal meanings. Our hypothesis is that the relationship of a metaphorical meaning to a literal meaning of a word remains a latently significant factor in the semantic system we learn as we acquire our native language or languages, and that for words with surviving literal and metaphorical meanings, native speakers will readily activate the creative metaphorical potential if the context or expressive purpose prompts such activation. In other words, the metaphor is not 'dead' but 'dormant'. When we learn words from an early age, we internalize them as part of a living system that encompasses metaphorical meanings created by processes of extension and transfer. We normally use them without being conscious of those processes, but new needs such as technological developments, a special communicative purpose or a spirit of poetic experimentation may prompt us to activate the creative potential and open up old pathways or invent new ones. In doing so, we can rely on our listener or reader having the lexical knowledge and the experience with metaphoric processes to respond with reciprocal creativity.

Investigating the Creative Power of Metaphor

Investigating creativity at the interface between cognition and language requires a wide range of approaches and research methodologies. The study of metaphor benefits from having a long history, starting with Aristotle and continuing in the long tradition of rhetoric and literary studies. Lakoff and Johnson's achievement was to shift the focus from metaphor as a feature of exceptionally crafted language to its ubiquitous role in our cognition and ordinary linguistic repertoire. This laid the basis for a burgeoning field of scientific investigation in cognitive linguistics, psychology and neuroscience, with experimental methods and interrogation of large corpora permitting systematic research on the cognitive processing and use of metaphor.

Scientific studies concerned with metaphorical creativity have focused on such questions as 'optimal innovation' (Giora, Fein et al. 2004: 116–20), and — drawing on fully automated metaphor generation — the criteria that need to be fulfilled in order for metaphors generated by artificial intelligence (AI) to be perceived as creative (Littlemore, Pérez Sobrino et al. 2018). There has however been a tendency in recent decades for research on metaphor to become overly reliant on approaches developed within cognitive science, and focused on investigating aspects of metaphor that lend themselves to testing by experimental methods, organization into clearly distinct categories, and interrogation of large corpora. Especially when investigating creative processes that may be unusual, singular and individual, however, it is useful also to involve interpretive methods used in the humanities. For example, the conceptual framework of rhetoric with its holistic and process-oriented concept of language in action is often better suited to capturing creative metaphoric processes than science with its rationalist heritage.

By focusing attention on metaphor as a feature of ordinary speech, cognitive linguistics has established a strong basis for elucidating processes by which novel metaphors are created using techniques such as extending, elaborating and combining conventional ones (Lakoff and Turner 1989, passim; Kövecses 2010: 53–56). An example is the metaphor created by Neil Armstrong when he became the first human being to set foot on the moon, an event in 1969 that was transmitted across the world by television. His purpose was to anchor the historic event in the public consciousness: 'That's one small step for a man, one giant leap for mankind' (NASA 2019). The statement built on his literal, visible physical action and the equally literal upward movement of space travel, and infused those processes with the conventional metaphor of upward movement as progress towards something better. What made the statement memorable was its palpable connection to the unique historic moment experienced and articulated by a heroic human being. The metaphoric processes Armstrong deployed were immediately understood by an audience of millions — all of them well versed in the use of metaphor.

Fig. 3 'That's one small step for a man, one giant leap for mankind' (Neil Armstrong). This is a photograph by Neil Armstrong of his fellow astronaut Buzz Aldrin on the Moon (1969). NASA. Wikimedia Commons, Public Domain, https://commons.wikimedia.org/wiki/File:Aldrin_Apollo_11_original.jpg#/media/File:Aldrin_Apollo_11_original.jpg

We can see similar mechanisms at work in Charles Baudelaire's poem 'Élévation' (1961: 10), addressed to his 'esprit', i.e. mind or spirit:

> Au-dessus des étangs, au-dessus des vallées,
> Des montagnes, des bois, des nuages, des mers,
> Par delà le soleil, par delà les éthers,
> Par delà les confins des sphères étoilées,
>
> Mon esprit, tu te meus avec agilité,
> [...].
>
> (*Above ponds, above valleys,* | *Mountains, woods, clouds, seas,* | *Beyond the sun, beyond the ether* | *Beyond the boundaries of starry spheres,* || *My spirit, you move with agility,* [...].)

He extends the conventional metaphor of mental 'agility' by means of personification as he implicitly animates his 'esprit' by casting it in the role of addressee, and elaborates on the metaphor by evoking a journey that sets out from a physical landscape and travels up into the firmament. In this process, he combines several conventional metaphors: ACTION IS MOVEMENT, THINKING IS A JOURNEY, RATIONAL IS UP. While the statement is novel, the familiar elements allow our mental agility to respond gradually as we accompany the spirit on its cosmic journey. The poetic process thereby involves the reader as a participant who enacts the process conveyed in the poetically memorable words. While the poem is addressed to the speaker's 'esprit', it engages the reader through shared bodily experience.

The creative power of metaphor is however by no means always generated in such a clearly structured process. Indeed, metaphor may attain special creative strength in spiritual discourse where the literal merges seamlessly into the metaphorical, or in artworks that integrate metaphor in a multi-sensory experience. Here it can hinder rather than aid understanding to use an approach that is predicated on isolating the contribution of metaphor to the whole.

The 'Sacred Funk' performance project *Yòrùbá Sonnets* created by Lékan Babalolá, Kate Luxmoore and Olu Taiwo and hosted by Creative Multilingualism for a performance in Oxford, exemplifies what is at stake (Babalolá 2019b and Creative Multilingualism (Slanguages: Yòrùbá Sonnets) 2019a). The work unites the ancient oral Yoruba tradition of Ifá sacred verse and divination with English translations, versions and creative elaborations. Occasional singing in Yoruba and incorporation of a Dorset folk song interweave with sustained English spoken word, articulated in formal British diction associated by Olu Taiwo with Shakespearean language, and accompanied by gesture, mime, dance and martial art moves. The performance is sustained by rhythms with cultural roots in West Africa while integrating musical elements from Trinidad and Brazil in a context of western funk (see Fig. 4). Invitations to dance by the spoken word performer encourage the listeners to involve their whole bodies in the experience of the work.

Fig. 4 The flyer announcing performances of *Yòrùbá Sonnets* in 2019 at Wolfson College, Oxford, and other venues visually and textually signals an exuberant fusion of ethnic heritage, cultures, traditions, languages and artistic forms. Babalolá et al. 2019c. Reproduced by kind permission of Lékan Babalolá.

Capturing the contribution of metaphor to this work of art is not straightforward. 'Master Wordsmith' Olu Taiwo highlighted the involvement of metaphor in the texts, in a post-performance exchange with the audience (Creative Multilingualism (Slanguages: Yòrùbá Sonnets) 2019c). Here, for example, is Verse 12: 'Victory over Suffering (if you feed the source of your birth you have victory)' (Babalolá 2019a: [15]). In listening to the comment on that verse, we can follow spiritual meanings unfolding from concrete things: 'It is from its roots that we feed the mighty African Teak! The Iroko tree [...]. For the people of heaven, celestial being, it is through ritual honour that we show our graceful face.' Yet the words are only one medium by which the work communicates its meaning. The resonant delivery enhanced by repetition and musical energy complements the meaning of the words, drawing associations with Yoruba spiritual ritual into the performance space.

Equally important are the metaphors generated among the audience members during a Q & A exchange following the performance. As well as being invited to give oral feedback, they were asked to provide written comments on feedback postcards (Creative Multilingualism (Slanguages: Yòrùbá Sonnets) 2019c and 2019b). One postcard commented on the 'Extremely immersive and profound experience' while another offered the following response: 'Fantastic mixture of poetry and music. Really strong visceral images. We need more of these cross-cultural collaborations.' Metaphor here becomes a means of articulating a holistic response to a multi-modal artform. It captures the nature of the experience as a communicative process that 'mixes' words with music, 'crosses' cultural boundaries and linguistic systems, and impacts on the very organs of the listener's body — both metaphorically and literally, we may surmise, given the elicitation of dancing participation. Another respondent used the metaphor of a 'journey' in their written response, articulating an experience of spiritual enrichment: 'Thank you for sharing this work. Feeling blessed by the wisdom and witticism of the Yoruba Sonnets! A beautiful journey.' The postcards also drew on metaphor to share personal cultural connections experienced in the course of participating: 'Thank you for taking me back to my homeland tonight', and — metaphorically complementing the music and the tree imagery — 'Resonates deeply with my roots'. Metaphor here works creatively at many levels in a holistic process involving participants in a shared experience.

The metaphors generated spontaneously by the audience members emerged from a specific shared moment in a particular spatial and cultural context while engaging individual cognitive, imaginative, cultural, bodily responses. Understanding such particular interactive processes is as important for researching the creative power of metaphor as analysing general patterns. Moreover, as with the conceptualization of space-time, researching metaphor is dependent on metaphorical thinking and language. To conceptualize and communicate how metaphor works, we need metaphors — sharing them and experimenting with them as much as analysing them. This should not trouble us — rather, we should embrace our dependence on metaphor. It is an intrinsic part of the human condition.

Exploring Metaphor Further

Metaphor is a fundamental human talent which allows us to make continual connections between the physical world we experience with our bodies, senses and minds, and the worlds we imagine. It is a talent with infinite potential for creative development of our lives as individual and social beings in our natural and technical environment, and understanding its importance can give us important means of shaping our world and engaging with the global challenges we collectively face.

Research on metaphor used to take place almost exclusively in the humanities, based on a tradition of theory and practice going back to the Greek philosophers, rhetoricians and poets. Following the publication of Lakoff and Johnson's landmark volume *Metaphors We Live By* in 1980, the field underwent a comprehensive shift and most research is currently being conducted in linguistics, psycholinguistics, psychology and neurosciences, with important work also being carried out on practical uses of metaphor in the social sciences.

A significant danger of the shift to the social sciences and sciences has been the — often invisible and unreflected — dominance of English and the high status accorded to research that focuses on the mental role of metaphor as the aspect with higher status than its verbal aspect. The rise of corpus linguistics has brought more emphasis on the role of big data to underpin empirical investigation, and there is now much greater appreciation of the need to include languages beyond English in research. But this is problematic especially with respect to corpus research because there tends to be lack of equivalence in availability and corpus quality across languages.

The way ahead rests with interdisciplinary research and giving a strong role both to the humanities and to qualitative research projects. They can provide an important corrective to some of the more optimistic expectations surrounding quantitative studies and foreground questions that may be in danger of becoming obliterated when one form of research gains dominance. They can also address types of metaphor that do not lend themselves to reliable tagging and that require interpretative methods — notably metaphors embedded in texts, and metaphors that are creative in unusual ways.

The future for metaphor studies lies in drawing on a diversity of methodologies, incorporating research on diverse languages and involving the respective communities in that research, and above all in productive dialogue between disciplines.

Works Cited

Babalolá, Lékan, et al. 2019a. 'Odu Eji Ogbe. Performance Text [for *Yòrùbá Sonnets*]'.

Babalolá, Lékan, et al. 2019b. *Yòrùbá Sonnets*. Performance of music from Lékan Babalolá's Sakred Funk Quartet with spoken word poetry and mime from Dr Olu Taiwo, organized by Creative Multilingualism under the aegis of Slanguages at Wolfson College, Oxford, on 15 February 2019.

Babalolá, Lékan, et al. 2019c. '*Yòrùbá Sonnets*: Tour 2019'. Flyer.

Baudelaire, Charles. 1961. Œuvres *complètes*, ed. by Y.-G. Le Dantec and rev. by Claude Pichois (Paris: Gallimard).

Boroditsky, Lera. 2011. 'How Languages Construct Time', in *Space, Time and Number in the Brain. Searching for the Foundations of Mathematical Thought*, ed. by Stanislas Dehaene and Elizabeth Brannon (London: Elsevier), pp. 333–41.

Boroditsky, Lera, and Alice Gaby. 2010. 'Remembrances of Times East: Absolute Spatial Representations of Time in an Australian Aboriginal Community', *Psychological Science*, 21(11): 1635–39, https://doi.org/10.1177/0956797610386621

Brown, Theodore L. 2003. *Making Truth: Metaphor in Science* (Urbana: University of Illinois Press).

Carroll, Sean. 2019. 'Woven from Weirdness', *New Scientist*, 14 September, 34–38.

Casasanto, Daniel. 2008. 'Who's Afraid of the Big Bad Whorf? Crosslinguistic Differences in Temporal Language and Thought', *Language Learning*, 58(s1): 63–79, https://doi.org/10.1111/j.1467-9922.2008.00462.x, http://www.casasanto.com/papers/Casasanto2008_BigBadWhorf.pdf

Creative Multilingualism. 2020. https://www.creativeml.ox.ac.uk

Creative Multilingualism (Slanguages: Yòrùbá Sonnets). 2019a. 'Yòrùbá Sonnets', web page with films and other materials relating to the event on 15 February (see Lékan Babalolá et al. 2019b), Creative Multilingualism, https://www.creativeml.ox.ac.uk/yoruba-sonnets

Creative Multilingualism (Slanguages: Yòrùbá Sonnets). 2019b. 'Yòrùbá Sonnets: Audience Feedback Postcards Completed during the Post-Performance Q&A on 15 February 2019' (see Lékan Babalolá et al. 2019b), unpublished. Selection: Creative Multilingualism, 19 February 2019, https://www.creativeml.ox.ac.uk/blog/exploring-multilingualism/yoruba-sonnets-audience-feedback

Creative Multilingualism (Slanguages: Yòrùbá Sonnets). 2019c. 'Yòrùbá Sonnets with Lékan Babalolá: Post-Performance Q&A', film of event (see Lékan Babalolá et al. 2019b), 19:42, posted online by Creative Multilingualism, YouTube, 12 September 2019, https://www.youtube.com/watch?v=9x982hY9I3E

Faust, Miriam, Elisheva Ben-Artzi and Nili Vardi. 2012. 'Semantic Processing in Native and Second Language: Evidence from Hemispheric Differences in Fine and Coarse Semantic Coding', *Brain and Language*, 123(3): 228–33, https://doi.org/10.1016/j.bandl.2012.09.007

Fauconnier, Gilles, and Mark Turner. 2008. 'Rethinking Metaphor', in *The Cambridge Handbook of Metaphor and Thought*, ed. by Raymond W. Gibbs, Jr. (Cambridge: Cambridge University Press), pp. 53–66, https://doi.org/10.1017/cbo9780511816802.005

Giora, Rachel, Ofer Fein et al., 'Weapons of Mass Distraction: Optimal Innovation and Pleasure Ratings', *Metaphor and Symbol*, 19(2) (2004): 115–41, https://doi.org/10.1207/s15327868ms1902_2

Kövecses, Zoltán. 2010. *Metaphor: A Practical Introduction*, 2nd edn (Oxford: Oxford University Press).

Lakoff, George, and Mark Johnson. 2003. *Metaphors We Live By*, 2nd edn (Chicago: University of Chicago Press), https://doi.org/10.7208/chicago/9780226470993.001.0001

Lakoff, George, and Mark Johnson. 2018. *Leben in Metaphern: Konstruktion und Gebrauch von Sprachbildern*, trans. by Astrid Hildenbrand, 9th edn (Heidelberg: Auer).

Lakoff, George, and Mark Turner. 1989. *More than Cool Reason: A Field Guide to Poetic Metaphor* (Chicago: University of Chicago Press), https://doi.org/10.7208/chicago/9780226470986.001.0001

Littlemore, Jeannette, Paula Pérez Sobrino et al. 2018. 'What Makes a Good Metaphor? A Cross-Cultural Study of Computer-Generated Metaphor Appreciation', *Metaphor and Symbol*, 33(2): 101–22, https://doi.org/10.1080/10926488.2018.1434944

NASA. 2019. 'July 20, 1969: One Giant Leap for Mankind', July 20, https://www.nasa.gov/mission_pages/apollo/apollo11.html

Thierry, Guillaume. 2016. 'Neurolinguistic Relativity: How Language Flexes Human Perception and Cognition', *Language Learning*, 66(3): 690–713, https://doi.org/10.1111/lang.12186

Werkmann Horvat, Ana, Marianna Bolognesi and Katrin Kohl. (a) 'Processing of Literal and Metaphorical Meanings in Polysemous Verbs: An Experiment and its Methodological Implications', in revision for *Journal of Pragmatics*.

Werkmann Horvat, Ana, Marianna Bolognesi and Katrin Kohl. (b). 'Demolishing Walls and Myths: On the Status of Conventional Metaphorical Meaning in the L2 Lexicon,' in preparation.

Find Out More

Casasanto, Daniel. 2013. 'Development of Metaphorical Thinking: The Role of Language', in *Language and the Creative Mind***, ed. by M. Borkent, J. Hinnell et al. (Stanford: CSLI Publications), pp. 3–18,** http://casasanto.com/papers/Casasanto_Development_of_Metaphorical_Thinking_2013.pdf

This article considers fundamental questions about the interplay between different types of cognitive metaphor and language.

Gibbs, Raymond W. 1994. *The Poetics of Mind: Figurative Thought, Language and Understanding* **(Cambridge: Cambridge University Press).**

The author shows how figurative language reveals the poetic structure of the mind, drawing on psychology, linguistics, philosophy, anthropology and literary theory.

Glucksberg, Sam. 2003. 'The Psycholinguistics of Metaphor', *Trends in Cognitive Sciences***, 7(2): 92–96,** https://doi.org/10.1016/s1364-6613(02)00040-2

An examination of how people create and understand metaphors such as 'lawyers are sharks', demonstrating that we process these as easily as literal meanings.

Kohl, Katrin, Marianna Bolognesi and Ana Werkmann Horvat. 2019. 'The Creative Power of Metaphor: Multimedia Output', Creative Multilingualism, https://www.creativeml.ox.ac.uk/creative-power-metaphor-multimedia-output

These videos look at different aspects of metaphor, focusing on linguistic diversity, emotion, communication and creativity. The videos draw on interviews with researchers who attended an international conference organized by the Creative Multilingualism research strand 'The Creative Power of Metaphor' in 2019.

Kohl, Katrin, Marianna Bolognesi and Ana Werkmann Horvat. 2020. 'The Creative Power of Metaphor', Research Strand 1 of Creative Multilingualism, https://www.creativeml.ox.ac.uk/research/metaphor

Research project on metaphor conducted as part of the Creative Multilingualism programme between 2016 and 2020. This chapter draws on that research.

Littlemore, Jeannette, and Graham Low. 2006. *Figurative Thinking and Foreign Language Learning* **(Basingstoke, UK: Palgrave Macmillan), https://doi.org/10.1057/9780230627567**

The authors look at the role of figurative speech and figurative thinking in language teaching and learning and discuss the need to attend to figurative extensions of meaning when teaching vocabulary.

Credits

Permission to include their contribution was kindly granted by the following:

Lékan Babalolá for the flyer announcing performances of *Yòrùbá Sonnets* in 2019 at Wolfson College, Oxford, and other venues (Fig. 4).

Peanuts for the cartoon image (Fig. 1).

2. Creating a Meaningful World
Nature in Name, Metaphor and Myth

Karen Park, Felice S. Wyndham, Andrew Gosler and John Fanshawe

> Language diversity protects biodiversity

Whether it is a natural law or merely a productive analogy, we don't yet know but we wish to assert the importance of the relationship between creativity in human languages and the creativity of a world that has not stopped diversifying since our ancestral life forms came into existence over three billion years ago.

The authors of this chapter work in linguistics, anthropology, ornithology and conservation. Our research is grounded in place, where the themes that constitute the different areas of our particular expertise — language, people, birds and nature — are intrinsically linked. Our work proceeds from the following principles:

Creativity inherent in language is related to creativity in life forms.

All people are creative; all people are multilingual.

The natural world is inextricably intertwined with, and serves as an infinitely productive source for, the creation of meaning in lexicons, cognition, world views and praxis.

It is a fundamental human right to express creativity: in one's languages, modes of production and relationships with other living beings and land/water-scapes.

While societies and their economies have relied upon drawing on the earth's creative capital in the past with few checks, we are in a new era in which people must conscientiously safeguard remaining linguistic and biological diversity and the processes that generate them.

We engage an association that has proved to be remarkably salient across two centuries and two separate scholarly narratives: there are parallels between the study of natural history and the study of languages. This association has its origins in synchronicities of linguistic and biological research of the nineteenth century exploring processes of evolution and change. In *The Descent of Man*, Charles Darwin described how he was using the same cognitive model for languages and species, noting that 'the formation of different languages and of distinct species, and the proofs that both have been developed through a gradual process, are curiously parallel' (Darwin 1871: 58). Now, in the twenty-first century, the commonalities between the creativity of biological evolution and the creativity of language have progressed to incorporate our knowledge of biological and cultural diversity, and a world in which endangerment and extinction are prevalent.

> **Biocultural Diversity**
>
> It's the true web of life: diversity in both nature and culture. It's a living network made up of the millions of species of plants and animals that have evolved on Earth, and of the thousands of human cultures and languages that have developed over time. Languages, cultures, and ecosystems are interdependent. They're bound together through the myriad of ways in which people have interacted with the natural environment. Through a diversity of cultural traditions and practices, in a great variety of natural environments, human communities have acquired invaluable knowledge of how to achieve harmony with nature. Biocultural diversity is both the source and the expression of all the beauty and potential of life on Earth.
>
> Terralingua, 'What Is Biocultural Diversity?' (2017).

Often the transformational ideas of a given era have a way of crossing disciplinary boundaries or, perhaps more accurately, bringing to light shared tendencies across diverse fields. In the mid-1990s scholars in

Fig. 1 Francis (?) Darwin (c. 1858). Drawing on the back of the original manuscript for Charles Darwin's *On the Origin of Species* (1859) by one of Darwin's children. Reproduced by kind permission of William Darwin.

linguistics, anthropology and biology observed correlations between linguistic diversity and biological diversity, uniting these observations under the umbrella term *biocultural diversity*. Broadly defined as an 'interdependence between biological and cultural diversity' (Maffi 2001: 11), biocultural diversity recognizes links amongst linguistic, cultural and biological variation (Stepp et al. 2002) and has led to scholarly and practical outputs that include mapping of language and species groups (Loh and Harmon 2005), investigation into the traditional ecological knowledge of Indigenous peoples (Singh et al. 2010) and correlations between linguistic and biological diversity (e.g. regions with high diversity of bird, plant and mammal species also tend to have high linguistic diversity) (Sutherland 2003).

There is, on one level, an intuitive logic to these observed correlations — namely, that both species and languages evolve in relation to place. Geographical, historical or other barriers that lead to speciation can also apply to linguistic diversification (Harmon 1996). A full description of the historical and evolutionary landscape of language change, however, is beyond the scope of this chapter. We focus here on a few select language-environment interactions to highlight the role of environments in linguistic creativity over time.

We work with the hypothesis that linguistic richness plays an important role in protecting and sustaining biodiversity through human-environment relations and, on a practical level, we explore mutual benefits of coordinating linguistic and biological conservation efforts. Integration of local language diversity and cultural knowledge systems with biological conservation practice is key to political engagement and decolonization, particularly within locally managed conservation frameworks. A more culturally rooted approach to biological conservation directly relates local land and resource rights with ontologies and creative lifeworlds, history, storytelling and poetics, in addition to the promise of increased effectiveness of conservation objectives on a local level.

> **To You They Are Birds, To Me They Are Voices in the Forest**
>
> I soon discovered that collecting and organizing information this way indicated basic weaknesses in my conception of how culture interprets nature. The fault was never better realized than by Jubi, who expressed it in a remark one afternoon. After months of constant work on bird taxonomy and identification, carried out observationally in the forest and more experimentally in the village, we came to an impasse trying to specify the zoological content of closely related Kaluli taxa. With characteristic patience, Jubi was imitating calls, behavior, and nesting. Suddenly something snapped; I asked a question and Jubi blurted back, 'Listen — to you they are birds, to me they are voices in the forest.' I was startled by this, not because it was so direct (Kaluli tend to be very direct, even confrontative, in face-to-face interaction) but because it so thoroughly expressed the necessity of approaching Kaluli natural history as part of a cultural system.
>
> Steven Feld, Sound and Sentiment (1990: 45).

What's in a Name?

Languages are infinitely creative systems. They provide frameworks for encoding human knowledge and experience, partitioning continua of sensory perception into a myriad of meaningful units. In a world with over seven thousand languages, each with its own geographic, social and cultural context, the creative flexibility of the linguistic system permits a vastly diverse and beautifully nuanced realization of human experience. The names of things are the currency of every language.

So what exactly are names, and how does one begin to study them? In the late fifth century BCE, Plato addressed this question with reference to the naming of things in his dialogue *Cratylus*. Socrates is called upon to settle a debate between Hermogenes, a conventionalist who argues that naming is simply a practice of social convention and custom, and Cratylus, a naturalist who asserts that names carry an intrinsic relation to the things they signify.

> **The Naming of Things**
>
> 'But if the primary names are to be representations of any things, can you suggest any better way of making them representations than by making them as much as possible like the things which they are to represent? Or do you prefer the theory advanced by Hermogenes and many others, who claim that names are conventional and represent things to those who established the convention and knew the things beforehand, and that convention is the sole principle of correctness in names, and it makes no difference whether we accept the existing convention or adopt an opposite one according to which small would be called great and great small? Which of these two theories do you prefer?'
>
> Socrates to Cratylus, in Plato, *Cratylus* (1926: 169).

Over two thousand years later, Ferdinand de Saussure, a Swiss linguist working at the turn of the twentieth century, established a basis from which modern linguists have tackled Plato's riddle. In his *Cours de linguistique générale*, Saussure introduced a number of principles that were designed to underpin a 'scientific' and structural approach to language study. Most relevant to the dialogue in *Cratylus* is his first principle of language — 'the linguistic sign is arbitrary' (Saussure 1983: 67).

> **First Principle: The Sign is Arbitrary**
>
> The link between signal and signification is arbitrary. Since we are treating a sign as the combination in which a signal is associated with a signification, we can express this more simply as: *the linguistic sign is arbitrary*.
>
> There is no internal connection, for example, between the idea 'sister' and the French sequence of sounds *s-ö-r* which acts as its signal.
>
> Ferdinand de Saussure, *Course in General Linguistics* (1983: 67).

There is a great deal of explanatory power in Saussure's argument for the arbitrary nature of the linguistic sign. At a conceptual level, words are simply a combination of meaning and the sounds (or, in the case of the roughly two hundred known signed languages, movements) used to express meaning. Independent of language, meaning exists on a continuum. The naming of things partitions this meaning continuum into individual units. As a result, the meaningful content of these units can vary across different languages. Take, for instance, Saussure's example of the word for *sister*. French and English are similar in that both languages have one word to refer to female siblings, *sœur* and *sister* respectively. Chinese, on the other hand, has two words, *jiějie* (姐姐) for older sisters and *mèimei* (妹妹) for younger sisters. Chinese, French and English parcel out the continuum of meaning differently. Whereas French and English note only the sibling relationship and the gender, Chinese includes the element of birth order. Equally arbitrary are the sounds we use to relay this meaning. Neither *mèimei* nor *jiějie* share sound patterns with the English word *sister* yet all of these combinations of sound are used to reference a similar meaning. French, *sœur*, and English, *sister*, on the other hand, do have an aural resemblance, but this is not proof of Cratylus's argument for naturalness in naming. Rather, the similarities between the French and English systems stem from the fact that the two words share a common ancestor. Arbitrariness in language thus offers linguists tremendous explanatory power in understanding the creative power of language, as well as how languages interrelate and change. The languages we speak may categorize our shared experiences of the world in different ways. In a further association between biological evolution and the development of language, the debate over the arbitrariness of the sign in linguistics resonates with a long-standing debate over the reality of species in biology and thence also whether a biological reality exists that can be expressed through taxonomy and nomenclature (Gosler 2017).

Yet, in our understanding of language and its creativity, there is room also for Cratylus and his naturalist perspective. The linguistic sign may be arbitrary, but the act of naming is not necessarily random. The study of neologisms finds that root creations — new words with no contextual or referential basis — are rare. More frequently new vocabulary enters a language with a pre-established context. Words are born of personal names (eponyms) or place names (toponyms) (Thornton 2012). They can be compounds of words already present within the language or portmanteaus, blends of sounds and meanings from other words. Our environments and senses can give us words in the form of onomatopoeia, sound symbolism and other forms of iconicity (Berlin 2006).

The naming of birds across unrelated languages gives us examples of iconicity in naming. It may seem arbitrary whether a bird is named after its voice, appearance, behaviour or the context in which it is encountered, but these at least in part result from the bird's salience within a particular community and, inasmuch as that might direct its naming, it will not be random (Hunn 1999, Gosler 2017). Furthermore, creative processes in language change are often reflected in bird names. These may specifically reflect what is culturally salient to a people at a particular place and time. For example, there are sixty-nine recorded English folk names for the Stonechat (*Saxicola torquata*), a small passerine bird strongly associated with heathland and gorse or furze (plants in the genus *Ulex*) in Britain. Whilst fifty-seven of these names are habitat-related, typically indicating where the bird is found, e.g. furze-chuck, furze-jack, furze-cheqer, furze-chucker, furze-chick, furze-chatterer etc. (Desfayes 1998), a further seven local names refer to horses: horse-snatcher, horse-matcher, horse-masher, horse-smatch, horsematch, horse-smitch and horse-mate (some of this variation is ideolectical). The association between this bird and horses may have arisen because the Stonechat's call, which recalls the sound of two stones struck together, also resembles the tongue-click commonly made to encourage a horse to walk on. Indeed, this is how one would imitate the bird's call (Gosler 2019). This is a good example of how local cultural practices can lead to name changes over time or in different places.

Fig. 2 Akkadian cuneiform on the wings of a stone bas-relief eagle-headed genie from Nimrud, Assyria. This giant figure was meant to magically protect a doorway. Held at the Ashmolean Museum, Oxford. Reproduced by kind permission of the Ashmolean Museum, Oxford (exhibit); photograph by Felice S. Wyndham (2014).

The names of birds cue ecological and cultural information. Cross-cultural comparative research within Europe (Desfayes 1998; Gosler and Jackson-Houlston 2012) and worldwide (Wyndham and Park 2018) gives insight into linguistic and cultural understandings of local environments. When names are mapped across countries, counties and even towns, patterns of use that reflect historical patterns of settlement and resettlement of the land emerge. For example, the English common name for *Turdus torquatus*, Ring Ouzel, makes a clear reference to an old name for the Blackbird (*Turdus merula*), the Ouzel, which appears to have been in use mainly in the north of England and Scotland. Where did 'Ouzel' come from? Among European names it resonates most closely with Germanic names such as *Amsel*. Does this imply an Anglo-Saxon origin in England or does its geographic distribution in fact indicate something else?

Language Ecologies: Naming the Local in Languages

Most cultures include in their mythologies and legends tales of the first language, exploring themes of origin and diversification. Frequently

> **To Name is to Create**
>
> Naming is also an act of creation. For example, the Yavapai culture heroes Widapokwi and Amchitapuka name the months and constellations. The Alsea black bear Suku names the rivers. The Kutenai figure Nalmuqtse is depicted as crawling about naming things. Of related interest are the Navajo figures Long Life Boy and Happiness Girl, who personify speech and thought.
>
> Sam Gill and Irene Sullivan, *Dictionary of Native American Mythology* (1992: 208).

these myths locate the language's genesis within a greater natural ecology. Over four millennia ago in China, Cangjie (倉頡), a historian for the Yellow Emperor, founded the Chinese writing system through a close study of nature; in the Abrahamic tradition the first man Adam was tasked by God with naming every living creature; and once upon a time in Mexico, a dove taught language to the children Coxcox and Xochiquetzal, the only Mexica to have survived a great flood (Zhang 2005; Turner and Russell-Coulter 2001).

> **The Language of the Toltecs and the Aztecs**
>
> Coxcox [and] his wife Xochiquetzal alone escaped the deluge. They took refuge in the hollow trunk of a cypress (*ahuehuete*), which floated upon the water, and stopped at last on top of a mountain of Culhuacan. They had many children, but all of them were dumb. The great spirit took pity on them, and sent a dove, who hastened to teach them to speak. Fifteen of the children succeeded in grasping the power of speech, and from these the Toltecs and Aztecs are descended.
>
> Susan Hale, *Mexico* (1891: 23).

Language exists in the mind as an infinitely creative cognitive system. It exists in human communities, inextricably intertwined with cultural and personal identities, places and times (Garner 2004). And it exists in the ideas and experiences that are relevant to our generation and the environments in which we live. The concept of language ecology, championed by linguist Einar Haugen in the mid-twentieth century

(Haugen 1972), adopts the metaphor of an ecosystem in order to locate language within the context of its larger geographic, social and cultural environment:

> Language ecology may be defined as the study of interactions between any given language and its environment [...] The true environment of a language is the society that uses it as one of its codes. Language exists only in the minds of its users, and it only functions in relating those users to one another and to nature, i.e. their social and natural environment. (Haugen 1972: 57)

Though the analogy implies a linguistic context that is systemic with inputs and outputs, its realization is more broadly interpreted as a framework for understanding how human languages relate to changing geographic and social contexts in which they are used.

Our lexicons reflect these changes. Many young people today struggle to readily name birds, trees, butterflies and flowers (for Britain, see Gosler 2018). In 2007 a hubbub erupted around the fact that the *Oxford Junior Dictionary* replaced a number of words for the natural world, including *acorn*, *bluebell*, *wren* and *pasture*, with words such as *blog*, *chatroom* and *database*, reflecting a rise in electronic interfaces in contemporary culture. On one level this is par for the course as languages change over time. Speakers of English now rarely use words such as *timwhisky*, *jinker* and *cariole* because automobiles have replaced horse-drawn carriages as a major means of transportation. Equally, effects of language contact and natural sound change have contributed to the fact that we no longer sound like Shakespeare, Chaucer or Æthelweard. But there is a reciprocal relationship in the process of language evolution as it relates to changing social contexts. Names, metaphors and stories give us a framework for conscious awareness of our surroundings. The backlash to the *Oxford Junior Dictionary*'s edits has led to a widespread conversation about the state of British nature knowledge, its vocabularies and its relevance to ecological challenges in the future. One particularly compelling and beautiful response has been the children's book *The Lost Words*, written by Robert Macfarlane and illustrated by Jackie Morris, which invokes several words for flora and fauna cut from the dictionary in a series of word poems and lush watercolour images.

Fig. 3 Children's mural depicting a kingfisher, leaves and river names, West Oxford Community Centre. Photograph by kind permission of Felice S. Wyndham (2019).

Reconnecting Kids with Nature is Vital, and Needs Cultural Leadership

We the undersigned are profoundly alarmed to learn that the *Oxford Junior Dictionary* has systematically been stripped of many words associated with nature and the countryside. We write to plead that the next edition sees the reinstatement of words cut since 2007.

We base this plea on two considerations. Firstly, the belief that nature and culture have been linked from the beginnings of our history. For the first time ever, that link is in danger of becoming unravelled, to the detriment of society, culture and the natural environment.

Secondly, childhood is undergoing profound change; some of this is negative; and the rapid decline in children's connections to nature is a major problem.

In all, the names for thirty species of common or important British plants and animals have been removed — such as acorn and bluebell — along with many words connected with farming and food. Many are highly symbolic of our cultural ties with the land, its wildlife and produce.

This is what the National Trust says in their Natural Childhood campaign: *Every child should have the right to connect with nature.*

Margaret Atwood et al., Letter to the Oxford University Press (2015).

Ecolinguistics has emerged as a framework for engaging with the interplay between language and environmental sustainability. It opens up a space for exploring the relationship between cultural change, language change and the natural world, for example through discourse analysis (Stibbe 2015). In addition to increased awareness and understanding, the framework has a practical motivation:

> Ecolinguistics explores the role of language in the life-sustaining interactions of humans, other species and the physical environment. The first aim is to develop linguistic theories which see humans not only as part of society, but also as part of the larger ecosystems that life depends on. The second aim is to show how linguistics can be used to address key ecological issues, from climate change and biodiversity loss to environmental justice. (The International Ecolinguistics Association)

Practical approaches to the ecological consequences of our language systems, however, do face translation challenges. Human engagement with the environment is not simply embedded in our systems of naming, it is present in how we talk about, classify and understand the world, a fact that can lead to translation conundrums at a cultural level. Whereas many urbanized cultures tend to interpret biological diversity and robustness of knowledge through the application of the scientific method and quantifiable results, many other cultures transmit this knowledge through everyday practices, stories, song and other varied arts.

> **Traditional Ecological Knowledge**
>
> A substantial part of any language is devoted to the description of biological phenomena, so that we cannot give a complete account of how any language functions without examining how it represents these in its vocabulary, grammar and phraseology. And, in an era when there is increasing appreciation of how much small-scale speech communities know about the natural world that have yet to be 'discovered' by mainstream biology, the study of little-documented languages is a natural key to unlocking the full dimensions of Traditional Ecological Knowledge.
>
> Nicholas Evans and Nicholas Thieberger, 'The Web of Words and the Web of Life' (2013).

It is no accident that Indigenous languages are often targeted first in programmes of national assimilation. Language engenders creativity, and creative flourishing threatens nationalizing and colonizing processes. Loss of language can sever continuity in the transmission of local ecological knowledge systems and, over generations, change peoples' relationships with environments and means of independent subsistence (Wyndham 2010). At the same time, by dispossessing peoples of land, colonizing systems rupture the environmental immersions and relationships that keep alive specialist vocabulary and social practices that communicate subtle ecological processes (Wyndham 2009). From a human rights perspective, scientists and scholars have an obligation and opportunity to work with local peoples as equals, to support initiatives to revitalize multilingual knowledge systems in parallel with the revitalization of rights to land, water and other resources.

From Local to Global: Creating a World that Values Biocultural Diversity

In 1988, a diverse community of scholars, practitioners and representatives from Indigenous and local communities gathered in Belém, Brazil for the First International Congress of Ethnobiology. An influential outcome of this gathering was the Declaration of Belém, which outlines eight steps towards integrating the needs, knowledges and contributions of Indigenous and local communities in global planning. In addition to providing an inclusive plan of action, the declaration clearly notes that 'native peoples have been stewards of 99 percent of the world's genetic resources; and that there is an inextricable link between cultural and biological diversity' (International Society of Ethnobiology 1988).

However, more often than not, the native peoples who do the day-to-day work of biocultural stewardship are minority groups in the larger national or global context. Achieving a precise count of the world's languages is challenging due to the difficulty involved in organizing a global framework for identifying speakers of unknown or less commonly known languages, regularly collecting information about languages on a global scale and even determining what exactly constitutes a

> **A Delicate Balance**
>
> Delicate tropical environments in particular must be managed with care and skill. It is indigenous peoples who have the relevant practical knowledge, since they have been successfully making a living in them for hundreds of generations. Much of this detailed knowledge about local ecosystems is encoded in indigenous language and rapidly being lost.
>
> Daniel Nettle and Suzanne Romaine, *Vanishing Voices: The Extinction of the World's Languages* (2000: 166).

language. To the best of our knowledge there are approximately 7,000 living languages in the world — of these, only 23 are spoken by more than half of the world's population and 40% are threatened or endangered (Endangered Languages Project; Ethnologue). The human rights contexts of these languages vary greatly, but many speakers of threatened languages face significant pressure to adopt a national language and/or abandon a native language. Some nations demand that individuals living within their boundaries speak a 'national' language and take extreme measures to prohibit the use of local languages. Equally, many speakers of minority languages see educating their children in a dominant language as a path to greater economic, intellectual or social influence and freedom. Dominant languages often spread at the expense of local languages, resulting in a loss of both sustainable local cultures and the important ecological knowledge contained within a language and a culture (Nettle and Romaine 2000).

> **Language Loss**
>
> Obviously we must do some serious rethinking of our priorities, lest linguistics go down in history as the only science that presided obliviously over the disappearance of the very field to which it is dedicated.
>
> Michael Krauss, 'The World's Languages in Crisis' (1992: 10).

Local stewardship of natural resources is also frequently challenged by a certain philosophy, particularly prevalent within the British and American conservation movements of the nineteenth century, that still permeates much of conservation practice to this day — the myth that our nature is a pristine wilderness untouched by human influence.

Most of what the West has labelled 'pristine wilderness' has, at some point in time, been named and shaped by people (Boivin et al. 2016). For example, according to the World Wide Fund for Nature, the Amazon rainforest is home to 'over three thousand indigenous territories' as well as 'over 10% of the planet's known biodiversity' (WWF). The establishment of the great American National Parks in the nineteenth century came at a tremendous cost to the Indigenous peoples who once lived in, and were systematically removed from, these lands — a heritage still preserved in names like Yosemite (*Yohhe'meti*, Southern Miwok or *Yos s e'meti*, Central Miwok), Appalachia (possibly *abalahci*, Apalachee or *apalwahči*, Muskogean) and Mississippi (*Misiziibi*, Ojibwe). As noted by Victoria Tauli-Corpuz, the United Nations Special Rapporteur on the Rights of Indigenous Peoples, the practice of removing local peoples from their native lands in the name of conservation continues to this day:

> The establishment of national parks and conservation areas has resulted in serious and systemic violations of Indigenous peoples' rights through expropriation of their traditional lands and territories, forced displacement and killings of their community members, non-recognition of their authorities, denial of access to livelihood activities and spiritual sites and subsequent loss of their culture. (Tauli-Corpuz 2016)

Just as a number of linguists and anthropologists are working towards a more biologically nuanced approach to language and culture, conservation initiatives have recognized for decades the core need to work closely with local peoples. BirdLife International, an integral collaborator in our work, is one such organization. Taking a local-to-global approach to bird conservation, BirdLife is renowned for its path-breaking governance system of bottom-up streaming of local bird conservation priorities into a global Partnership and Secretariat, which, in turn, lobby on behalf of local voices. Likewise, the 2019 report of the Intergovernmental Science-Policy Platform on Biodiversity and Ecosystem Services (IPBES) is the first global assessment ever to systematically include Indigenous and local knowledge, issues and priorities.

> **There are People in the Park**
>
> Traditional Indigenous territories encompass around 22 per cent of the world's land surface and they coincide with areas that hold 80 per cent of the planet's biodiversity. There is increasing recognition that the ancestral lands of Indigenous peoples contain the most intact ecosystems and provide the most effective and sustainable form of conservation.
>
> Victoria Tauli-Corpuz, 'Statement of Ms. Victoria Tauli-Corpuz, Special Rapporteur on the Rights of Indigenous Peoples' (2016).

Fig. 4 Abel Rodríguez, *Ciclo anual del bosque de la vega* (2009–2010). Details of ecological relations with land animals and fish, drawn from memory by Abel Rodríguez, Nonuya Indigenous man from the Middle Caquetá River. He is a great authority on the world of plants and forests, and considered a leading light for the exchange of knowledge with the academy and the art world, based on his interaction of more than three decades with researchers in the tropical forest. Reproduced by kind permission of Abel Rodríguez.

In the hundred and fifty years since Darwin wrote of the 'curious parallels' between species and languages, his observation has expanded to encompass our understanding of biodiversity, linguistic diversity, endangerment and revitalization. Through scholarship and practice oriented towards biocultural diversity and recognition of the rich systems of knowledge and stewardship often maintained by local peoples, practice in conservation and scholarship is taking a more nuanced approach to our complex social and natural ecologies. However, at the global level much of this work remains compartmentalized within the spheres of expertise of different disciplines and practices.

Our work brings together local knowledge holders, anthropologists, biologists, linguists and conservationists to craft a more comprehensive approach to engaging biocultural diversity in practice. We are pursuing both on-the-ground local networks and providing accessible digital tools geared towards citizen science through the Ethno-ornithology World Atlas (EWA), public awareness and the local-to-global sharing of knowledge and expertise (Wyndham et al. 2016).

Working together across disciplines in recognition of the interrelatedness of people, language and place, we have the potential to develop global networks that can lead to better systems of language documentation and a more nuanced understanding of local knowledge in conservation practice, as well as provide a global platform from which local communities can actively engage in dialogue around their cultures and environments.

Fig. 5 Logo of the 2019 symposium *Intersections of Language and Nature*, organized by Karen Park, Felice S. Wyndham, John Fanshawe and Andrew Gosler. It brought together scholars from Indigenous communities, conservation practice, the arts, and academia to address the parallel and intersecting threats facing linguistic and biological diversity (www.iln2019.com). Reproduced by kind permission from Karen Park.

Works Cited

Atwood, Margaret et al. 2015. 'Reconnecting Kids with Nature is Vital, and Needs Cultural Leadership', Letter to the Oxford University Press., http://www.naturemusicpoetry.com/uploads/2/9/3/8/29384149/letter_to_oup_final.pdf

Berlin, Brent. 2006. 'The First Congress of Ethnozoological Nomenclature', *Journal of the Royal Anthropological Institute*, 12(s1): S23–S44, https://doi.org/10.1111/j.1467-9655.2006.00271.x

Boivin, N., et al. 2016. 'Ecological Consequences of Human Niche Construction: Examining Long-Term Anthropogenic Shaping of Global Species Distributions', *Proceedings of the National Academy of Sciences of the United States of America*, 113(23): 6388–96, https://doi.org/10.1073/pnas.1525200113

Creative Multilingualism. 2020. https://www.creativeml.ox.ac.uk

Darwin, Charles. 1871. *The Descent of Man, and Selection in Relation to Sex* (London: John Murray), https://doi.org/10.5962/bhl.title.2092

Desfayes, Michel. 1998. *A Thesaurus of Bird Names: Etymology of European Lexis through Paradigms*, 2 vols (Sion, Switzerland: The Museum of Natural History).

Endangered Languages Project. 2020. www.endangeredlanguages.com

Ethnologue. 2020. https://www.ethnologue.com

Ethno-ornithology World Atlas. 2020. https://ewatlas.net

Evans, Nicholas, and Nicholas Thieberger. 2013. 'The Web of Words and the Web of Life', 3rd International Conference on Language Documentation and Conservation, 23 February, University of Hawai'i, Hawai'I, https://scholarspace.manoa.hawaii.edu/handle/10125/26184

Feld, Steven. 1990. *Sound and Sentiment*, 2nd edn (Durham, NC: Duke University Press).

Garner, M. 2004. *Language: An Ecological View* (Oxford: Peter Lang).

Gill, Sam, and Irene Sullivan. 1992. *Dictionary of Native American Mythology* (Santa Barbara, CA: ABC-CLIO).

Gosler, Andrew G. 2017. 'The Human Factor: Ecological Salience in Ornithology and Ethno-Ornithology', *Journal of Ethnobiology*, 37(4): 637–62, https://doi.org/10.2993/0278-0771-37.4.637

Gosler, Andrew G. 2018. 'Knowledge of Nature and the Nature of Knowledge,' Paper presented at the International Society for Ethnobiology Conference, 9 August, Belém, Brazil.

Gosler, Andrew G. 2019. 'What's in a Name: The Legacy and Lexicon of Birds', *British Wildlife*, 30: 391–97.

Gosler, Andrew G., and Caroline M. Jackson-Houlston. 2012. 'A Nightingale by Any Other Name? Relations Between Scientific and Vernacular Bird Naming', *Proceedings — Ecosystem Services: Do We Need Birds?*, Proceedings of the British Ornithologists' Union's 2012 Annual Conference, 3–5 April, University of Leicester, Leicester, https://www.bou.org.uk/bouproc-net/ecosystem-services/gosler&jackson-houlston.pdf

Hale, Susan. 1891. *Mexico* (New York: G. P. Putnam's Sons).

Harmon, D. 1996. 'Losing Species, Losing Languages: Connections Between Biological and Linguistic Diversity', *Southwest Journal of Linguistics*, 15(1&2): 89–108.

Haugen, Einar. 1972. *The Ecology of Language* (Stanford: Stanford University Press).

Hunn, Eugene S. 1999. 'Size as Limiting the Recognition of Biodiversity in Folk Biological Classifications; One of Four Factors Governing the Cultural Recognition of Biological Taxa', in *Folkbiology*, ed. by D. Medin and S. Atran (Cambridge, MA: Harvard University Press), pp. 47–69.

Intergovernmental Science-Policy Platform on Biodiversity and Ecosystem Services. 2019. *Global Assessment Report on Biodiversity and Ecosystem Services*, https://ipbes.net/global-assessment

International Ecolinguistics Association. 2020. http://ecolinguistics-association.org

International Society of Ethnobiology. 1988. 'Declaration of Belém', http://www.ethnobiology.net/what-we-do/core-programs/global-coalition-2/declaration-of-belem/

Krauss, Michael. 1992. 'The World's Languages in Crisis', *Language*, 68(1): 4–10, https://doi.org/10.1353/lan.1992.0075

Loh, Jonathan, and David Harmon. 2005. 'A Global Index of Biocultural Diversity', *Ecological Indicators*, 5(3): 231–41, https://doi.org/10.1016/j.ecolind.2005.02.005

Macfarlane, Robert, and Jackie Morris. 2017. *The Lost Words* (London: Hamish Hamilton)

Maffi, Luisa (ed.). 2001. *On Biocultural Diversity: Linking Language, Knowledge and the Environment* (Washington, DC: Smithsonian Institution Press).

Nettle, Daniel, and Suzanne Romaine. 2000. *Vanishing Voices: The Extinction of the World's Languages* (Oxford: Oxford University Press).

Plato. 1926. *Cratylus*, in *Cratylus. Parmenides. Greater Hippias. Lesser Hippias*, trans. by Harold North Fowler, Loeb Classical Library 167 (Cambridge, MA: Harvard University Press), pp. 1–193.

Saussure, Fernand de. 1983. *Course in General Linguistics*, ed. by Charles Bally and Albert Sechehaye, trans. and annotated by Roy Harris (London: Duckworth).

Singh, Ranjay, Jules Pretty and Sarah Pilgrim. 2010. 'Traditional Knowledge and Biocultural Diversity: Learning from Tribal Communities for Sustainable Development in Northeast India', *Journal of Environmental Planning and Management*, 53(4): 511–33, https://doi.org/10.1080/09640561003722343

Stepp, J. R., F. S. Wyndham and R. K. Zarger (eds). 2002. *Ethnobiology & Biocultural Diversity* (Athens: University of Georgia Press).

Stibbe, Arran. 2015. *Ecolinguistics: Language, Ecology and the Stories We Live By* (Abingdon: Routledge).

Sutherland, William J. 2003. 'Parallel Extinction Risk and Global Distribution of Languages and Species', *Nature*, 423(6937): 276–79, https://doi.org/10.1038/nature01607

Tauli-Corpuz, Victoria. 2016. 'Statement of Ms. Victoria Tauli-Corpuz, Special Rapporteur on the Rights of Indigenous Peoples, at the 71st session of the General Assembly', 17 October, New York, https://www.ohchr.org/EN/NewsEvents/Pages/DisplayNews.aspx?NewsID=20748&LangID=E

Terralingua. 2017. 'What Is Biocultural Diversity?', https://terralingua.org

Thornton, Thomas F. (ed.). 2012. *Haa Leelk'w Has Aani Saax'u / Our Grandparents' Names on the Land* (Seattle: University of Washington Press).

Turner, Patricia, and Charles Russell-Coulter. 2001. *Dictionary of Ancient Deities* (Oxford: Oxford University Press).

WWF, 'Protected Areas and Indigenous Territories', http://wwf.panda.org/knowledge_hub/where_we_work/amazon/vision_amazon/living_amazon_initiative222/protected_areas_and_indigenous_territories/

Wyndham, Felice S. 2010. 'Environments of Learning: Rarámuri Children's Plant Knowledge & Experience of Schooling, Family, and Landscapes in the Sierra Tarahumara, Mexico', *Human Ecology*, 38(1): 87–99, https://doi.org/10.1007/s10745-009-9287-5

Wyndham, Felice S. 2009. 'Spheres of Relations, Lines of Interaction: Subtle Ecologies of the Rarámuri Landscape in Northern Mexico', *Journal of Ethnobiology*, 29(2): 271–95, https://doi.org/10.2993/0278-0771-29.2.271

Wyndham, Felice S., Ada M. Grabowska-Zhang, Andrew G. Gosler, Karen E. Park, John Fanshawe, David Nathan, Heidi Fletcher and Josep del Hoyo. 2016. 'The Ethno-ornithology World Archive (EWA): An Open Science Archive for Biocultural Conservation', *Revista Chilena de Ornitología*, 22: 141–46.

Wyndham, Felice S., and Karen Park. 2018. '"Listen Carefully to the Voices of the Birds": A Comparative Review of Birds as Signs', *Journal of Ethnobiology*, 38(4): 533–49, https://doi.org/10.2993/0278-0771-38.4.533

Zhang, Shudong. 2005. 中华印刷通史 (*A General History of Chinese Printing*) (Taipei: XingCai Literary Foundation).

Find Out More

Ethno-ornithology World Atlas. 2020, https://ewatlas.net

EWA is an online space that promotes nature and language conservation: a place where communities can record and share their knowledge, language traditions and understandings of nature. EWA is about building relationships between Indigenous and local communities, conservationists, academics and their institutions, to promote bird and language conservation through the engagement with, respect for and celebration of diverse cultural traditions of knowledge.

Evans, Nicholas. 2010. *Dying Words: Endangered Languages and What They Have to Tell Us* (Oxford: Wiley-Blackwell).

Nicholas Evans writes with eloquence and insight on language diversity, bringing into stark focus what we stand to lose in a time of massive language extinction.

Gosler, Andrew, Karen Park and Felice S. Wyndham. 2020. 'Creating a Meaningful World: Nature in Name, Metaphor and Myth', Research Strand 2 of Creative Multilingualism, https://www.creativeml.ox.ac.uk/research/naming

Research project on naming conducted as part of the Creative Multilingualism programme between 2016 and 2020. This chapter draws on that research.

Loh, Jonathan, and David Harmon. 2014. *Biocultural Diversity: Threatened Species, Endangered Languages* (Zeist: WWF-Netherlands).

A clear and concise overview of biocultural diversity, engaging with the topic on the themes of evolution, decline and status.

Macfarlane, Robert, and Jackie Morris. 2017. *The Lost Words* (London: Hamish Hamilton).

In response to the 2007 decision by the editorial team of the *Oxford Junior Dictionary* to replace several words for the natural world with words for the Internet age, author Robert Macfarlane and illustrator Jackie Morris created *The Lost Words*. The book is both a work of art and a compelling reminder of the magic and power of language.

Maffi, Luisa (ed.). 2001. *On Biocultural Diversity: Linking Language Knowledge and the Environment* **(Washington, DC: Smithsonian Institution Press).**

This compilation of papers from an interdisciplinary group of leaders working in academia, advocacy and Indigenous communities provides a compelling discussion of connections across biological, linguistic and cultural diversity.

Saussure, Fernand de. 1983. *Course in General Linguistics,* **ed. by Charles Bally and Albert Sechehaye, trans. and annotated by Roy Harris (London: Duckworth).**

Cours de linguistique générale (1916) was foundational to modern linguistic theory, introducing a 'scientific' approach to language study and establishing both the study of semiotics and structural linguistics. Though introduced over a hundred years ago, Saussure's general principles remain widely accepted as fundamental to linguistic research, including naming.

Credits

Permission to include their contribution was kindly granted by the following:

The Ashmolean Museum (exhibit) and Felice S. Wyndham (photograph) for the Akkadian cuneiform on the wings of a stone bas-relief eagle-headed genie from Nimrud, Assyria (Fig. 2).

William Darwin for the drawing by Francis Darwin (?) (c. 1858), drawn on the back of the original manuscript for Charles Darwin's *On the Origin of Species* (1859) by one of Darwin's children (Fig. 1).

Karen Park for the logo of the 2019 symposium *Intersections of Language and Nature,* organized by Karen Park, Felice S. Wyndham, John Fanshawe and Andrew Gosler (Fig. 5).

Abel Rodríguez and Tropenbos, Colombia for his drawing *Ciclo anual del bosque de la vega,* 2009–2010 (Fig. 4).

Felice S. Wyndham for the photograph of the children's mural depicting a kingfisher, leaves and river names, West Oxford Community Centre, 2019 (Fig. 3).

3. Not as 'Foreign' as You Think

Creating Bridges of Understanding across Languages

Martin Maiden, Chiara Cappellaro and Aditi Lahiri

> We're more multilingual than we think

One of the authors of this chapter grew up in the south of England in the 1960s. Just about the only language he could ever hear spoken was the one he, too, spoke all the time — English. Foreign languages were just that, 'foreign'. They were 'foreign' in the sense that they were spoken by 'foreigners', people who were not British and lived outside Britain. You heard foreign languages if you went abroad, say, on holiday. Those languages were also 'foreign' in the sense that they all seemed quite alien, impossible to understand, at best strange speech-sounds to which no meaning could be attached. Indeed, so difficult and strange were they that some of them, such as French or German, were formidable subjects on the school timetable, alongside, for example, maths or biology. Another of the authors grew up in the north-east of Italy, speaking Italian. But Italian was not the only language she heard. Older members of her family spoke a different language, Friulian, the traditional heritage language of the region, and one that was fairly remote from Italian. She understood it, but nobody ever expected her to speak it. And if she went a few kilometres from her native town, she could hear yet another, far more different, language, Slovenian — today the national language of the Republic of Slovenia, which shares a border with Italy.

The third author grew up in Kolkata (India), where it was normal to hear and actively speak two or three languages, such as Bengali, Hindi and English.

Now the real 'oddity' here is the author who grew up in England. Most human beings who have ever lived have grown up in a world where 'other' languages are not 'foreign' languages, where it is simply normal to hear other languages spoken around you — and normal to understand and speak some of those languages. There is a widespread tendency to assume, by the way, that there is a natural, one-to-one match between a country and a language. In fact, this is true only in the rarest of cases (Iceland might be an example, where the entire native population speaks Icelandic — but is nowadays almost entirely competent in a foreign language, namely English). Virtually all national states are multilingual. India, for example, is estimated to have over 700 languages; even the United Kingdom, despite the predominance of English, nowadays also has, in addition to languages which are native to Britain, such as Welsh, Scots Gaelic, or Ulster Scots, numerous immigrant languages such as Bengali, Hindi, Italian, Polish, Portuguese, Punjabi or Romanian — yet in the United Kingdom it has often been possible to be confined to an entirely English-speaking world, in which other languages may seem to be bizarre intrusions from outside.

Those of us who have grown up in this way are in fact missing a golden opportunity for contact with another language and possibly with another culture, and often we do not realize that we are much closer to that apparently impenetrable other language than we think. Indeed, if one has grown up in a 'monoglot' world (i.e. one where only one language is used), exposure to other languages — actually the normal situation for most human beings — can even become awkward, or uncomfortable, or downright threatening. At its worst, exposure to multilingualism can be perceived as menacing and make members of monoglot societies feel isolated and hostile towards speakers of those other languages. Such feelings of alienation can be alleviated if societies are aware that 'foreign' languages are not inaccessible barriers to comprehension, that many doors into other languages are already open, and that what seems alien may be much more familiar than might at first appear. The impression of alienation can turn into something much worse: real alienation and exclusion. To the extent that we do not know some language, we are indeed 'locked out' of the societies and the cultures that express themselves through that language, indeed we might very well claim that people have a *right* to be introduced to other languages, and that any properly functioning education system has a *duty* to assist children to gain access to those languages. There is a crudely statistical way of representing this fact, taking as an example the place of English and German in Europe: at a conservative estimate there are in Europe 70 million native speakers of English and about 95 million native speakers of German. It follows that if you speak *both* languages you have the potential to understand and/or communicate directly with 165 million people on our continent; if you only speak English you have less than half that capacity. The monoglot is simply less 'free', less 'powerful', than the person who has even a small command of another language. For centuries, whole lives are and have been lived in, for instance, German (or countless other languages), with the entire range of human activities — cultural, routine, commercial — conducted in German. If we have no access to the language, then the only way that we can ever have access to the world expressed in it is through the kind indulgence of German-speakers (for example) who have taken the trouble to learn English. We are reduced to mere dependency on the linguistic skill of others.

We can create solutions to this kind of disadvantage, and we can do this particularly via children of school age who are naturally endowed with the kind of linguistic flexibility which, if properly cultivated, can make them veritable linguistic 'acrobats', able to jump with fluent ease from one language to another. It is *never* too late to learn a foreign language, even in late old age, but our children are those best equipped to do it, and our schools have a responsibility to show that bridges into other languages can be built in ways that are perhaps not expected. A very useful starting point is to make children realize that they may already be able to *understand* more of a foreign language than they suspect, and that they can build on that understanding to understand — and eventually to express — even more.

Finding Long-Lost Relatives

All human beings have relatives. Some may be close, like sisters, brothers, mothers or fathers. Others can be more distant, such as cousins, or cousins once removed, or any number of times removed. Sometimes, even distant relatives look familiar simply because they have a common ancestor with us, and it can be a pleasant surprise to discover that we have

Fig. 1 Félix Gallet, 'Arbre généalogique des langues mortes et vivantes [...]' ('Genealogical tree of dead and living languages [...]') (Paris, c. 1800). Bibliothèque nationale de France. Public Domain, https://gallica.bnf.fr/ark:/12148/bpt6k8546015

something in common with them. Languages are not so very different, and genetic relationships across languages — as with families — have often been visualized as trees (for one of the first examples of such an idealization, see Fig. 1, produced in France around 1800, and for a more schematic representation see Chapter 8 in this volume).

Other languages that are apparently 'foreign' to us may turn out to have more in common with a language we already speak than we ever suspected. They may actually contain hidden links that we can use to create bridges between our own language and them. They may turn out to be less 'foreign' after all.

If you are British, you probably think of Dutch, German, Danish, Norwegian, Swedish or Icelandic as truly 'foreign' languages. One of these, German, used to be widely taught as a 'foreign language' in British schools. It is surprising that it no longer is so commonly studied, because, as we have seen, it has a good claim to being the 'biggest' language in Europe, having the largest number of native speakers. If one's starting point is English, German certainly sounds foreign. Yet English and German, and all the other languages mentioned above (plus numerous, lesser-known, languages such as Frisian, or Faroese, or Afrikaans) all have a common *ancestor* language, labelled 'proto-Germanic'. And these languages are related to other 'families' of languages such as 'Romance languages' (French, Spanish, Portuguese, Italian, Romanian and others) or 'Slavonic languages' (e.g., Russian, Polish, Bulgarian) or 'Indo-Aryan languages' (e.g., Punjabi, Hindi, Gujarati, Bengali). These families in turn have a common ancestor, called 'proto-Indo-European', spoken five to six thousand years ago in an area of Europe around Ukraine and neighbouring regions in the Caucasus and southern Russia. Speakers of this language and their descendants gradually spread out over large areas of northern Europe. As these communities drifted apart, their speech gradually changed, so that over the centuries there emerged different languages, and speakers of one would have found it increasingly difficult to understand the speech of the other. In fact, it is estimated that just under half of the modern population of the earth speaks an 'Indo-European' language. Exactly how closely related different languages are to each other is often unclear and controversial, but the relationship for the modern Germanic family goes something like this:

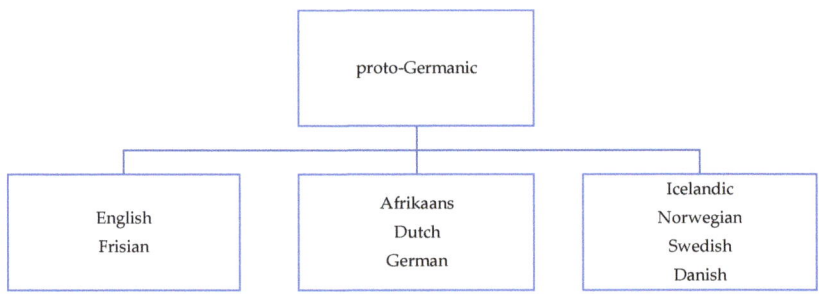

There is a similar story for another group of Indo-European languages widely spoken in Europe, the so-called *Romance* languages, which get their name because they all descend from the Latin spoken by ordinary people in the *Roman* Empire, nearly two thousand years ago. All of Portuguese, Spanish, Catalan, French, Italian, Romanian and many other languages that are probably less well-known (such as Occitan, Romansh, Sardinian, Ladin, Friulian), have a common origin in Latin. Their relationship is something like this:

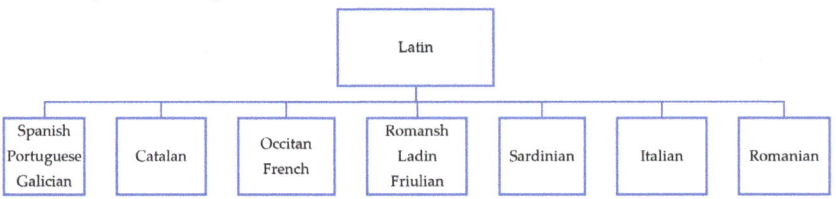

If we take some basic everyday notions, for example names of body parts, the 'family' resemblance between these languages becomes apparent pretty fast (especially if we see the words in writing, but also when we hear them spoken). In each case, the resemblance is a consequence of these languages having inherited words from a common ancestor:

Table 1 Germanic languages

English	Dutch	German	Icelandic	Norwegian	Swedish	Danish
hand	*hand*	*Hand*	*hönd*	*hånd*	*hand*	*hånd*
finger	*vinger*	*Finger*	*fingur*	*finger*	*finger*	*finger*
nail	*nagel*	*Nagel*	*nagli*	*negl*	*nagel*	*negl*
leg	*been*	*Bein*	*fótur*	*bein*	*ben*	*ben*
knee	*knie*	*Knie*	*hné*	*kne*	*knä*	*knæ*
foot	*voet*	*Fuß*	*fótur*	*fot*	*fot*	*fod*
tooth	*tand*	*Zahn*	*tönn*	*tann*	*tand*	*tand*
eye	*oog*	*Auge*	*auga*	*øye*	*öga*	*øje*

Table 2 Romance languages

Portuguese	Spanish	Catalan	French	Italian	Romanian	
mão	*mano*	*má*	*main*	*mano*	*mână*	hand
dedo	*dedo*	*dit*	*doigt*	*dito*	*deget*	finger
unha	*uña*	*ungla*	*ongle*	*unghia*	*unghie*	nail
perna	*pierna*	*cama*	*jambe*	*gamba*	*picior*	leg
joelho	*rodilla*	*genoll*	*genou*	*ginocchio*	*genunchi*	knee
pé	*pie*	*peu*	*pied*	*piede*	*picior*	foot
dente	*diente*	*dent*	*dent*	*dente*	*dinte*	tooth
olho	*ojo*	*ull*	*œil*	*occhio*	*ochi*	eye

It is clear, of course, that not all the languages listed have always inherited the same word. With the word for 'leg' in Portuguese and Spanish, versus the word in Catalan, French and Italian, versus the Romanian word, we are clearly dealing with a different word altogether. The same is true of the word for 'leg' in English versus Icelandic versus the other Germanic languages. In such cases we simply have to make the effort to learn the word and its meaning. But some of the differences between languages are actually *predictable*, if one knows certain 'tricks'.

Some 'Detective' Tricks: How Different Sounds May Hide the Same Word

In the history of languages, what was originally the same word can split into different forms which may end up losing their apparent connection. That can come about because sounds change, not randomly but in quite regular and systematic ways. This makes it possible for the learner to 'play detective', to realize that replacing a sound in one language with a sound in another may suddenly make an unfamiliar word familiar. Note the German word for 'tooth' in Table 1. Where English (and all the other sister languages) has 't', German has 'z' (pronounced 'ts'). This pattern of difference occurs again and again across the two languages. There are other patterns too, such as English 'th' tending to correspond to German 'd', or English 'd' tending to correspond to German 't'. These sound resemblances do not always work, and the details are rather more complex than we have made them appear here, but it is striking how often they do work. Given this knowledge, it is not difficult to guess the meaning of the following German words:

- *zwei* (a number); *zehn* (a number); *Zunge* (a part of the body); *Herz* (a part of the body); *sitzen* (opposite of 'stand'); *Zweig* (part of a tree).

- *drei* (a number); *Ding* (an object); *dünn* (physical appearance); *dick* (opposite of *dünn*); *danke* (what you say when someone gives you something); *denken* (verb for a mental activity).

- *tief* (an adjective that might be used when talking about water); *trinken* (something you might do with water); *Tropfen* (also involves water); *tot* (the opposite of alive); *Tür* (an entrance); *rot* (a colour).

To take some similar examples from Romance languages, it is very often the case that words that in Italian have 'p', 't', 'c' (where 'c' is pronounced 'k') between two vowels have 'b', 'd', and 'g' in Spanish. We see an example of this in Table 2 (Italian *dito* 'finger' versus Spanish *dedo*). So, if we know Italian *sapere* 'know', *potere* 'be able', *dico* 'I say' we can easily recognize the meanings of Spanish *saber*, *poder*, or *digo* (and vice versa). Another example of a systematic correspondence across languages applies to certain consonants followed by *l*: French *clé* 'key', Spanish *llave* 'key', Italian *chiave* 'key'. Given this, if one knows, say, French *pleuvoir* 'rain', *plein* 'full', *flamme* 'flame', one can easily recognize the meaning of Spanish *llover, lleno, llama* and Italian *piovere, pieno, fiamma*.

Hidden Resemblances between Unrelated Languages

It is possible that all human languages are ultimately related, and that they descend from one common ancestor language. This question is much argued over by linguists, but what is certain is that even if all languages are related, many of them are so distant from each other now that the kind of 'family resemblances' we mentioned earlier are lost. While we know that languages such as English and German, French and Portuguese, Russian and Czech, Welsh and Irish, Hindi and Bengali, Greek or Albanian, all descend from a common Indo-European ancestor language, there are other major language 'families' which are not related to Indo-European or to each other. Japanese, for example, is not obviously related to any other language, Arabic and Hebrew are related to each other and to a number of other languages of western Asia and northern Africa, but these groups are not obviously connected with Indo-European, or with Japanese, or with anything else — and so forth.

One might think that this means that if we speak a language of a different 'family', we do not have the kind of 'foot in the door' that we have been illustrating for more closely related groups of languages. This is not necessarily true, although the 'foot in the door' may be of a different kind, because when speakers of different languages come into contact, they also tend to *converge* linguistically. In effect, those people 'create bridges' between languages by 'borrowing' words (and some grammatical structures) from one language into another. This is especially true when speakers of one language bring to speakers of another language the names for things which simply do not exist in the culture of the latter group, such as foodstuffs or beverages originally peculiar to a particular part of the world which have then become spread by trade and other forms of contact across the world. We cannot go into the history of such terms here (although they are often fascinating stories), but the kind of effects we are talking about can be seen, for example, across German and Swedish, Spanish and Romanian, Russian and Bulgarian, modern Arabic or Japanese, etc. These are all

Table 3 Borrowing

German	Swedish	Spanish	Romanian	Russian	Bulgarian	Arabic	Japanese
Tomate	tomat	tomate	roșie	помидор (pomidor)	домат (domat)	طماطة (ṭamāṭa)	トマト (to ma to)
Tee	te	té	ceai	чай (chai)	чай (chai)	شاي (shāy)	お茶 (o cha)
Schokolade	choklad	chocolate	ciocolată	шоколад (shokolad)	шоколад (shokolad)	شوكولاتة (shukulata)	チョコレート (cho ko rē to)
Avocado	avokado	aguacate	avocado	авокадо (avokado)	авокадо (avokado)	أفوكاتو (afukatu)	アボカド (a bo ka do)
Kartoffel	potatis	patata	cartof	картошка (kartoshka)	картоф (kartof)	بطاطس (batatis)	じゃがいも (ja ga i mo)
Kaffee	kaffe	café	cafea	кофе (kofe)	кафе (kafe)	قهوة (qahwa)	コーヒー (kō hī)

clearly different languages that are more, or less, closely related (Arabic and Japanese are not related to any of the other languages listed, for example), but all or some of them often share what is recognizably the 'same word' for certain culturally diffused objects and concepts. Thus Table 3:

If your native language is English and you read the table from left to right, you can probably guess the meanings already from the first column (which happens to be German); in the case of the fifth row, you may have to wait until the second and third columns (Swedish and Spanish) to discern the meaning 'potato'. Some of the words may not be recognizable to English-speakers, but we will notice that they are shared across a number of languages which are not necessarily related or directly in contact with each other (for example, words beginning 'kart-' for 'potato'), or the Romanian, Russian, Bulgarian, Arabic and Japanese words for 'tea', all of which share a common origin. Compare also the now old-fashioned English 'a cup of *cha*', of the same origin. Ultimately, in fact, both the 'tea' type and the 'cha' type share a common origin, and reflect original dialectal variants of the same word in Chinese: for more about this point, see Dahl (2005). Sometimes, of course, there really are 'local' words with no obvious point of contact with other languages, such as the Japanese word for 'potato', or the Romanian for 'tomato'. It is worth saying that even here we can create paths to understanding; for example, the Romanian word *roșie* means 'red', so in the context of talking about vegetables you might still be able to guess that it means 'tomato' (and from there you might guess that a vegetable called a *vânătă* — literally, a 'purple' — is an 'aubergine'!). And sometimes, just a little knowledge of the sound system of the language may still help us to recognize old friends. Arabic does not have the sound 'p', and tends to replace it in foreign words with 'b' (which makes *batatis* 'potato' becomes a bit more familiar): so which European capital city is Arabic 'Baris'? Japanese systematically replaces 'f' with 'h' before the vowel sound 'i', so we can tell that *kōhī* is borrowed from English *coffee*. Japanese does not have the sound 'l', and usually replaces 'l' before a consonant in foreign words with 'ru'. Now that we know that, what is a フィルム (pronounced hirumu)?[1] Finally, the more languages one knows, the easier it can get to spot 'familiar faces': Russian помидор

---

1   A 'film'.

(pomidor) 'tomato' looks quite isolated on our list, but it is not originally a Russian word, and if we were to include Italian in the list we would immediately recognize a loanword from the Italian *pomidoro* 'tomatoes' (more commonly *pomodori* in modern Italian), which literally means 'fruits (*pomi*) of (*d'*) gold (*oro*)'.

Sometimes, languages borrow in more subtle ways, so that at first sight the resemblance is not obvious. What can happen is that word-like expressions from one language can be translated into another: if you know the meaning of the words that make up the expression, you may suddenly be able to recognize the meaning from your knowledge of another language in such cases of 'loan translation' (also known as 'calquing') (see previous page).

Table 4 Calques

Spanish	French	Italian	Romanian	Dutch	German	Swedish
luna de miel	lune de miel	luna di miele	lună de miere	—	—	—
gratacielos	gratte-ciel	gratta-cielo	zgârie-nori	wolken-krabber	Wolken-kratzer	skyskrapa
ferrocarril	chemin de fer	ferrovia	cale ferată	spoorveg	Eisenbahn	järnväg
OVNI	OVNI	—	OZN	—	—	—

To work out what these mean, one needs to have already learnt the following words:

| luna/lune/lună = moon; de/di = of; miel/miele/miere = honey |
| grata/gratte/gratta, zgârie, skrapa = scrape; krabber/Kratzer = scraper; ciel(o) = sky; Wolken, nori = clouds |
| ferro/fer = iron; ferată = made of iron; Eisen/järn = iron; carril, spoor, Bahn = track; chemin, cale, via, veg, väg = way, road, track |
| O = objeto / objet / oggetto / obiect = object; N = no / non = not, un-; N = neidentificat unidentified; I = identificado / identifié / identificato = identified; V = volador / volant, Z = zburător = flying |

Sometimes *parts* of words may look very different across languages, but they may occur over and over again in such a way that we can readily recognize them once we know they are equivalent. Take, for example, the word for 'electricity' in the following European languages:

Table 5 The word for 'electricity' across some European languages

Portuguese	Spanish	Catalan	French
electrici*dade*	electrici*dad*	electrici*tat*	électrici*té*

Italian	Romanian	Dutch	German
elettrici*tà*	electrici*tate*	elektrici*teit*	Elektrizi*tät*

Given this pattern, we will have no trouble in recognizing — indeed we should actually be able to create — some words: what are Portuguese *sociedade*, French *société*, Italian *società*, Romanian *societate*? With this knowledge, you can actually create on your own the Portuguese, Spanish, Catalan, French, Italian, Romanian, Dutch and German words for 'university', and you can probably make a useful guess about the form of many other words whose English equivalent ends in -*ty*.

Another lesson that some of the examples in Table 3 have to teach us is about *writing*. A foreign language will appear more foreign when the writing system is unfamiliar. French and German appear to English speakers to be more easily accessible than Greek or Russian, simply because the visual symbols are unlike one's own. But most of the world's writing systems represent speech sounds, so that if we can hear what the written form represents, then we may be able to recognize a familiar term. If we see the Russian, Bulgarian or Arabic words for 'chocolate' written down, and we cannot read the alphabets, we have no idea what they mean, but if we heard them spoken we might recognize them.

Actually, one's native orthography may also be relatively opaque — think of the unpredictable pronunciations of 'ough' in English 'tough', 'bough', through' and 'cough' — but we tend to forget this when faced with a 'frightening' foreign script. But any writing system can be put to use to write any language. Arabic is generally written in the Arabic alphabet, yet Maltese (actually a dialect of Arabic) is written using the Latin alphabet, while the Arabic alphabet is used to write Persian, which is unrelated to Arabic. To tell the truth, no language is necessarily any more easy or difficult than any other, either in its sound system or in its orthography. So even making the effort merely to learn a new writing system is a creative tool for insight into another language.

There is more. Sometimes, knowing about orthography can come in handy for more sophisticated linguistic 'detective work'. Underlying linguistic contrasts as well as the orthography provide cues to different loan adaptation preferences. The letter <t> is not articulated in the same way in English and Portuguese and this difference is captured by Bengali speakers who have two different <t> sounds — a front 'dental' [t̪] <ত> (as in French) and one pronounced further back in the mouth, a 'retroflex' [ʈ] <ট>, closer to that of the English sound.[2] This is manifested in the orthography when adapting the loans. The words *taxi* and *towel* are both borrowed in Bengali; although both words are written in the Latinate orthography with the letter <t>, they differ in the Bengali script. The reason for the difference in spelling is due to the original pronunciations of the loanwords: *taxi* is borrowed with the back consonant more appropriate to the alveolar <t> sound in English, while *towel* is from Portuguese with a more fronted dental 't'. Thus, the adaptations are dependent on the original pronunciations and the Bengali writing system reflects the difference: words borrowed from English like *taxi* are written with a retroflex ট্যাক্সি, while the Portuguese *toalha* is written with the front dental <t> as তোয়ালে.

The Climb towards Understanding

People very often view the process of learning a language as being like climbing a mountain. You cannot say that you have 'climbed Everest' until you have actually reached the top. But what is the 'top' in understanding (and in speaking) another language? One could say that the 'summit' had been reached when you were as good doing those things as a native speaker of the language, when you understand not only the 'gist' of what was being said, but immediately grasp every last nuance of what a native speaker was saying. This is a really excellent aim to have, but very few people ever make it all the way, and it is undoubtedly hard work,

---

2 Sounds are represented in writing by using the IPA (International Phonetic Alphabet) symbols standardized by the International Phonetic Association. Further information and a full IPA chart can be found at http://www.internationalphoneticassociation.org/content/ipa-chart

requiring a lot of time spent with native speakers, and true discipline and attention not only to vocabulary and pronunciation but, of course, to grammatical structure as well. In fact, even native speakers of a language often stumble, failing to create understanding between themselves and others. Actually, none of us understand, or speak, a language perfectly. Yet, everyone possesses the capacity to get somewhere in understanding a foreign language and, more often than we realize, the first steps are already carved out for us, because there may be hidden and helpful similarities between languages that we know and others that we don't know. Young people, in particular, are capable of remarkable plasticity and flexibility in acquiring other languages, well into their teens, and the kind of 'footholds' in new languages that we have pointed out can act as encouragement to embark on learning other languages at school.

Our thinking here is certainly not original, and there exist sophisticated and carefully worked models for the general approach we indicate, drawing on the discovery of patterns of 'family relationship' between languages as a creative means of gaining understanding of multiple foreign languages. An impressive model of this kind is the so-called 'Seven Sieves' series of manuals (aimed at adults rather than schoolchildren, however), which take Germanic languages (e.g. Hufeisen and Marx 2014) or Romance languages (McCann et al. 2003; Peris et al. 2005) and teach learners through a series of stages (e.g. obviously cognate words, sound and orthographical correspondences, techniques of word-formation) how the apparently unfamiliar can be transformed into the familiar.

Whatever means they use to do it, it is our belief that those shaping policy in foreign language learning in our schools should be trying to stimulate interest in and enthusiasm for foreign languages by showing how students can use what they already know, their capacity to exploit patterns of correspondence, to create bridges of understanding into other languages.

Works Cited

Creative Multilingualism. 2020. https://www.creativeml.ox.ac.uk

Dahl, Östen. 2005. 'Tea', in *The World Atlas of Language Structures*, ed. by Martin Haspelmath et al. (Oxford: Oxford University Press), pp. 554–57.

Hufeisen, Britta, and Nicole Marx (eds). 2014. *EuroComGerm — Die sieben Siebe: Germanische Sprachen lesen lernen*, 2nd edn (Aachen: Shaker).

International Phonetic Association. 2020. *Full IPA Chart*, http://www.internationalphoneticassociation.org/content/ipa-chart.

McCann, William J., Horst G. Klein and Tilbert D. Stegmann. 2003. *EuroComRom — The Seven Sieves: How to Read All the Romance Languages Right Away*, 2nd edn (Aachen: Shaker).

Peris, Ernesto, Esteve Clua et al. 2005. *EuroComRom — Los siete tamices: un fácil aprendizaje de la lectura en todas las lenguas románicas* (Aachen: Shaker).

Find Out More

Edwards, John. 2012. *Multilingualism: Understanding Linguistic Diversity* **(London: Continuum).**

An excellent short introduction to the diversity of languages, and to the emergence and consequences of multilingualism.

Janson, Tore. 2012. *The History of Languages: An Introduction* **(Oxford: Oxford University Press).**

This book offers an approachable and attractive introduction to how languages may be related historically, and to the nature and history of linguistic diversity.

Lewis, M. Paul. 2009. *Ethnologue: Languages of the World* **(Dallas: SIL International), http://www.ethnologue.com**

A comprehensive and regularly updated catalogue of all the known living languages in the world.

Maher, John. 2017. *Multilingualism. A Very Short Introduction* **(Oxford: Oxford University Press), https://doi.org/10.1093/actrade/9780198724995.001.0001**

A wide-ranging account of the nature and consequences of linguistic diversity and multilingualism in the modern world.

Maiden, Martin, Aditi Lahiri and Chiara Cappellaro. 2020. 'Creating Intelligibility across Languages and Communities', Research Strand 3 of Creative Multilingualism, https://www.creativeml.ox.ac.uk/research/intelligibility

Research project on intelligibility conducted as part of the Creative Multilingualism programme between 2016 and 2020. This chapter draws on that research.

McCann, William J., Horst G. Klein and Tilbert D. Stegmann. 2003. *EuroComRom — The Seven Sieves: How to Read All the Romance Languages Right Away*, **2nd edn (Aachen: Shaker).**

The project offers a detailed and thought-provoking model of how 'family resemblances' can be used as a means of creating bridges across languages.

Robinson, Andrew. 2009. *Writing and Script: A Very Short Introduction* **(Oxford: Oxford University Press), https://doi.org/10.1093/actrade/9780199567782.001.0001**

A fascinating introduction to the origins of writing systems and their development across millennia.

Thomason, Sarah Grey. 2001. *Language Contact: An Introduction* **(Edinburgh: Edinburgh University Press).**

This useful and informative account of the nature and effects of language contact includes coverage of how unrelated languages in contact can come to converge over time.

Weinreich, Max. 1963. *Languages in Contact: Findings and Problems* **(The Hague: Mouton).**

A fundamental and classic work on language contact and its effects on the structure of languages.

4. A Breath of Fresh Air... Ivan Vyrypaev's *Oxygen* (2002)

From Moscow to Birmingham via Oxford

Rajinder Dudrah, Julie Curtis,
Philip Ross Bullock and Noah Birksted-Breen

> Language diversity inspires creativity in performance

How might a Russian play be translated and adapted through hip-hop and related genres on the British stage? What might such a process reveal about doing creative multilingualism beyond conventional language learning contexts, and via collaboration between scholars and artists in the creative industries? Our chapter explores how these questions emerged, and how the act of translating, adapting and performing the Russian play *Oxygen* came about.

The idea for re-working *Oxygen* through aspects of UK hip-hop and grime occurred during an event organized by Rajinder Dudrah, which brought the rap, hip-hop and grime artists RTKal, Ky'Orion and Royalty from Birmingham to perform at Oxford's Taylor Institution in 2017. In their performance, they played with greetings from different languages, and drew on patois via a Rastafarian frame of reference, further energized through their spoken-word art form.

This provided a lightbulb moment for Julie Curtis and Noah Birksted-Breen, who looked at each other, and wondered what would happen if they introduced such artists to Ivan Vyrypaev's work... The initial moment of inspiration eventually led to artistic collaboration with the two UK hip-hop artists Lady Sanity and Stanza Divan from Birmingham

Fig. 1 Left to right: Simon Redgrave from Punch Records and artists Ky'Orion and RTKal, speaking after a performance at the first Creative Multilingualism conference, Taylor Institution, University of Oxford, 28 January 2017. Reproduced by kind permission of Kyle Greaves aka Ky'Orion, Joshua Holness aka RTKal and Simon Redgrave. Photograph by John Cairns (2017), CC BY-NC.

and Leicester respectively, culminating in a performance on 11 October 2018 at Birmingham City University.

Fig. 2 Left to right: Lady Sanity, Rajinder Dudrah, Stanza Divan and Noah Birksted-Breen at a Q & A following the Research and Development performance of *Oxygen* at Birmingham City University, 11 October 2018. Reproduced by kind permission of Noah Birksted-Breen, Rajinder Dudrah, Liam Lazare-Parris aka Stanza Divan and Sherelle Robbins aka Lady Sanity. Photograph by Katy Terry (2018), CC BY-NC.

In what follows, Julie Curtis offers a contextual overview of *Oxygen* and its importance not only in Russia but also beyond, highlighting the versatility that makes the play particularly well suited to translation and contemporary interpretation. Philip Ross Bullock provides an analysis of the language and musicality in the play, alongside its 'Russian-ness', as the musicality allows another entry point for different languages to exist, be spoken and performed alongside each other. Noah Birksted-Breen presents an account of the challenges and possibilities of taking up the form, ideology and musicality that Curtis and Bullock describe, particularly in re-imagining these for contemporary UK audiences. Rajinder Dudrah introduces the genre of grime, with part of its antecedents in rap and hip-hop, and reflects on the process of collaboration in putting together an artistic enterprise as a thinking and doing piece in the creative industries. What we offer, then, is not a linear or uniform diary of our events. Instead, we offer perspectives on the original play through translation and adaptation, a process which led to eclectic collaborative research and the development of *Oxygen* through UK hip-hop theatre.

On *Oxygen*

Julie Curtis

As an informal group of researchers, we have been working for some years now to explore the impact academic interventions can have in facilitating the staging of contemporary Russian drama in Britain. The Creative Multilingualism project has provided an ideal framework for such an investigation, allowing us to contextualize this undertaking more broadly and to understand the role languages play in the creative economy, and their significance for performance. In this case study we show how one of the best-known Russian plays of this century still encounters hurdles in reaching British audiences, and investigate how translation can grow into transposition, to give a foreign text new life in entirely different cultural contexts.

The Russian playwright Ivan Vyrypaev (born 1974) came to prominence in Moscow early in the twenty-first century as a leading figure in the 'New Drama' movement, which has shaped the most inventive and courageous theatre-making in Putin's Russia. Vyrypaev grew up in Eastern Siberia but moved to Moscow, and in his late twenties he saw his play *Kislorod* (Oxygen) premiered by one of the few independent theatre companies there, Teatr.doc. The play was translated by Sasha Dugdale with the title *Oxygen* in a version which remained remarkably true to the original while preserving its musicality. This was staged as a rehearsed reading at the Royal Court Theatre in London in 2004, and it has been taken up in other countries since then. In 2009/10 it was fully staged for just a handful of performances by the Royal Shakespeare Company (RSC). Vyrypaev also made a Russian film version of the play under the same title, *Kislorod* (2009), which is probably the most widely-known version of the work for Russian speakers.

The play is structured around the Ten Commandments, which are cited in turn at the beginning of each 'Composition', the musical term used to designate each section of the play. The text is made up of a dialogue between a She and a He, principally recounting the love affair between Sasha from Serpukhov (Alexander) and Sasha from Moscow (Alexandra), which begins with the male Sasha battering his wife to death with a spade. Sasha justifies his actions by his longing for 'oxygen', which his wife lacks and the female Sasha offers. The male Sasha lives in the town of Serpukhov, a couple of hours by train south of Moscow, a place so run-down that nowadays they can make films about the 1917 Revolution there without building any special sets. The play encompasses the hopeless lives of the young people, many of them alcoholics or drug addicts, who live in Serpukhov, and contrasts that with the more cosmopolitan outlook of Moscow. But there is also a great deal about the wider world, in particular the Arab-Israeli conflicts and the events of 9/11. This elevates the play's preoccupation with violence to a higher level, offering a meditation on the ways in which great love (sexual attraction, or religious belief) can lead to great evil.

The play's ten Compositions are performed with a sing-song manner of speech often involving syncopated rhythms, echoed patterning or repeated phrases in the dialogues.

Extracts from *Oxygen*

Композиция 1. Танцы

1 куплет:

Он

Вы слышали, что сказано древним: не убивай; кто же убьет, подлежит суду? А я знал одного человека, у которого был очень плохой слух. Он не слышал, когда говорили, не убей, быть может, потому, что он был в плеере. Он не слышал, не убей, он взял лопату, пошел в огород и убил. Потом вернулся в дом, включил музыку погромче, и стал танцевать.

Composition No. 1 'Dances'

1st couplet:

He

Have you heard what was said to the people in ancient times: 'Thou shalt not kill: he who is killed will be judged'? But I know one man, who couldn't hear properly. He didn't hear when they said 'Thou shalt not kill', perhaps because he was listening to his Walkman. He didn't hear 'Thou shalt not kill', and he took a spade, and went into the vegetable garden, and he killed. Then he came back into the house, turned the music up, and began to dance.

The play shocked Russian audiences by its unflinching representations of violence in the domestic and the public sphere. Authorial comment on this appears in the finale, which is a plea for people to take note of the dilemmas facing the new generation, born in the 1970s, which has reached adulthood in the twenty-first century. Some of the language is archaic, redolent of the Bible, and occasionally it becomes beautiful and poetic. But the play is also filled with obscenities, and in this respect was one of the first to transgress a taboo that had remained firmly entrenched throughout the Soviet era, and had continued even since the collapse of the USSR in 1991. Since 2014, the sharp turn towards social conservatism in Russia has seen obscenity banned by new legislation from film, literature and theatre, so that any performances of the play in Russia today would technically be breaking the law.

The depiction of young people's lives in the play is partly achieved through the references to music and dancing: just as in Vyrypaev's 2002 production at Moscow's Teatr.doc, the 2003 Royal Court production in London involved a DJ, the playwright Debbie Tucker Green, to provide backing tracks to score the sections. The 2009 RSC production brought over from Russia the 2008 world champion breakdancing team Top 9, whose performance brilliantly punctuated the text with breakdancing sequences loosely inspired by the unfolding of the narratives. Vyrypaev's text prompts performers to speak some of the text as rap, and for his 2009 film he commissioned a whole range of Russian musicians to set each of the ten Compositions to music, and he too used breakdancers.

The play *Oxygen* has the potential to speak to audiences worldwide about the disconnectedness young people may feel about the world events they watch on their screens, the challenges of finding a moral compass in the modern era and the difficulties of escaping the stifling suffocation — or lack of spiritual oxygen — in their lives. At a public discussion in 2015, Vyrypaev, by now an ardent follower of Mohandas K. Gandhi, argued that the advent of the Internet has simply rendered it impossible for us to live separately and to be indifferent: the world has come together, irrespective of our politics and religions, and obliges us to seek what unites us universally. In 2017, he also wrote about the urgent need to offer values to the young that differ from those which still prevail in Russia as a legacy of the Soviet era.

However, significant questions arise about the possibilities and limitations of 'domesticating' a play like *Oxygen* in order to communicate the concerns it raises to an English-speaking audience, or for it to function successfully as drama in any other setting outside Russia. Non-linguistic forms of communication such as music, rapping and breakdancing can facilitate the 'translation' of the text to a new environment. Nevertheless, Sasha Dugdale has warned of other challenges which the play offers to a British director — specifically when it comes to disentangling racist and sexist attitudes expressed by the characters, and interpreting the author's stance on these matters (Dugdale 2006: 46). Our project responds to these challenges creatively, through a process of prismatic translation, by inviting UK hip-hop artists from the Midlands to rework the play — one of the most important to emerge from Russia in the new century — for a British audience which will be unfamiliar with the Russian social and political background to the play, but responsive to the urgent moral questions it asks.

The Rhythm of Life

Philip Ross Bullock

Audiences of *Kislorod* and the English translation *Oxygen* are perhaps most likely to be struck by Vyrypaev's use of language, particularly his distinctive fusion of quotations from the Bible with profanity and explicit references to sex and drugs. Certainly, much of *Oxygen*'s impact rests on its transgressive and even blasphemous tone, an effect which is heightened by its schematic plot and the lack of psychological depth in the characterization. What is equally crucial to the play, however, is its inventive structure, which is in many ways akin to musical form. The significance of sound in *Oxygen* is present from the outset of the play, in which we encounter a young man with poor hearing who dances in time to the music he listens to on his Walkman. Around halfway through the play, Vyrypaev scripts a brief episode of rap. Even where there is no explicit reference to music, the use of frequent repetitions — whether of individual words, whole lines or even entire paragraphs — means that the play's provocative content is placed in a carefully structured, quasi-musical context, which is one of the main sources of its surprising beauty.

Indeed, the play as a whole is set out in terms which are explicitly musical and can perhaps be interpreted as a kind of 'theme and variations' in which Vyrypaev, as composer-playwright, develops his material by the subtle use of repetition and development. Take, for instance, the use of words such as *kompozitsiya* (composition), *kuplet* (verse), *pripev* (chorus) and *final* (finale) which are used to describe and demarcate the play's ten individual sections:

Composition No. 1 ('Dances'):
    1st verse
    Chorus
    2nd verse
    Chorus
    3rd verse
    Chorus
    Finale

Composition No. 2 ('Sasha loves Sasha'):
    1st verse
    Chorus
    2nd verse
    Chorus
    3rd verse
    Chorus
    Finale

Composition No. 3 ('No and yes'):
    1st verse
    Chorus
    2nd verse
    Chorus
    Finale

Composition No. 4 ('Moscow rum'):
    1st verse
    Chorus
    2nd verse

Composition No. 5 ('The Arab world'):
    1st verse
    Chorus
    Finale

(Rap)
2nd verse
Finale

Composition No. 6 ('How without feelings')

Composition No. 7 ('Amnesia'):
    1st verse
    2nd verse
    Chorus
    Finale

Composition No. 8 ('Pearl'):
    1st verse
    Chorus
    2nd verse
    Chorus

Composition No. 9 ('For the main thing'):
    1st verse

Composition No. 10 ('Listening to his Walkman'):
    1st verse
    2nd verse

As the above scheme illustrates, the play derives much of its force from the various iterations of its individual building blocks. Moreover, it not only repeats key structural devices, but develops them by combining them in different ways so that each composition differs from the preceding one (with the exception of the first and the second). Important as the play's verbal material might be, its impact derives as much, if not more, from the quasi-musical framework that Vyrypaev employs. As Susanna Weygandt has recently argued, 'musically and rhythmically inclined, Vyrypaev sees the world through organized rhythm' (Weygandt 2018: 205).

Yet if the structure borrows techniques that are more familiar from music, it is much less explicit when it comes to the actual music that might be used in a performance (other than the brief passage of scripted rap in 'Composition No. 5', and even that is marked as being at the discretion of the director). The implicit musicality of the play thus gives its performers considerable licence when it comes to interpreting it at any given moment in time (as in the 2009 film version of the play). The original play text of *Kislorod* (2002) is seemingly stable, yet the realization of its musical form is one way in which a new staging can respond to Vyrypaev's demand that *Kislorod* is a work 'which should be produced here and now', just as a translation into a foreign language permits for a re-accenting of the original Russian to conform to the circumstances of a new production. At the same time, however, the play's musicality places it in dialogue with the theatrical traditions of the past. Stage music has long been part of the world of drama — think, for instance, of the 'noises, sounds, and sweet airs, that give delight and hurt not' that suffuse Shakespeare's *The Tempest* (Shakespeare 2013: 187). Or Felix Mendelssohn's score for a production of Shakespeare's *A Midsummer Night's Dream* from 1842 (Mendelssohn 2000), or the music that Tchaikovsky provided for a run of *Hamlet* in 1891 (Tchaikovsky 1892). Such scores are perhaps more familiar nowadays from concert performance, but they attest to the ways in which music and the word have long been entwined in dramatic theatre.

There is, though, another way of looking at Vyrypaev's *Oxygen* and its relationship to music. Throughout the twentieth century, many dramatists have managed to draw on the expressive potential of music as a means of coping with the apparent emptiness of language and the existential bleakness of modern existence. In Anton Chekhov's plays, for instance, characters often talk past each other and find themselves confined to the most meaningless banalities. Music, however, seems to belong to another emotional realm, somehow expressing — despite its abstraction — crucial features of a play's emotional world. The verbal texture of *Uncle Vanya* (1899) is often punctuated with instances of real music — songs sung or hummed to the accompaniment of a guitar — and the play's final moments are full of an intense musicality where humdrum words and activities are suffused with the atmosphere of another world (Chekhov 1988: 184–85). In *The Cherry Orchard* (1904) too, sound serves to structure the play, even when words fall short. In a famous moment in Act II (Chekhov 1988: 315), the action is interrupted by a strange sound which is variously interpreted by one character as the call of a heron, by another as the sound of an owl, and by a third as what may be the snapping of a cable in a distant mineshaft. Then, the end of the play resonates with the sound of trees being cut down. Chekhov was, of course, using sound to convey atmosphere and verisimilitude. But he was doing more than that; he was investing ordinary human language with something mysterious and evocative that resists ready verbal description. This 'musicality' was central to the development of European drama in the decades that followed, not least in the works of Samuel Beckett, where music and language sit creatively, yet uneasily together, and where music often supplants words altogether, as in the case of his 1976 television play, *Ghost Trio*, with its explicit use of a number of extracts of Beethoven's work of the same name (Beckett 1977: 39–47).

So, the role of music in Vyrypaev's *Oxygen* is not just a gesture to the kind of popular culture which was so central to post-Soviet literature; neither is it merely an extension of the play's seemingly nihilistic treatment of sex, drugs and violence. *Oxygen*'s soundtrack is central to how the play structures form and time, and invests its verbal meanings with something more intangibly mysterious and immaterial. Our reading of the play will be impoverished if we consider only its 'content' or propositional logic; instead, we must attend to its musicality, its rhythms and its form — to the oxygen which gives the play its life and animates its constituent parts.

A Statement of Creative Intent: Directing Vyrypaev's 'Impossible Play'

Noah Birksted-Breen

As has already been indicated, many new Russian plays are experimental. I have heard Russian directors accuse Russian playwrights of writing 'an impossible play' on more than one occasion. Julie Curtis has elaborated on the challenges of form and ideology in *Oxygen*, while Philip Ross Bullock notes that music offers the possibility of a non-verbal 'message' — which the director must interpret in their staging. In this section, I explain the approach taken to imagining *Oxygen* for British audiences. This was developed in a collaboration between UK hip-hop artists Lady Sanity and Stanza Divan, the producer and curator Rajinder Dudrah, and myself as director.

Over my dozen years of translating and staging new Russian plays in London, I have observed a general tendency in British theatre in relation to new foreign plays. Almost without exception, UK theatres create 'niches' for translated plays. The audience is prepped for an encounter with the foreign 'other'. Even before the spectators turn up, the marketing prepares the spectators for what lies ahead, with the subtext: 'this is from a *different* country, be warned!'.

The perceived need for prepping is understandable. British audiences have proven themselves to be cautious about plays which are stylistically at odds with what they know. Vicky Featherstone, current Artistic Director of the Royal Court, has stated that 'we are not traditionally a country that is good at looking beyond our shores. [...] Our island geography, coupled with our imperialist nature, has encouraged a culture of splendid isolation' (Aston and O'Thomas 2015: 185). This is not a new state of affairs. The founder of the Royal Court, George Devine, attempted unsuccessfully to make contemporary foreign-language plays a major part of the company's repertoire from the mid-1950s (ibid.: 5). Nevertheless, over decades, the Court has been one of a small number of British theatres advocating and producing international work. So, I celebrate the Royal Court and producers at other theatres daring enough to stage *some* contemporary foreign-language drama.

The fact remains that in order to drum up audiences and critical interest, most new foreign plays are produced under the banner of foreign 'otherness' — labelled by their nationality and presented in studio spaces for specialist audiences (those familiar with experimental work). As a consequence, audiences are encouraged to experience foreign cultures as being fundamentally different to British culture, rather than similar — or even as a combination of similar/different. Contemporary translated plays should offer a nuanced 'dialogue', not a binary 'us and them'.

At its core, this conservative approach to new foreign dramas is monocultural. British programmers tend to seek out new Russian plays which can be translated directly into an 'equivalent' and familiar British genre, performed by British-trained actors, directed in conventional British directing styles. Yet this representation of new Russian plays does not correspond to their multicultural composition. Many Russian playwrights are, naturally, influenced by a range of cultures. Their inspirations are diverse, including UK traditions: Vasilii Sigarev's iconic hit play *Plasticine* (2001) was partly inspired by Stephen King's *The Body* (1982); the Presnyakov Brothers wrote their plays at least partly under the influence of *Trainspotting*, the novel (1993) and the film (1996); while talented playwright Irina Vas'kovskaya — who has won several awards since 2014 — draws upon Harold Pinter's *oeuvre* for stylistic inspiration. To understand 'foreign' work, it is vital to perceive it through a multicultural lens, and consider what that might mean for theatrical practice. A multilingual translation is likely to respond better to the diverse cultural 'layers' within each drama.

It is time to pioneer new approaches at all stages of the production process in:

- The selection of plays: experimentation could extend to more daring choices of foreign texts — those which are least similar to the dominant naturalistic 'new writing' traditions in Britain;

- Translation practice: a move towards multilingual adaptations would generate new conceptual approaches;

- The staging of foreign dramas: directors and actors could embrace performance styles which acknowledge the original *theatrical* context of the translated play as opposed to solely its socio-political context.

The project which I proposed for our research strand 'Languages in the Creative Economy', in my dual capacity as artistic director of Sputnik Theatre Company and postdoctoral researcher, engages with each of these three areas by:

- Working with a non-realist text, Ivan Vyrypaev's *Oxygen*, which offers a significant formal departure from dominant British 'new writing' traditions based largely on realism;

- Engaging hip-hop artists to adapt an existing translation, shifting the emphasis from the original Russian context into a British narrative storyline — He and She became Jordan (a young black man living near the Grenfell Tower) and Jordan (a young woman in London running a beauty blog, an Instagrammer);

- Staging the work through a complete adaptation using hip-hop lyrics instead of a conventional playtext, to accentuate the 'Russianness' of the play's tonality and non-linear structure, while emphasizing striking similarities between youth subcultures in Russia and the UK, most notably their political dispossession.

For ten days in September and October 2018, Sanity and Stanza worked with Sasha Dugdale's literary and monolingual translation in a collaborative process with myself and Rajinder in order to adapt *Oxygen* as a multilingual piece. The adapted version draws upon urban black youth speech, English 'received pronunciation', archaic English and even some Russian words (woven into the sampled musical tracks). In a future iteration of this work, we hope to add Caribbean-influenced patois and other languages beyond English through video-projections of overseas hip-hop artists speaking in their own languages.

Extract from *Oxygen*

Adapted by Lady Sanity and Stanza Divan

Track 1

Thou shall not kill...
Thou shall not kill...
Comes like man's deaf nowadays
Lost in streams and audio plays

I knew a man
Stuck in those same ways.
Switched up his cards
And took a life for trade

I knew a man — Jordan — that killed
...Went back to his yard and blazed,
Skanked out to music, one man rave
But this guy's movement was off, staggered 'n strange

Chorus

In each person there's two dancers the right-hand and left-hand and both need
'Oxygen!'
In a Relationship you have two partners, one on either side who should both be
'Oxygen!'
Politicians should be philosophically brilliant, serving and giving their citizens pure
'Oxygen!'

This approach we have adopted offers two main benefits over conventional translation practice:

- It captures the artistic complexity of *Oxygen* by speaking to its Russian philosophical roots while re-imagining the drama as a dystopian vision of life in Britain today. In this way the adapted play opens up shared ground between Russia and the UK, rejecting the notion that they are separated by 'foreignness'.

- It responds creatively to the musicality of the original. The hip-hop lyricism and music directly embody the play's spiritual yearning for a more utopian society which would cease to suffocate the younger generation.

This project does not offer a one-size-fits-all formula for translation of new plays. Indeed, it challenges the very notion that a standardized approach is appropriate. Instead, it serves as a constructive example of how theatres and translators might reconceptualize play translation in a more holistic manner — in an ethos of creative multilingualism.

Creating Multilingual Grime and Hip-Hop

Rajinder Dudrah

Grime — urban, gritty, digital, youthful, representing where you are from, and uncompromising in its engagement with social issues. With anything between 130 and 140 breakbeats per minute, the music genre has been likened in the British musical trade press to the originality and potential for disruption of British punk from earlier decades. Hailing initially from the East End of London in the early 2000s, it developed out of the pirate radio scene and electronic music genres of UK garage and jungle, dancehall, rap and hip-hop. It has marked out a regional scene beyond the capital, most notably in Greater Birmingham, and inspired international re-workings in East Asia and North America.

From London, artists including Wiley, Dizzee Rascal, Kano, Lethal Bizzle, Ghetts, Jme, Skepta and Stormzy have brought grime to the attention of mainstream musical circles in the UK since 2003, leading to its global spread. Birmingham artists including The Streets, Devilman, Trilla, Slash, C4 and Lady Leshurr have also contributed to the genre's development in the UK and beyond.

More recently, grime gained further national and international attention when the artist Stormzy received two of the biggest awards at the 2018 Brit Awards at the London O2 Arena for British Male Solo Artist and Best Album of the Year with his *Gangs, Signs & Prayer*. In his freestyle rap performance during the show's finale, he reminded the ceremony's global audience of the urban social roots and critical commentary prevalent in the music. Stormzy critiqued the coalition government headed by Prime Minister Theresa May for their lack of response to the Grenfell fire in West London, and slammed the *Daily Mail* newspaper for its anti-black representations: 'Theresa May, where's the money for Grenfell?' he asked, adding that the government 'just forgot about Grenfell, you criminals, and you got the cheek to call us savages, you should do some jail time, you should pay some damages, we should burn your house down and see if you can manage this' (Stormzy 2018).

Grime artists like Stormzy are based in urban locales from where they draw their musical and lyrical inspirations. Regional, national and international inflections signal diasporic routes of migration and settlement, working-class upbringings and ecumenical religious backdrops (Stormzy 2017), engaging with the world and telling it like it is through an 'in-yer-face' no nonsense approach. The musical worlds of grime are eclectic, multicultural, hybrid and fusion-based, with local and regional UK dialects and accented catchphrases thrown in as markers of area postcodes. These worlds are often further invoked in MC or lyrical clashes, competitions or collaborations with other artists from around the country and elsewhere overseas.

Grime and associated genres are an important and exciting fit to the work in our 'Languages in the Creative Economy' strand where artists not only engage creatively with different languages and mediums of expression, but also illustrate the possibilities for selfhood formation through livelihoods shaped by creative endeavours. Using popular music forms such as grime and hip-hop opens up new possibilities for playing with languages, artistic forms and the written content of formal text. This allows us to explore the creative uses of multilingualism in settings beyond conventional classroom and language-learning contexts.

In this spirit, Joshua Holness aka RTKal from Birmingham worked with me to devise and perform a piece around 'word, sound and power' at the first Creative Multilingualism conference on Languages and Creativity at the Taylor Institution in January 2017 in Oxford. His performance with fellow artists Ky'Orion (Kyle Greaves) and Royalty (Reece Wilson-Haughton), also from Birmingham, drew on his spoken word background, rap and grime performances, Rastafarian beliefs, and multicultural and multilingual upbringing in the city. By drawing on word, sound and power as inter-related concepts of communication and performativity, RTKal and his colleagues demonstrated the liveness of language, its embodied nature and the vibrations of sounds made through speaking different snatches of languages with a rhythmic beat.

Fig. 3 RTKal performing at the first Creative Multilingualism conference, Taylor Institution, University of Oxford, 28 January 2017. Reproduced by kind permission of Joshua Holness aka RTKal. Photograph by John Cairns (2017), CC BY-NC.

In the roundtable discussion that followed between the artists, Simon Redgrave (Head of Creative Development from Punch Records, Birmingham, and one of our research strand's cultural partners), Julie Curtis, audience members and myself, ideas of creativity and multilingualism were critically interrogated, whilst also affirming their potential for social good. Questions posed in this vein included the following: 'How is creativity in the creative industries able to flourish in different urban and multicultural settings?' and 'Are young people from different socio-economic and ethnic backgrounds experiencing, and able to access, creativity equally or differentially?'

Working with such artists inevitably means thinking through together the possibilities and challenges the play *Oxygen* will reveal in terms of cultural translation, transfer and performance. It means asking questions not only about the text and how best we are able to work with it afresh, in part or whole, for our strand-related performance, but also about the process of collaboration and the working practices between the artists and researchers. Working collectively in workshop or lab-style processes of dialogue, co-design, experimentation, discovery and public performance requires us to consider further the ways in which our research and practices are being informed and/or developed in the process of working together.

The unique collaboration at the heart of our project was designed to generate new creatively multilingual possibilities, and to simultaneously draw attention to pressing social issues that concern young people today. In this way it responds directly both to the subject matter of the play *Oxygen* and to the subject matter that inspires hip-hop, grime and associated genres.

When people think of plays written in contemporary Russia, they may not immediately think of diverse and multicultural urban settings and community languages in Britain. With the Research and Development of *Oxygen*, we hope to have showcased the exciting potential of mixing and playing with the artistic languages of the contemporary UK through theatre and popular music. In doing so, we also hope to have inspired others to consider multilingualism across cultures, languages and genres as a constructive trajectory for new creative endeavours.

Works Cited

Beckett, Samuel. 1977. *Ends and Odds: Plays and Sketches* (London: Faber and Faber).

Chekhov, Anton. 1988. *Plays*, trans. by Michael Frayn (London: Methuen).

Creative Multilingualism. 2020. https://www.creativeml.ox.ac.uk

Curtis, Julie. 2015. Notes from public discussion at Liubimovka Festival, with Ivan Vyrypaev.

Dugdale, Sasha. 2006. 'Oxygenating Theater: A Translator's Note', *Theater*, 36(1), 45–47, https://doi.org/10.1215/01610775-36-1-45

Featherstone, Vicky. 2015. 'Afterword', in *Royal Court: International*, ed. by Elaine Aston and Mark O'Thomas (Basingstoke: Palgrave MacMillan), pp. 185–86, https://doi.org/10.1057/9781137487728_6

Kislorod. 2009. Dir. by Ivan Vyrypaev (Ded Moroz).

Mendelssohn-Bartholdy, Felix. 2000. *Musik zu Ein Sommernachtstraum von Shakespeare, op. 61* (Wiesbaden: Breitkopf & Härtel).

Punch Records. 2020. https://www.wearepunch.co.uk/ [See also 'Punch Records', Creative Multilingualism, https://www.creativeml.ox.ac.uk/about/partners/punch-records]

Shakespeare, William. 2013. *The Tempest*, ed. by David Lindley (Cambridge: Cambridge University Press), https://doi.org/10.1017/cbo9781139109369

Stormzy. 2017. 'Blinded by Your Grace Pt. 2', *Gang Signs & Prayer* (Merky Records).

Stormzy. 2018. 'Stormzy — Blinded by Your Grace Pt. 2 & Big For Your Boots [Live at the Brits '18]', 4:51, posted online by Stormzy, YouTube, 22 February 2018, https://www.youtube.com/watch?v=ReY4yVkoDc4

Tchaikovsky, Petr. 1892. *Hamlet (de W. Shakespeare). Ouverture, mélodrames, fanfares, marches et entr'actes pour petit orchestre, op. 67* (Moscow: Jurgenson).

Vyrypaev, Ivan. 2002. *Kislorod*, performed by Teatr.doc, Moscow, October.

Vyrypaev, Ivan. 2004. *Oxygen*, trans. by Sasha Dugdale, staged as an internal rehearsed reading (date not recorded), Royal Court Theatre, London.

Vyrypaev, Ivan. 2006. '*Oxygen*', trans. by Sasha Dugdale, https://doi.org/10.1215/01610775-36-1-49

Vyrypaev, Ivan. 2009/10. *Oxygen*, trans. by Sasha Dugdale, dir. by Deborah Shaw, Royal Shakespeare Company/LIFT, Institute of Contemporary Arts, Stratford-upon Avon (17 September 2009); London (15–18 July 2010).

Vyrypaev, Ivan. 2017. 'Open Letter in Support of Kirill Serebrennikov', *Snob.ru*, 24 August, https://snob.ru/profile/26058/blog/128291

Vyrypaev, Ivan. 2018. *Oxygen*, trans. by Sasha Dugdale, adapted and performed by Lady Sanity and Stanza Divan, dir. by Noah Birksted-Breen, produced by Sputnik Theatre Company, Birmingham City University and Creative Multilingualism, 11 October.

Weygandt, Susanna. 2018. 'Revisiting *Skaz* in Ivan Vyrypaev's Cinema and Theatre: Rhythm and Sounds of Postdramatic Rap', *Studies in Russian and Soviet Cinema*, 12(3): 195–214, https://doi.org/10.1080/17503132.2018.1511260

Find Out More

Birksted-Breen, Noah. 2020. 'Vassily Sigarev and the Presnyakov Brothers: Staging the New Russia', in *Contemporary European Playwrights***, ed. by Maria Delgado, Bryce Lease and Dan Rebellato (London: Routledge), pp. 168–84.**

A chapter about the plays of two iconic Russian playwrights, whose work was critically acclaimed in Russia and the UK in the early 2000s.

Birksted-Breen, Noah, and Rajinder Dudrah. 2018. 'Translating a Russian Play into Hip-hop Theatre: A Conversation', Creative Multilingualism, 28 November, https://www.creativeml.ox.ac.uk/blog/exploring-multilingualism/translating-russian-play-hip-hop-theatre-conversation

A discussion of the dilemmas faced by the director and the curator of *Oxygen*, from Russian page to British stage.

Creative Multilingualism (Slanguages: Oxygen). 2018a. 'Oxygen: A Hip-hop Translation', web page with films and other materials relating to the event on 11 October, Creative Multilingualism, https://www.creativeml.ox.ac.uk/oxygen-hip-hop-translation

This web page brings together a film about the adaptation of *Oxygen*, the recording of the performance, and related material by the participants.

Creative Multilingualism (Slanguages: Oxygen). 2018b. '*Oxygen* Translated into Hip-hop Theatre: The Full Performance', 1:03:38, posted online by Creative Multilingualism, YouTube, 10 December 2018, https://www.youtube.com/watch?v=bozjOgLLR-U

A video showing the workshop performance of *Oxygen*, including a post-performance discussion with the adaptors, director and curator.

Curtis, Julie. 2018. 'Collaboration and Ownership in Cross-Cultural Creativity', Creative Multilingualism, 28 November, https://www.creativeml.ox.ac.uk/blog/exploring-multilingualism/collaboration-and-ownership-cross-cultural-creativity

This blog post gives an academic perspective on the process of adapting *Oxygen* for a UK audience.

Dudrah, Rajinder, Philip Bullock, Julie Curtis and Noah Birksted-Breen. 2020. 'Languages in the Creative Economy', Research Strand 4 of Creative Multilingualism, https://www.creativeml.ox.ac.uk/research/creative-economy

Research project on language diversity in the creative arts conducted as part of the Creative Multilingualism programme between 2016 and 2020. This chapter draws on that research.

Slanguages. 2020. A project under the aegis of 'Languages in the Creative Economy', Research Strand 4 of Creative Multilingualism, https://www.creativeml.ox.ac.uk/projects/slanguages

The process of adapting *Oxygen* into a hip-hop drama was carried out in the framework of Slanguages, which is both a project and a way of conceptualizing creativity through the prism of diverse ethnic-minority languages.

Credits

Permission to include their contribution was kindly granted by the following:

Noah Birksted-Breen (Fig. 2).

Rajinder Dudrah (Fig. 2).

Kyle Greaves aka Ky'Orion (Fig. 1).

Joshua Holness aka RTKal (Figs 1 and 3).

Liam Lazare-Parris aka Stanza Divan (Fig. 2).

Simon Redgrave (Fig. 1).

Sherelle Robbins aka Lady Sanity (Fig. 2).

5. Multilingualism and Creativity in World Literature

Wen-chin Ouyang

> Languages travel and migrate

One of the most important features of world literature is 'multilingualism'. Multilingualism in poetry and stories written in any language around the world may best be described as 'languages in dialogue'. Languages travel, talk to each other and interact. This can take place across languages, and even within a language, which makes each language multilingual. Multilingualism is both the sign and site of creativity in world literature, as will be seen in examples from Arabic, Chinese and English stories. These stories represent creative multilingualism in two overlapping ways. They have travelled around the world through literary translation and cinematic adaptation, bringing their languages, world views, motifs and characters into dialogue with other cultures, languages and literatures. More importantly, they are born in translation and adaptation, in inter-cultural, inter-lingual and inter-literary dialogues.

> Language Lives
> **Languages in Dialogue**
>
> Wen-chin Ouyang
>
> I speak Mandarin peppered with English to my Chinese friends. In Arabic I use one of the spoken registers and intersperse it with classical Arabic as

well as English words, phrases and even sentences to chat with my Iraqi, Lebanese and Syrian colleagues at SOAS. When I speak to my brother in Taiwanese, it is saturated with Arabic, English and Mandarin. Arabic, Mandarin and English, the three languages I know well, are normally seen as three discrete and distinct languages, but they have blended into each other in my speech patterns. I pick and choose from each language and mix them up depending on my audience and what I want to say. Everybody I know is multilingual but not in exactly the same way. My brother is the only person I know who understands my three main languages and their inflections: standard Arabic and her[1] spoken regional variations (such as Libyan, Egyptian, Levantine and Gulf); Chinese Mandarin and Taiwanese; and English, in particular the US variety. The way I speak to him reflects his languages. My Arab colleagues and friends are fluent in Arabic and English. I am bilingual around them. European Arabists tend to know two or three Middle Eastern languages as well as two or three European languages. I can even put my smatterings of French and Persian to good use in conversations with them. Chinese Arabists often know only Arabic and Chinese. I speak to them in Mandarin, which is the lingua franca among the Chinese today, and only turn to Arabic names and terms when we discuss Arabic culture and literature. Certain concepts and practices are culture-specific.

Wen-chin Ouyang, Professor of Arabic and Comparative Literature at SOAS University of London, leads the 'Creativity and World Literatures' strand of Creative Multilingualism.

Fig. 1 Wen-chin Ouyang. Reproduced with her kind permission. Photograph by Dai Yazhen (2018).

---

[1] You may notice that 'language' appears as 'she' in this chapter — a reflection of its gender in Arabic (and in some other languages, e.g. German).

One of the most obvious traces of languages in dialogue is found in mentions of food. English, for example, is full of foreign-sounding words such as *spaghetti, couscous, falafel, hummus, kebab* or *ramen* (see 'The Multilingual Life of Food' in the Introduction to this volume).

Food has a way of integrating itself and the culture of its production and consumption seamlessly into the fabric of any language. Even the most innocuous food items can have a global history. *Harry Potter* (Rowling 1997–2007) is not big on food or drink. However, breakfast, lunch, tea, dinner and even feasts do mark the time of the day or give a sense of space when adventures or misadventures happen. Dialogues or adventures take place during mealtimes, or where meals are served. Meals and teas are respite from misadventures. Similarly, staple food, spice and drink in the seven novels give this world-famous series a background in British as well as European imperialism and colonialism. Harry, Ron and Hermione's all-time favourite is chocolate, whether in the form of chocolate frogs, a mug of hot chocolate, or medicinal chocolate blocks Madam Pomfrey makes her young patients eat. It comes from South America and has been travelling around the world through the production, trade and consumption networks created and supported during the age of European empires between the sixteenth and twentieth centuries. The potato — boiled, roasted or fried — has made its way into English cuisine from the Americas. Pumpkin, which goes into pumpkin pasties and Harry's favourite drink, iced pumpkin juice, comes from North America. Pepper in Madam Pomfrey's 'Pepperup potion', which 'left the drinker smoking at the ears for several hours' (Rowling 1998: 128), is native to Kerala in southwestern India. Coffee, favoured by the Muggles, originated in tropical Africa, Ethiopia and the Sudan. Merchants took it along on their travels around the world beginning in the fifteenth century, and it arrived in England in the sixteenth century through the efforts of the British Levant Company and East India Company as well as the Dutch East India Company. The brew for all occasions in *Harry Potter* is tea, which is native to Southeast China. The British East India Company brought it to England in the seventeenth century. The appearance of these food items and drinks in *Harry Potter* tells us that the English language is a seasoned traveller, that it is not only an important world language but also that it has absorbed into its very fabric its encounters with other languages around the world.

Multilingualism of the English Language

Britain has engaged with Asian, European and Middle Eastern empires diplomatically, economically and militarily for thousands of years. English is multilingual, locally and globally. At home, she sports regional, class, ethnic, gender and professional inflections, to name but a few examples. In the world, she engages in dialogue and mutual enrichment with the languages she encounters in her travels. These two characteristics of English, or for that matter any language, are visibly hard at work creatively in world literature. In Julian Barnes' acclaimed novel *England, England* (1998), the satire of the search for an authentic English identity and tradition is effective and poignant precisely because the fabric of its language undermines any notion of authentic, sovereign Englishness. England is not a desert island, the novel shows, but a part of the world in the past and at present. English cultural institutions, such as the Royal Family, Big Ben, the Houses of Parliament, Manchester United Football Club, the Class System, Pubs, the Union Jack, the West End, the BBC, Shakespeare, the Cup of Tea, Stonehenge, Marmalade, the Tower of London, the Bowler Hat, Oxford/Cambridge, Harrods, Double-Decker Buses, Black Cabs, Alice in Wonderland, Winston Churchill, Marks and Spencer, Magna Carta, have to be extracted carefully from her history of imperialism (Barnes 1998: 83–85). The characters who partake in the process of excavation speak what sounds like 'pure' English but they switch registers depending on the occasion, and spew out 'foreign' words and phrases without a second thought. Words like *faux, jouissance, marquee, mauve, portico, wigwam*, or phrases like *noli me tangere, soixante-huitards, eau de toilette, bon mots, je ne sais quoi, capito, coup d'état, lèse-majesté* and *feng shui* appear everywhere in the novel.

Feng shui 風水 is perhaps the most recent addition to the English language compared with the other 'foreign' words and phrases quoted above, and its foreignness is immediately detectable. Denoting a Chinese world view concerned with the unobstructed flow of air and water in the organization of living spaces, it is seamlessly blended into the English prose that describes a character, Jerry Batson, who always avoids confrontation:

> 'Your *brain*, my money.' Sir Jack's correction was an amiable growl. You didn't jerk someone like Jerry Batson around, but the residual instinct to establish dominance never left Sir Jack. He did so by his heartiness, his

embonpoint, his preference for staying on his feet while others sat, and his habit of automatically correcting his interlocutor's first utterance. Jerry Batson's technique was different. He was a slight figure, with greying curly hair and a soft handshake he preferred not to give. His manner of establishing, or contesting, dominance was by declining to seek it, by retreating into a little Zen moment where he was a mere pebble washed briefly in a noisy stream, by sitting there neutrally, just feeling the *feng shui* of the place. (Barnes 1998: 34–35)

Feng shui serves as an example of how languages interact with each other in generating new expressions, here, in English. It is not relevant whether the English expression gets the Chinese concept of *feng shui* right or, for that matter, its broader context, which is here referred to as *Zen*; rather, it is more important to see how the two terms, *Zen* 禪 and *feng shui*, by now vaguely familiar in English, can quickly, effectively, and poignantly portray a personality and his mode of action in adversity: Jerry Batson is usually calm and tends to go with the flow. They at the same time activate the visualizing capacity of language, conjuring up a scene of a monk meditating in complete stillness and silence amidst winds blowing in trees and waters running in streams.

Languages Travel and Interact with Other Languages

Languages have been travelling with people and things since time immemorial, not only across different parts of a city, as London buses do today, but also around the globe and across empires in caravans along the Silk Roads by land from China through Central Asia and the Middle East to Europe all the way to England, and by sea from the Pacific Ocean via the Indian Ocean and the Red Sea to the Mediterranean. They encounter other languages on their travels, interact with them, and pick up from them ideas, motifs and even entire world views, such as *Zen*, *feng shui*, and democracy, which, in time, become seamless parts of their adoptive language.

A language thrives on dialogues with other languages, for in these dialogues a language refuels, gains new energy and gets creative. It discovers novel ways of expressing old ideas. More important, it finds new things to say. If language is the stuff of literature, multilingualism is the stuff of world literature. World literature comprises not only novels that travel from one nation to another through translation, but also poems and stories whose literary worlds are multilingual, shaped by languages in dialogue, and populated by ideas, motifs and even world views circulating around the globe. Barnes' novel *England, England* is a brilliant example. He skilfully weaves these into the fabric of his very English prose. His English is a language that has been around and is packed with goods from the languages and cultures with which it has come into contact.

> **Parseltongue: Humans Who Converse with Animals**
>
> Harry Potter converses with snakes, but he is not the first or only person who can do so. A farmer in 'The Tale of the Ox and the Donkey' in *The Arabian Nights* understands every word his animals say. The Queen of Serpents, Yamlīkha, in another *Nights*' story, 'The Tale of Ḥāsib Karīm al-Dīn', speaks human language.

Fig. 2 Yamlīkha, who tells the young Ḥāsib a story in 'The Tale of Ḥāsib Karīm al-Dīn' from *The Arabian Nights*, is a serpent queen, a common motif in world literature. Nuwa, the Chinese goddess of creation depicted here, is imagined as a serpent queen. Illustration from Edward T. Chalmers Werner. 1922. *Myths and Legends of China* (New York: Harrap). Wikimedia Commons, Public Domain, https://commons.wikimedia.org/wiki/File:Nuwa2.jpg#/media/File:Nuwa2.jpg

Ideas, motifs and world views travel easily from one cultural sphere to another, with and through language, or above, beyond and around language. These are at the heart of creativity in cultural expressions of all kinds, in literature written for adults and children, and in popular culture including movies, comics and games. They are exchanged at various points and through diverse means of cultural encounter within global networks of circulation of people and things, such as the Silk Roads, and they always pick up traces from the places where they have been. They also interact cross-culturally and, in due course, become multilingual as well.

The figure of the monk, a Buddhist spectre of whom flickers in Barnes's prose, is a good example. He is a globetrotting shape-shifter traceable to multiple religious traditions and their attendant popular cultures, including Buddhism, Christianity, Daoism, Hinduism and Islamic Sufism. While they have in common the renunciation of material pursuits and commitment to spiritual contemplation, they each have their distinct world views and practices. Buddhist and Hindus are celibate and vegetarians. Buddhists shave their heads and beards but Hindus and Sufis (except perhaps for Persian Qalandars) do not. Christians and Daoists drink alcohol but Buddhists, Hindus and Muslim Sufis are not supposed to. However, by the time they have travelled around the world and come into contact with each other, they can look uncannily alike.

Worldly Itineraries of the Monk

The archetype of Barnes' Buddhist monk may be traced to the Tang scholar pilgrim Xuanzang 玄藏 (602–64), whose historical journeys from China to India in search of Buddhist sutras are famously fictionalized as a series of demon-conquering adventures starring his disciple the Monkey King, Sun Wukong 孫悟空, in the sixteenth-century Chinese classic novel *Journey to the West* 西遊記 by Ch'eng-en Wu (1961, trans. by A. Waley; 1977–1983, trans. by A. Yu). An itinerant monk is melded from this Buddhist archetype overlapped with the Daoist archetype, and put on the centre stage of action in *Ji Gong Quan Zhuan* 濟公全傳 (Life and Deeds of Ji Gong). Ji Gong 濟公 (1130–1209), a historical figure nicknamed the living Buddha, is one of the most popular monks in Chinese culture. He is revered among Buddhists and Daoists alike.

Guo Xiaoting 郭小亭, a Qing dynasty (1644–1911) author, refashioned his life and deeds from popular legends into a novel. *Ji Gong* is a fictional biography made up of fantastic tales about a mad monk with supernatural powers who wanders around Song China. He eats meat and drinks alcohol but cures illnesses and saves lives. He also exorcises demons from bodies and homes. He is in this the nemesis of all Buddhist and Daoist charlatans.

Itinerant Buddhist and Daoist monks are staple minor characters in popular Chinese fiction. They are inspired by real life mendicants, who also smack of Hindu monastics. Having renounced material pursuits and committed themselves to a simple, celibate and vegetarian life of meditation and spiritual contemplation, they depend on donated food and charity for their needs. Some live a settled life in monasteries but many wander from place to place. These wandering monastic mendicants pop up everywhere in storytelling around the world. In Chinese fiction, such as *Ji Gong*, they appear as charlatans who make a living out of conning hapless people into giving them shelter, food and gifts. In Chinese 'martial arts' or 'chivalric' novels, comics, films and television series, Buddhist (Shaolin 少林) and Daoist (Wudang 武當) monks are 'knights errant' who right wrongs and defend the poor and powerless against rich bullies and corrupt government officers.

In Arabic, a wandering monastic, al-Nāsik, makes his first appearance in a collection of tales of Indian origins said to have been translated from Middle Persian into Arabic in the eighth century by Ibn al-Muqaffaᶜ (died c. 756/759) under the title of *Kalīla wa-Dimna*. Al-Nāsik in this collection of stories, known in English as the *Fables of Bidpai* or *Pilpay*, offers wise counsel to the perplexed. He appears as a mendicant in Arabic didactic 'Mirror for Princes' literature in the tenth century. For example, in the central Asian book *Kitāb Naṣīḥat al-mulūk* (1983) (misattributed to al-Māwardī, d. 1058), which provides counsel for kings, he takes up temporary residence in the homes of the rich and powerful and admonishes them in regular daily sessions. He is also a recurring character in popular epics in the Islamicate world, such as *Ḥamzanāma*, also known as the *Dastān of Amīr Ḥamza*, which is a foundation myth of Islam in Central, South and South East Asia. It is structured around the fanciful exploits of Muḥammad's uncle, Ḥamza ibn ᶜAbd al-Muṭṭalib, who in history died before Islam was established but in popular storytelling spread Islam in Asia east of the Arabian Peninsula. The stories of Amīr Ḥamza have been circulating in Arabic, Balinese, Georgian, Hindi, Javanese, Persian, Turkish, Urdu and other languages, and in these stories the nāsik plays an instrumental role in revealing God's plans for humanity, particularly the conquering Muslims. Con artists impersonate this mendicant monastic sage in *Alf layla wa-layla* (*The Thousand and One Nights*), known in English as *The Arabian Nights*, and show up dressed as itinerant Sufis who, like Buddhist and Daoist charlatans in Chinese fiction, pretend to be able to tell fortunes, cure barrenness and exorcise demons.

Fig. 3. Sun Wukong, the hero of *The Journey to the West*, transforms his hair into miniature monkey kings. Screenshot from *The Monkey King* 西游記之大鬧天宮. 2014. Directed by Cheang Pou-soi.

Chivalric monks have no presence in Arabic stories. They do make frequent appearances outside Chinese fiction, in Shaolin monk movies in Hollywood cinema and American comics and games. Tibetan monks have generated a particular kind of interest for both cultural and political reasons. *Bulletproof Monk* (2003), albeit a box office flop, provides another brilliant example of how creativity works cross-culturally. The story, based on the comic novel of the same title written by Brett Lewis and illustrated by Michael Avon Oeming (1998), begins in 1943 and ends sixty years later. A Tibetan monk is entrusted with protecting a scroll containing knowledge that can make its reader powerful, young and immune to injury. He is given the power of the scroll and told to find successors and pass on the scroll in the future. The scroll becomes the object of a quest for the Nazis, who pursue it even after the fall of Nazi Germany. They initially try to rob the Tibetan monk of the scroll at the Tibetan monastery in 1943, and are in hot pursuit when he reappears in what looks like New York City sixty years later to look for his successors. The scroll turns out to be a smokescreen and the knowledge is actually tattooed, in Tibetan, on the monk's body. The monk finds his successors, Kar, an American low life, and Jade, a Russian crime lord's daughter, and transfers the writing on his body to them, half to Kar's body and another half to Jade's, before he disappears.

Bulletproof Monk has the feel of both Hollywood Holy Grail films and Chinese *Wuxia*. However, it is more like a quest for the Holy Grail than a tale of Shaolin chivalry in Chinese *Wuxia* 武俠 and *Kungfu* 功夫 films, resembling *Indiana Jones and the Last Crusade* (1989) rather than *A Touch of Zen* 俠女 (1971), in which a Tibetan monk makes an appearance. It is created out of genre fusion and conceptual blending. The Holy Grail is overlapped with the Tibetan scroll, and Hollywood action adventure with Chinese *Kungfu* extravaganza. It tells the familiar story of the quest for power, youth and immortality, but does so in an intercultural way, showing that despite our divergent expressions we all share some core concerns, and that regardless of our differing cultural, political and religious backgrounds, we have in common our sense of justice and ability to distinguish right from wrong. Kar and Jade need not be monks in order to appreciate their responsibility as the guardians of Tibetan secret knowledge. Whether Tibetan language and the knowledge it contains are intelligible or not is beside the point. Even as they rely on language to acquire and convey meaning, some ideas, motifs and world views can travel outside language via other means of communication. They can travel visually through comics and films, or through a combination of smatterings of languages, visual representations, sounds and gestures when they are put to use creatively in order to effect dialogue, communication and mutual understanding. This corresponds to what we found in *England, England*, where Julian Barnes deploys multilingualism inherent in English to situate England in the world, and to mock those who insist that it is a desert island.

> *Language Lives*
> ## Multilingualism and Multiculturalism
>
> Wen-chin Ouyang
>
> I mix languages because I can. But more often than not I bring one language into another in order to express an idea that exists in one language but not the other. How do I convey the Chinese culture of politeness, *keqi* (客氣)? Initially the expected conduct befitting a guest, it has over the centuries come to frame the ways the educated Chinese interact with each other in society. A Chinese guest does not make demands on his host; rather, he goes with the flow and puts himself at the disposal of his host. Similarly, no Chinese would impose himself on others in speech or action. On the contrary, he will always give way to others — after you, at your service, your humble servant, I don't need anything, what makes you happy also makes me happy.
>
> This culture of politeness is manifest in the language of social interaction, *ketao* (客套), which is formal, self-effacing, and distant. The closest to Chinese *keqi* is Persian *taʿārof*. I have yet to find their equivalent in the other languages I know. Clearly, when I explain the Chinese culture of politeness to Iranians, I immediately turn to *taʿārof*. If I have to explain *taʿārof* to the Chinese, of course I invoke *keqi*. *Keqi* and *taʿārof* are not exactly equivalent cultural codes, but they do evoke likeness in social behaviour and language. What if my interlocutor does not know Chinese or Persian? I explain in our common language, as I have done in English, quoting the concepts in Chinese or Farsi, describing the cultural contexts and giving examples. I can do so because both the Chinese and Persian concepts of *keqi* and *taʿārof* are an integral part of my thought and language. Even if I choose to communicate in a single language, such as English, it embeds Arabic and Chinese.

Translation and Adaptation are Creativity in Multilingualism

Multilingualism has always been an important source of creativity in world literature. I have mentioned three examples from pre-modern times which continue to resonate with readers around the world today: *Ḥamzanāma*, *Kalīla wa-Dimna* and *Alf layla wa-layla*. These three major literary works are effectively international collaborative projects that initially garner creative imaginings from a plurality of languages and traditions of storytelling along the Silk Roads and then re-convey the stories in different languages each in a unique formulation. The youngest, *Ḥamzanāma*, treasured by the Mughals in India and found written down in an enormous illustrated manuscript (in 46 volumes and 48000 pages) commissioned by Emperor Akbar in about 1562, is based on multiple sources in numerous languages used among the Muslims. It exists in diverse renditions. According to Ibn al-Nadīm (1988: 364), who authored the famous tenth-century catalogue *al-Fihrist*, the oldest *Kalīla wa-Dimna* was of either Indian or Persian origin, and was translated into Arabic in the eighth century by a famous man of letters. This work cannot be traced to any original authoritative text in any language. It exists in multiple versions in multiple languages, such as Syriac, Persian and Turkish in addition to Arabic. Each version is unique, but all versions overlap. Their inherent ideas, motifs and world views can be traced to multiple sources in Arabic, Greek, Persian, Turkish and Sanskrit.

The most global of the three works, *Alf layla wa-layla*, was of Persian origin according to the same *al-Fihrist* (363–64) and was translated into Arabic at the same time as *Kalīla wa-Dimna*. It was most popular among Arabic speaking men of letters, who collected stories and compiled books in a similar fashion. However, there is no definitive Arabic text. There is rather a variety of texts which contain a core of common stories as well as different stories. European orientalists, through translation into French first and English later, collated a variety of Arabic and Turkish texts, brought them together with oral storytelling, and fashioned them into the so-called full text in the nineteenth century, of course with the help of Arab 'editors'. Two of the most famous stories, 'Aladdin' and 'Ali Baba', are very likely the result of Arab-European collaboration. Even today, *The Arabian Nights* is available as adult or children's literature in different languages and versions, with no two identical renditions. If you look carefully, you will find two forms of multilingualism at work in each version, even in a 'European' concoction such as 'Aladdin': firstly, that the tale was created, and exists, in a multilingual environment; and secondly, that its language, be it Arabic, Chinese, English, French, Italian, Japanese, Korean, Persian, Turkish or Swahili, is multilingual. Set in China but permeated with Arabic and Persian details, and in whichever language you hear or read it, you can tell that genie is unquestionably Arabic (the word was imported from Arabic *jinnī* via the similar-sounding French word *génie*) and that the magical ring is old Hebrew, traceable to Solomon legends in ancient biblical folklore.

> **Transfiguration, Transmogrification**
>
> 'Animagus' is a wizard who can change from human into animal form in *Harry Potter* (Rowling 1997–2007). A wizard can also learn from lessons on transfiguration how to transform humans into animals or animals into humans. Transmogrification (*maskh* in Arabic and *bian* 變 in Chinese) is a well-known motif in popular stories around the world. The nine-tail-fox in Chinese legends famously transforms herself into a seductress woman and causes empires to fall. The Monkey King (齊天大聖孫悟空) can transform himself into seventy-two different living beings. Sakhr, a demon in Solomon legends, transforms himself into Solomon and rules on his behalf for forty days. Humans are regularly turned into animals and back again in *The Arabian Nights*.
>
>
>
> Fig. 4 'Nine Tails Fox', from the Chinese *Classic of Mountains and Seas* (山海經), which has existed since the fourth century. Image by Hu Wenhuan 胡文煥 (1596–1650) in 山海經圖 (sixteenth century). Wikimedia Commons, Public Domain, https://commons.wikimedia.org/wiki/File:%E5%8D%97%E5%B1%B1%E7%B6%93-%E4%B9%9D%E5%B0%BE%E7%8B%90.svg

Transmogrification, or transfiguration in Harry Potter speak, or adaptation in the language of literary criticism, is the creative impulse behind the 'worlding' of the figure of the monk, as we have seen, and of what is perhaps the most popular story in *The Arabian Nights*, 'The Tale of Sindbad the Mariner', known in English as 'The Adventures of Sinbad the Sailor'. This already multilingual and multicultural story becomes even more so as it travels around the world one more time, in this instance moving from the Middle East to Europe, North America and Asia through translation, and by means of adaptation from popular story to literary novel, and from literature to music, film, cartoon, graphic novel and anime. As it travels across cultures, genres and media, the original *Nights* pick up even more cultural and linguistic layers. Each tale is not only transformed in translation but also in adaptation. Translation is creative (see Chapter 6 in this volume), as is adaptation. Adaptation, like translation, is premised on conversations across languages in addition to genres, media and cultures.

No two renditions of 'Sinbad the Sailor' are the same (this is also true of 'Aladdin' and 'Ali Baba'). If the seven voyages of Sindbad the Mariner in *Alf layla wa-layla* repeat the same story of 'relief after hardship' to urge the devout to have faith in God while doing their best, they come to be an important part of an Egyptian 'national allegory' in Naguib Mahfouz's novel *Layālī alf layla* (1979; *Arabian Nights and Days*, 2001). In North America, the eighth voyage of Sinbad the Sailor becomes a 'fantastic' tale of American fascination with modern technology in Edgar Allan Poe's 'The Thousand-and-Second Tale of Scheherazade' (1845) and in John Barth's *The Last Voyage of Somebody the Sailor* (1991), a parody of post-modernist storytelling about the rise and fall of an American tycoon. Sinbad sheds his literary masks in cinema, television and comic books. He is a pirate prince who goes on adventures, saves a princess, and becomes king in Hollywood action adventures, starting with *Sinbad the Sailor* (1947) through DreamWorks' animated *Sinbad: Legends of the Seven Seas* (2003) to even more recent cinematic and TV adaptations. He is an adventurous boy in Japanese animation, starting with the TV series *Arabian Nights: Sinbad's Adventures* (1975) and continuing with the TV film *Magi: Adventure of Sinbad* (2016) and the film trilogy *Sinbad* (2015–2016), in which the hero travels around the world and learns about freedom, love, friendship, loyalty, responsibility and justice.

All the retellings of Sinbad the Sailor, as we have seen in the example of the itinerant monk, take the character from *The Arabian Nights*, set him in a different linguistic and cultural environment and send him off on a fresh series of adventures. He acquires a wardrobe, gallivants around in his new personality, Sinbad, and performs the tasks the readers and viewers expect of him in the new environment. He learns 'foreign' languages, such as English or Japanese, and integrates himself into the storytelling of the literary novel or short story, or the graphics of comics or anime, or the moving images of film and television. However, remnants of Arabic and the 'original' story saturate the very fabric of all the 'foreign' languages Sinbad speaks and the new arenas of his action. The transformation of Sindbad into Sinbad requires creative fusion of the 'original' with the new environment, in which languages, genres, media and cultures not only come into contact with each other but also actively engage with each other in dialogue. New works of art are born. Multilingualism, in the form of languages in dialogue, is at the heart of world literature.

Fig. 5 Douglas Fairbanks Jr. in *Sinbad the Sailor* (1947). Directed by Richard Wallace. Visualization of Sinbad in this film is arguably a creative fusion of Arabic storytelling, European translation, orientalist fantasy and Hollywood filmmaking.

Perspectives on Researching World Literatures

The researchers involved in the 'Creativity and World Literatures' strand of Creative Multilingualism have also pursued a range of other projects that illuminate how language diversity enriches the creative possibilities enacted in world literature.

Researching the Borders of Languages in Literature

Jane Hiddleston

Having worked for a long time on postcolonial literatures in French, I have been interested in the ways in which writers try to capture and express colonized culture within the language of the coloniser. Writers from North Africa, such as Assia Djebar and Abdelkebir Khatibi, often either intersperse their French with Arabic terms, or theorize the presence of Arabic within French in a range of subtle and transgressive ways. Francophone Caribbean writers such as the Martinican poet Aimé Césaire also stretch the French language by including great lexical diversity, or reflect on the interpenetration of French with Creole.

My close engagement with translanguaging strategies in postcolonial writings has led to a deeper questioning of the borders of languages, which are very often far more porous than it might at first appear. This reflection on the porosity of languages generates a further questioning of cultural hierarchies and power struggles. But it also invites us to think about how language far exceeds the framework of the nation, and even of the verbal, as multilingual writers experiment with multiple forms of expression in order to challenge our assumptions about how we frame and define language itself.

Jane Hiddleston, Professor of Literatures in French at the University of Oxford, is a Co-Investigator on the 'Creativity and World Literatures' strand of Creative Multilingualism.

Researching Language Differences in Literary Texts

Laura Lonsdale

I have always been interested in the expression of language differences in literary texts. In the last few years this has taken me to study the way writers experiment both stylistically and conceptually with the possibilities of the multilingual. Literature that incorporates more than one language challenges us to be aware of the boundaries of our own language, to realise that the world can be perceived and described in ways that both differ and coincide. In the process it can explore a range of cultural, political and even ecological questions, from migration to biodiversity, while at the same time enriching the store of words and figures available to a given language.

Laura Lonsdale, Associate Professor of Spanish at the University of Oxford, is an Associated Researcher on the 'Creativity and World Literatures' strand of Creative Multilingualism.

Researching Multilingualism as a Lens through which to Read Power Dynamics

Nora E. Parr

Do ideas mean the same thing in different languages? What happens to an idea when it travels across languages? This is what I explore, and through the often loaded, and always sensitive idea of 'trauma.' Existing theory on trauma says humans, when they are suddenly exposed to something violent, are shocked — so shocked they often do not have words to describe or explain what has happened. The solution for trauma is formed against this idea, and aims to give people and societies words, practices, and actions that help to deal with and integrate the experience of violence into a new everyday living.

My project looks at Palestinian literature on the *Nakba*. The word (meaning 'catastrophe' in Arabic) first indicated the violent shock of Palestinians being uprooted from their homeland and dispossessed of their land and material heritage as Zionist forces expelled them and declared the State of Israel on their land. More than seventy years have passed and the Palestinians are still waiting to return home. They have come to see *Nakba* as an ongoing process. The 'shock' of violence has come to shape and inform their everyday lives for generations, and the forces that saw to that first eruption of violence have not disappeared or dissipated.

So, is 'trauma' in English (and Spanish, and French, and German, all of which *do* use the same word and idea behind it) the same as it is in Arabic? My research suggests no. To complicate matters, the word in Arabic for 'trauma' is a calque for the nineteenth century English concept. 'Trauma'was rendered by Arabic translators as *ṣadma*, meaning 'impact,' collision, or sudden surprise — an excellent rendering of a foreign term. But trauma is the norm for many Palestinians. When there is no 'after', when violence shapes or constitutes the everyday, 'trauma' needs to be re-defined. In my project, multilingualism means reading the Arabic word, *ṣadma*, as an 'English' (European) idea. I mean being sensitive to the fact that the two terms, 'trauma' in English and '*ṣadma*' in Arabic, are not equivalent, and that work must be done to offer a new and better definition of trauma in Arabic based on its wider cultural use and understanding.

Multilingualism provides a lens through which to read power dynamics and the unequal weight of one idea across different languages. Contextualizing concepts and terms that cross linguistic borders and historical contexts, multilingualism allows for any analysis to be sensitive to words whose definitions have been occluded through uneven circulation.

Nora Parr, SOAS University of London, is a Postdoctoral Researcher on the 'Creativity and World Literatures' strand of Creative Multilingualism.

Works Cited

The Adventures of Amir Hamza. 2007. Trans. by Musharraf Ali Farooqi (New York: The Modern Library).

Al-Māwardī, Abū al-Ḥasan ʿAlī ibn Muḥammad ibn Ḥabīb. 1983. *Kitāb Naṣīḥat al-mulūk* (Kuwait: Maktabat al-Falāḥ).

Alf Layla wa Layla, see *The Arabian Nights*.

The Arabian Nights. 1990. Trans. by Husain Haddawy (New York: Norton).

The Arabian Nights II: Sinbad and Other Popular Stories. 1995. Trans. by Husain Haddawy (New York: Norton).

Arabian Nights: Sinbad's Adventures [アラビアンナイト シンドバットの冒険]. 1975. Dir. by Fumio Kurokawa (Nippon Animation). [Anime television series.]

Barnes, Julian. 1998. *England, England* (London: Jonathan Cape).

Barth, John. 1991. *The Last Voyage of Somebody the Sailor* (Boston: Little, Brown and Company).

Bulletproof Monk. 2003. Dir. by Paul Hunter (MGM).

The Classic of Mountains and Seas [山海經]. 1999. Trans. by Anne Birrell (Harmondsworth: Penguin).

Creative Multilingualism. 2020. https://www.creativeml.ox.ac.uk

Dastān of Amīr Ḥamza, see *The Adventures of Amir Hamza*.

Fables of Bidpai [or: *Pilpay*], see *The Instructive and Entertaining Fable of Pilpay*.

Guo, Xiaoting [郭小亭]. *Ji Gong Quan Zhuan* [濟公全傳] (The Adventures of Monk Ji). [Published regularly in many editions in the Chinese-speaking world, and freely available online, http://www.dushu369.com/gudianmingzhu/jgqz/]

Ḥamzanāma, see *The Adventures of Amir Hamza*.

Ibn al-Nadīm. 1988. *Al-Fihrist* (Cairo: Dār al-Masīra).

Ibn al-Muqaffaᶜ. *Kalīla wa-Dimna*, see *The Instructive and Entertaining Fable of Pilpay*.

Indiana Jones and the Last Crusade. 1989. Dir. by Steven Spielberg (Paramount).

The Instructive and Entertaining Fable of Pilpay, an Ancient Indian Philosopher: Containing a Number of Excellent Rules for the Conduct of all Ages, and in all Stations, under Several Heads. [*Kalīla wa-Dimna.*] 1987. Trans. by Gilbert Gaulmin (London: Darf).

Ji Gong Quan Zhuan [濟公全傳]. See Guo Xiaoting.

Kalīla wa-Dimna, see *The Instructive and Entertaining Fable of Pilpay*.

Kitāb Naṣīḥat al-mulūk, see Al-Māwardī.

Lewis, Brett, and Michael Avon Oeming. 1998. *Bulletproof Monk* (Portland/Oregon: Image Comics).

Magi: Adventure of Sinbad [マギ シンドバッドの冒険]. 2016. Dir. by Yoshikazu Miyao (Lay-duce). [Anime television series.]

Mahfouz, Naguib. 1979. *Layālī alf layla* (Cairo: Maktabat Miṣr).

Mahfouz, Naguib. 2001. *Arabian Nights and Days*. Trans. by Denys Johnson-Davies (Cairo: American University in Cairo).

The Monkey King [西游记之大闹天宫]. 2014. Dir. by Cheang Pou-soi (Filmko Entertainment).

Panchatantra, see *The Instructive and Entertaining Fable of Pilpay*.

Poe, Edgar Allen. 1845. 'The Thousand-and-Second Tale of Scheherazade', in *Godey's Lady's Book*, February 1845.

Rowling, J. K. 1997–2007. *Harry Potter and the Philosopher's Stone* (1997), *Harry Potter and the Chamber of Secrets* (1998), *Harry Potter and the Prisoner of Azkaban* (1999), *Harry Potter and the Goblet of Fire* (2000), *Harry Potter and the Order of the Phoenix* (2003), *Harry Potter and the Half-Blood Prince* (2005), *Harry Potter and the Deathly Hallows* (2007) (London: Bloomsbury).

Sinbad [シンドバッド]. 2015–2016. Dir. by Shinpei Miyashita (Nippon Animation).

Sinbad: Legend of the Seven Seas. 2003. Dir. by Patrick Gilmore and Tim Johnson (DreamWorks).

Sinbad the Sailor. 1947. Dir. by Richard Wallace (RKO Radio Pictures).

The Thousand and One Nights, see *The Arabian Nights*.

A Touch of Zen [俠女]. 1971. Dir. by King Hu (Union).

Werner, Edward T. Chalmers. 1922. *Myths and Legends of China* (New York: Harrap).

Wu, Ch'eng-en [吳承恩]. 1961. *Monkey* [西遊記]. Trans. by Arthur Waley (London and New York: Penguin).

Wu, Ch'eng-en [吳承恩]. 1977–1983. *The Journey to the West* [translation of 西遊記]. Trans. by Anthony Yu (Chicago and London: Chicago University Press).

Find Out More

Multilingualism

Gramling, David. 2016. *The Invention of Monolingualism* (London: Bloomsbury Academics), https://doi.org/10.5040/9781501318078

A cogent account of the process through which our multilingualism has been reduced to monolingualism.

Lennon, Brian. 2010. *In Babel's Shadow* (Minnesota: University of Minnesota Press), https://doi.org/10.5749/minnesota/9780816665013.001.0001

Lennon exposes the problems globalization generates with regards to translation and publication of multilingual literature.

World Literature

Damrosch, David. 2003. *What Is World Literature?* **(Princeton: Princeton University Press).**

A very accessible introduction to the idea of world literature as literature that travels and how to read it.

Helgesson, Stefan, and Pieter Vermeulen (eds). 2016. *Institutions of World Literature: Writing, Translation, Markets* **(New York and Abingdon: Routledge).**

This volume explores the creative, cultural and financial forces that go into the translation and circulation of national literatures, and the making of world literature.

Hiddleston, Jane, and Wen-chin Ouyang (eds). [Forthcoming: 2021.] *Multilingual Literature as World Literature* **(London: Bloomsbury).**

The essays in this volume display ways in which literatures that juxtapose and blend what are usually considered to be sovereign linguistic systems contest the very category of 'national literature', while raising questions about the concept and definition of language.

Moretti, Franco. 2005. *Graphs, Maps, Trees: Abstract Modes for Literary History* **(London: Verso).**

World literary history is presented in this volume in the form of maps, graphs and trees.

Ouyang, Wen-chin, Jane Hiddleston, Laura Lonsdale and Nora Parr. 2020. 'Creativity and World Literatures: Languages in Dialogue', Research Strand 5 of Creative Multilingualism, https://www.creativeml.ox.ac.uk/research/world-literatures

Research project on world literatures conducted as part of the Creative Multilingualism programme between 2016 and 2020. This chapter draws on that research.

Sinbad and *The Arabian Nights*

Irwin, Robert. 1994. *The Arabian Nights: A Companion* (**London: Penguin**).

A comprehensive account of the history of *The Arabian Nights* in Arabic and European translations.

Ouyang, Wen-chin. 2005. 'Whose Story Is It? Sindbad the Sailor in Literature and Film', in *New Perspectives on [the] Arabian Nights: Ideological Variations and Narrative Horizons,* **ed. by Wen-chin Ouyang and Geert Jan van Gelder (London and New York: Routledge), pp. 1–16.**

This essay relates *The Arabian Nights* to classical Arabic literature and provides an account of the globalization of 'Sindbad the Sailor'.

Warner, Marina. 2011. *Stranger Magic: Charmed States & the Arabian Nights* (**London: Chatto & Windus**).

Warner analyzes the impact of *The Arabian Nights* in European literature and culture.

Credits

Permission to include their contribution was kindly granted by the following:

Wen-chin Ouyang for the photograph of herself (Fig. 1).

6. Prismatic Translation

*Matthew Reynolds, Sowon S. Park
and Kate Clanchy*

> Translation is inherently creative

Here are the key principles of 'Prismatic Translation', one of Creative Multilingualism's research strands:

Translation generates multiple new texts: it is inherently creative.

Translation works differently with different kinds of languages: for instance, in the 'Chinese scriptworld', speech and writing do not interact in the same way as with European languages, so translation has other processes and results.

Translation can merge with other modes of writing and re-writing: poetry and fiction are nourished by the fresh perspectives that come from thinking and feeling across languages.

In what follows, three participants in the strand outline the new perceptions and practices that arise from their approach. Matthew Reynolds explains the prismatic conception of language and translation, and shows what you can discover when you look at a book — in this case Charlotte Brontë's *Jane Eyre* — that has been translated multiple times into many different tongues. Sowon Park then shows that paying attention to different kinds of script can change how we think about what a language is, and therefore what translation does. For instance, in Europe, writing and speech typically relate to one another quite differently than in East Asia: the meaning-making practices that we name with one word — 'language' — are, in fact, very varied, and translation has to be correspondingly creative as it moves across them.

Finally, Kate Clanchy describes what happened when she introduced elements of translation and multilingual imagining into her poetry workshops at a comprehensive school, Oxford Spires Academy. A prismatic understanding of language and translation helped generate brilliantly creative work in the classroom.

Two Ideas of Translation

In the first idea, translation is a matter of right or wrong. You are doing a test at school: you either know the French for 'teacup' or you don't. You are a diplomat negotiating an international treaty: you need a text that holds both countries to the same obligations. You are a reader making your way through a book called the *Divine Comedy*: you want to know that you are getting an accurate picture of what goes on in Dante's *Commedia*. You take it for granted that the source text has something called 'a meaning' which can be carried across into the new language: any differences are errors to be deplored and, if possible, corrected. In this idea, translation is like a channel.

In the second idea, translation inevitably generates change. Even a word like 'ναι', which a dictionary will tell you is the Greek for 'yes', is not exactly the same as the English word: it has different nuances and is used in slightly different ways. How much more will a whole sentence shift when it is re-made in another language, especially if it is a sentence from a literary novel or a poem. In this idea of translation, a source text does not have a given meaning that can be extracted and relocated in another language. Rather, its significance at any moment is generated in collaboration with readers who — if they then translate — make an approximation to the source in new words which inevitably generate new meanings. These differences reveal the creative aspect of human linguistic interaction. People are varied; communication requires change; and change entails creativity. In this idea, translation is like a prism.

These two contradictory ideas probably always co-exist in thinking about translation. People use translations as equivalents of their source texts; and they also (at least, when they stop to reflect) recognize that translation and source are different. But the balance between the two ideas varies according to circumstances. With an international treaty, there will always in fact be differences of nuance between the text in one language and the text in another; but a legal and administrative structure will be in place to try to make sure that their interpretation does not differ in ways that matter in practice. With a poem, variances in translation are more likely to be relished: this is why there have come to be hundreds of translations from the *Commedia* into English, and many more than that in all the languages of the world.

The nature of the languages involved matters too, as does the medium in which the translation is done. With standardized, national languages such as French or German, grammar books and bilingual dictionaries impose the idea that there is a clear distinction between right and wrong ways of using the words, and therefore correct and incorrect translations. The medium of print reinforces this notion, because print produces identical, static copies: it is easy to slip into treating a translated book as though it were just another copy of the source text.

But there are very many situations where language-use is more fluid, so that the differences between languages become difficult, if not impossible, to distinguish from variations of dialect, register and idiom. Speech is more variable than print: speakers everywhere — in Oxford or Cornwall just as much as Delhi or Hong Kong — shift across languages, varieties and styles as they change topic, audience, or whim. In this kind of language-use, the question of what is or is not acceptable is not so much a matter of correctness as of what works in a given context.

Traditionally, this fluidity in language has been easier to hear than to see. It could manifest itself in handwriting, but it was generally excluded from the domain of print by the stringent processes of correction — of punctuation, spelling and grammar — to which manuscripts were subjected on their way to being fixed in type and published. But now, new media have shifted the relationship between the aural and the visual aspects of language: you need only glance at a text message or go to a chatroom to see all sorts of idiosyncratic, non-standard ways with words; and the Internet makes a lot of varied language-use from around the world readily available to anyone who looks for it. This alters how translation can be done, and thought about. The Prismatic Translation project responds to these new circumstances, and reconceptualizes translation in the light of them.

> **Translation and Interpreting**
>
> The difference in English, and some other languages, between 'translation' and 'interpreting' implies a strong distinction between writing and speech. We 'translate' written texts, and 'interpret' when someone is speaking. The word 'interpret' has connotations of freedom which harmonize with the fluidity of spoken language by contrast with print — as when a musician interprets a piece of music or a ballerina interprets a dance. Friends with different languages who interpret for one another in informal conversation might adopt a similar liberty, and the way they re-word one another might become part of an expression of sympathy or humour.
>
> But often interpreting happens in formal contexts such as an asylum interview or a session of an international body like the United Nations. In these circumstances, the interpreter's use of language is strongly regulated, as we can see from the guidelines for interpreters in the Finnish immigration service:
>
>> The asylum seeker's matter must be interpreted into another language comprehensively and accurately, so that the authority can reach a fair decision in the matter of a person seeking international protection. Therefore the interpreter is in a key position, communicating messages in situations which have a bearing on the rest of the asylum seeker's life. (Finnish Immigration Service Refugee Advice Centre 2010: 9)
>
> This shows the role of context and purpose in determining what an interpreter can do. The same is true of written translation: part of the reason why literature is often more freely translated than other texts is that literature spans many contexts and has complex purposes.

The Prism in Action: *Prismatic Jane Eyre*

The Prismatic Translation project combines several domains: critical theory, literary research, and the writing of poetry in schools. In all of them, we explore the creativity of translation in a world of linguistic fluidity.

In the domain of theory, we emphasize that translation necessarily generates difference. Once you accept this, you can see that the hundreds of translations of Dante are not a by-product of a process which fundamentally aims to achieve equivalence; they are not the detritus of a repeated failure of translations to match up to the original. Neither is it sufficient to explain them as symptoms of historical change. Rather, they arise from the mutability of language, and the variety in how people experience and inhabit it. Each reader will see something slightly different in the *Commedia* and, if they then translate, they will remake it in their own ways in their own idioms and cultures. Of course, sometimes there are changes that can be called mistakes; but more often there are variances which reveal the differences between people using language differently in different places and times, and thereby open up the wealth of potential meaning in the source text, its signifying energy.

This means that we can use translations not only to get a sense of books in languages we do not know, but to learn more about works that we can already read in our own tongue(s). Like Dante's *Commedia*, Charlotte Brontë's *Jane Eyre* is massively translated worldwide: so far, we have identified five hundred and ninety-two different translations, including three into Armenian and thirty into Persian. What can we discover by studying them?

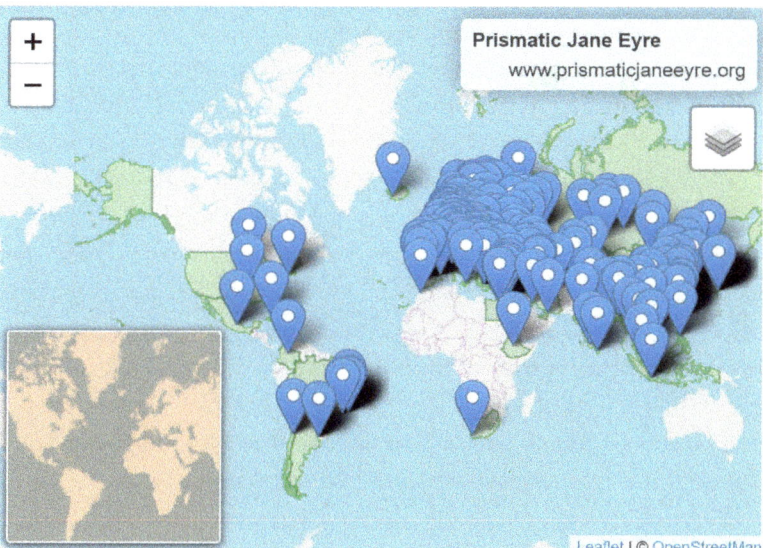

Fig. 1 This map shows the global distribution of translations of *Jane Eyre*, from the first one in 1848 to the present day, in *Prismatic Jane Eyre: An Experiment in the Study of Translations*, https://prismaticjaneeyre.org/maps/. Reproduced by kind permission of Matthew Reynolds and Giovanni Pietro Vitali.

Even changes to the title are suggestive. In 1904, an anonymous Italian translation re-titled the book *Jane Eyre, o le memorie di un'istitutrice*, which might be back-translated as 'Jane Eyre, or the Recollections of a Governess'. In 1941, a Portuguese version by João Gaspar Simões (under the pseudonym 'Mécia') saw a different story in the novel: *A paixão de Jane Eyre* ('Jane Eyre's Passion'). In Slovenia, in 1955, France Borko and Ivan Dolenc's translation offered another emphasis: *Sirota iz Lowooda* ('The Orphan of Lowood'), echoing the titles of Hungarian and German film versions, which in turn re-use the sub-title of many German translations from 1853 onwards. Jump to the 2001 Chinese translation, by Li Daming 李大明 and Li Jing 李晶, and we find yet another key, one which exploits the distinctive resources of the Chinese writing system. The title *jiǎn ài* 简· 爱 sounds like 'Jane Eyre', but the characters also mean 'simple love'. For details of these translations, and to discover more titles, go to https://prismaticjaneeyre.org/prismatic-title/. The information relayed here has been provided by participants in the project: Alessandro Grilli, Ana Teresa Marques dos Santos, Claudia Pazos Alonso, Jernej Habjan and Yunte Huang — working on multiple translations requires multifaceted collaboration!

How should we think about these prismatically varied titles? They are all different from the source; but they are not mistakes. Their divergences show that language is always embedded in contexts and communities: to translate is to remake, not only in a new language with its different nuances and ways of putting words together, but in a new culture where readers are likely to be attracted by different themes: orphanhood, governesses, passion, simple love. Tracing variants in translation can be a precise mode of cultural studies. But the multiple titles also open up a fundamental ambiguity about what kind of text *Jane Eyre* is, and what sort of story it tells. This ambiguity was already hinted at in the English titles. When it was first published in English, in 1847, the book was called *Jane Eyre: An Autobiography. Edited by Currer Bell* (Charlotte Brontë's name did not appear). The second edition, a year later, introduced a small but startling change: *Jane Eyre: An Autobiography. By Currer Bell*.

This makes the title utterly self-contradictory. If it is 'by Currer Bell' then it cannot be Jane Eyre's autobiography; if it is Jane Eyre's autobiography then it cannot be by Currer Bell. The paradox points to related questions of identity which run throughout the novel: whom should we think of as writing it? How far is it autobiographical? Is it realism or romance? How much is it about orphanhood and being a governess, and how much a timeless story of love? These uncertainties are brought into the open and crystallized by the prismatic spread of translated titles. Similar things happen to ambiguities everywhere in the book, in pretty much every turn of phrase: to show this, the Prismatic *Jane Eyre* project has taken twenty-six keywords, from 'passion' and 'conscience' to 'walk', 'elf' and 'glad', and tracked how they shift in translations into twenty languages. The source text reveals new colours of meaning when seen through the creative prism of translation. To open up this phenomenon for readers, we have created an interactive website: https://prismaticjaneeyre.org/. Please visit, explore and enjoy!

Language Lives
True to My Linguistic Reality

Eleni Philippou

In the 1940s, my grandparents emigrated from Cyprus and Greece to South Africa. My parents were raised in Greek-speaking homes, but like many first-generation children adopted their host country's language as their primary tongue. In our familial home, we spoke English to each other, but it was an English peppered with Greek phrases or words, thrown into conversation haphazardly. I went to a Greek secondary school in Johannesburg, where most pupils had the same background as myself: my friends and I used the same sort of pastiche language, English with a very light sprinkling of Greek.

As an academic I strictly use standard English, but in conversation with Greek friends and family, I still sometimes switch languages, and it is in my poetry that the mixture flourishes most creatively. I write in English, but throw in Greek words or expressions, and never translate them: that would feel disingenuous, not true to my linguistic reality. Sometimes using Greek gives a poem a different rhythm or sound, or plays with a poem's visual fabric. I believe that my poems' multilingualism forces the Anglophone reader into an active reading experience — if the reader wants to understand everything in the poem, they must search out the meaning!

My poems have been translated into Greek, Polish and German. The Polish and German translations have kept their polyglottal dimension, retaining the original Greek. To remove the Greek aspect of the poems would flatten or eviscerate them.

Here is an extract from a work in progress, entitled 'Simera':

In Attica,
from the hotel rooftop
I watch the erection of tents.

Your people carrying banners and rough signs.
They come in waves and wash the grey cement
with the paraffin grit of Molotovs.

They break upon the shoreline
of police shields,
the tainted words *drachmi* and *dollaria*.
evro.

*

As you enter the ward you pay your *fakelaki* —
pearl-white casing for an ashen owl face —
and the doctor listens to the watery murmur in your chest,
and it beats and it beats,
but only because you paid to make it beat.

Eleni Philippou is a Post-Doctoral Research Assistant on the 'Prismatic Translation' strand of Creative Multilingualism.

Fig. 2 Eleni Philippou. Reproduced with her kind permission. Photograph by Keith Barnes (2019).

Scriptworlds

A particular problem with the 'channel' view of translation is that it fails to distinguish between spoken language and written language and ignores the problems that emerge from the conflation of speech and text.

Admittedly the distinction between spoken language and written language is one that very few people are concerned to make because it has seemed self-evident that spoken language is the primary structure from which writing is derived. Thus, what we call 'language' is often presumed to be synonymous with speech, of which writing is a phonetic copy. The relation between speech and writing is quite straightforward in this way of thinking.

Ignoring the specific properties of writing does not pose an obvious problem when we are translating between literatures in European languages, which have uniformly used the sound-based Roman alphabet for writing. But when we broaden our view to the literatures of the world, and especially when we are translating between them, it becomes obvious that the relation between writing and speech is much more complicated than that which arises from within the European frame.

In contrast to how European languages are written, many 'national' languages are written in more than one script in other parts of the world, especially in the southern hemisphere. To put it technically, the national languages are 'digraphic'. Contemporary Konkani is written in Devanagari, Kannada, Perso-Arabic, the Roman alphabet and Malayalam. Azerbaijani was written in the Runic alphabet (fourth to eighth century), Arabic (seventh to twentieth century), the Roman alphabet (1929–1939), and then Cyrillic (1939–1991), before returning to a modified version of the Roman alphabet after 1992. Vietnamese was written in *Chữ Nôm* and classical *Hanzi* (*Chữ Hán*) before transitioning to the Roman alphabet in the early twentieth century. As these examples illustrate, spoken language and written language do not correlate with each other along the official borders of standardized national languages.

The lack of alignment produces a basic problem in translation. When, say, a 'Korean' poem is translated into English, anthologized and categorized as being translated from Korean, it gives a very vague and confusing indication of what it refers to, since there is no such thing as *a* Korean written language — or *a* literature written in *a* Vietnamese written language, or *a* Turkish writing system. Stating that a *Gasa* has been translated from 'Korean' into English without specifying whether it was from *Hangul* or *Hanmun* misses the fundamental details of the piece from which the translation was made. Script is not a transparent medium for transcribing spoken language as is conventionally thought.

Erasing the particular features of script is to miss the ways in which the author negotiated with the writing systems of that literary culture. For the script in which a text is written indicates whom it aimed to address. So, for example, when we read *The Tale of Genji* in English, we have an idea that it is translated from Japanese, but this does not tell us very much. In order to understand who it is addressed to, we need to know that it is mostly written in phonetic *Hiragana* and not classical *Kanji*. We can then see that Murasaki Shikibu intended it for an intimate female circle of readers in the imperial court rather than the elite male class of eleventh century Kyoto. Or we might think about the fact that Ho Chi Minh wrote the stirring *Declaration of Independence* (1945) of the Democratic Republic of Vietnam in the Roman alphabet and not *Chữ Nôm* or classical *Chữ Hán*. The alphabetic writing alone reveals the pedagogic apparatus of an internationalist literary culture in which the document is steeped.

Script is not just a medium for transcribing spoken language with no independent features in itself. Not only does it disclose the text's immediate readership, it also reveals whom it intended to exclude. Paying attention to the form of written language leads us to differentiate between the levels of readership it was intended to reach as well as to situate it in its generic and literary tradition. There are political dimensions, historical dimensions, class dimensions and dimensions of literary craft. Understanding script choice is often a precondition for appraising the nature and value of specific literary practices in most non-European literatures.

Understanding the system by which a literary culture encodes its multiple spoken languages offers a comparative perspective on how different 'scriptworlds' organize and disseminate knowledge. In a basic sense, this is because writing systems reveal the institutional educational processes by which literacy is acquired. But in a more fundamental sense, writing systems offer insight into the cognitive processes by which literature is produced and interpreted. For written word recognition not only enables the transmission of culture but also inscribes culture in our brain, as the neuroscience of reading has demonstrated in recent years. Gaining an awareness of its functions equips us with an understanding of how distinct cognitive worlds are created through different writing systems.

In addition, the opportunities presented by a more precise understanding of script allow us to move constructively beyond studies of literature based on national boundaries and national languages. World literature anthologies have become more diverse than before. But national classifications such as 'Polish literature', 'Azerbaijani literature' and 'Vietnamese literature' sustain and reproduce the modern myth of separable national languages. Statements such as 'Kazuo Ishiguro's *Never Let Me Go* has been translated into forty languages' reaffirm the presupposition of languages as discrete and distinct systems and assumes that the act of translation crosses over the gaps. Exactly what counts as a language is normally unquestioned. It is assumed that languages just exist, as biological species are assumed to exist, and need no further definition.

But the lines that divide languages are debatable and often disputed, particularly by the specialists. The old Hindi proverb that 'language changes every eighteen or twenty miles' or the often-repeated jibe that 'a language is a dialect with an army and a navy' (see also Chapter 10 in this volume) point to the hazy and often arbitrary line between dialects and languages and the equally arbitrary line between speech and writing.

Once we delve into writing systems, we soon encounter problems that force us to think through fundamental ideas which are often taken as axiomatic. One conspicuous feature of 'language' that is laid bare by scrutinizing writing systems is the extent to which the borders of a language are regulated by the structures of a nation state that legitimate and enforce them, erasing differences between the extraordinarily diverse range of spoken and written forms of language. The model of a singular standardized national language is inseparable from the sociolegal constructions of the modern nation state that polices and patrols all the scripts and dialects that the standard is supposed to constitute. The lens of script allows us to see that there is always a gap between speech and the written sign which defies the standard classification.

Translation provides an excellent site for drawing out each of the properties that distinguish writing from spoken language, and for re-orienting the relationship between them. By moving away from naturalized phonocentrism, the Scriptworlds project explores the nature and significance of both writing and spoken language on their own terms.

One of the focuses compares literature written in 'ideographic' scripts (e.g. Chinese) with those written in phonetic scripts (e.g. the Roman alphabet) and contests the controversial idea that the ideographic Chinese produces 'nominalist' thought on account of its 'graphic wealth' and 'phonetic poverty', while the phonetic Roman alphabet lends itself to the kind of abstract thinking that produced western 'realist' philosophy.

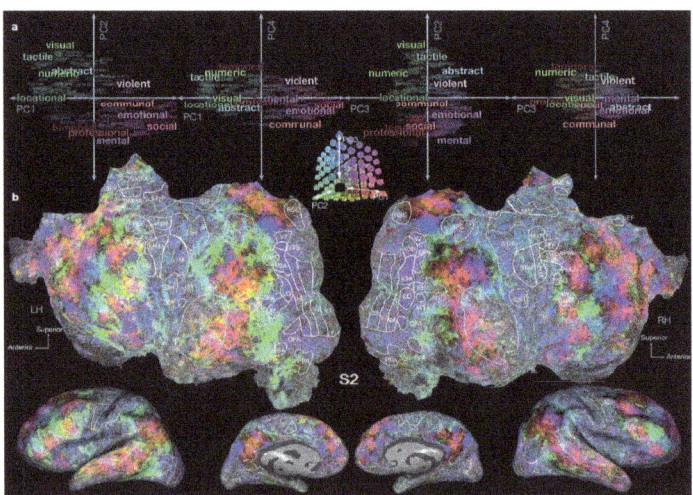

Fig. 3 'Semantic Selectivity', Alexander G. Huth et al. (2016). This figure presents a 'semantic atlas' of the human brain. Using fMRI, the authors mapped which brain areas respond to the meanings of each word, discovering that these maps are highly similar across individuals speaking the same language. © Alexander Huth / The Regents of the University of California.

Another looks at how recent developments in technology and cognitive neuroscience can help us think about language, literature and translation. With the support of the Digital Arts and Humanities Commons at the University of California, Santa Barbara, the Arnhold Program (2018–2019) scrutinized how ideas about writing can influence both our close and distant reading. Ten undergraduate and two graduate fellows researched the use of visual experimentation in the International

Concrete Poetry movement (1960–1980) archived at the Getty Research Institute. The Arnhold students translated and produced shape poems, which were exhibited in the Digital Arts and Humanities Commons (DAHC). The project enabled students to animate new links between existing scholarship on concrete poetry and the notable advances that have been made in the study of visual communication in digital technology and cognitive neuroscience. Overall, Scriptworlds creates new ways of thinking about world literature beyond the traditional rubric of nation, state and national language by examining language and literature through the lens of script, giving a more adequate account of what we call a 'language', and providing a more prismatic view of translation.

Creative Writing across Language-Difference in School: The Prismatic Workshops

Oxford Spires Academy (OSA) in Oxford is a comprehensive school with two special characteristics. One is its ethnic mix. OSA is the chosen school of Oxford's many migrants: both the asylum-seeking families who come in from nearby Heathrow and Campsfield, and the 'economic migrants' who man the city's huge hospitals and thriving car plant. The school has only about 25% White British pupils: the rest come from all over the world and speak more than thirty languages. Our second specialism is poetry: we annually sweep the board in national poetry competitions and we've made a Ted Hughes Award nominated radio documentary. Now we reach millions with our tweeted poems and we've had an anthology, *England, Poems from a School* (2018), published by Picador.

These two things are clearly related. Many of our best poets have another language at home. Very often, they went through a period of dislocation in their childhood when they lost their native language and, as one of my students once put it, 'silence itself was my friend'. That locked-down period may be painful, but it feeds the inner voice. Many of the second language students also have a strikingly good ear for the musicality of English words. Perhaps this is because, in the same way that children can learn to speak a new language without an accent because their ears and brain are still open to all the sounds and rhythms of another speech, they are also especially able to hear and reproduce the sounds of English poetry.

Language Lives
Connecting to People

Mukahang Limbu

I came to England from Nepal, when I was six years old, and although I had been learning English beforehand, it wasn't until I lived here that I truly mastered the language. I still speak Nepalese every day at home, to talk to my mother. When I am translating something, I am amazed at how the tones, and how the word orders are so different. The message is still the same, but the stresses are at different destinations. Nepal is also geographically in the middle of many countries so it is a melting pot of languages, and therefore I can also converse in Hindi and Urdu. These tongues have such a vital presence in our culture. I also taught myself very basic Korean, Japanese and Mandarin because I enjoy connecting to people from different backgrounds and I love celebrating the beauty of their words. In school I have been learning German for five years, and this has reached a point where I can write better in German than in Nepalese! Earlier on, I think there were definite barriers between the languages (my prepositions still suffer to this day), but now they co-exist, and allow me to look through different specs, aiding me in my essays, writing, drama. Every language feels like a distinct part of my identity. It feels like wearing a different mask or a persona, every time I move from one to the other.

Mukahang Limbu, who went to school at Oxford Spires Academy, is a winner of the First Story National Writing Competition, the Out-Spoken Prize for Poetry, the Peregrine Prize for Young Writers and the Forward/emagazine Student Critics Competition.

Fig. 4 Mukahang Limbu (2018). Reproduced with his kind permission. Photograph by Helen Bowell (2018).

The shapes of the student's mother language show through their English: that is part of their freshness and originality, in the way that passing a simple metaphor through Google Translate, and back again, may turn it into poetry. But the word 'mother' also matters: it is no coincidence that many of my best poets have at least one story-telling, poem-singing, non-English speaking, magical parent. When I started a Ghazal Club with Arabic-, Bengali-, Urdu- and Farsi-speaking students, and explained this ancient form, one of the Afghan girls said: 'I didn't know that ghazals were proper poems. I thought it was just something my mum knew.' But her illiterate, brilliant, mother knew, as so many Afghan women do, how to use pictures and sound to tell a salty story, create comedy and set a memory, and she had passed that ability to her daughter, who passed it into English. We wrote some wonderful ghazals because the students were able to write as more themselves with their home tongues pressing in their mouths, their magical mothers at their shoulders.

Since working with Creative Multilingualism, we've been able to bring poets in those mother languages into school. Once a term we've brought in a home language poet to work with students who speak that language. So far, we've hosted Arabic, Polish, Portuguese and Swahili poets and the results have been amazing. The students find it exciting and liberating to work in their home languages and have often started writing and translating independently afterwards. The Arabic workshop was so successful that we have had to run extra ones. One Syrian student subsequently won the John Betjeman Competition, and Mohamed Assaf, who is twelve, has had his poems retweeted more than 10,000 times on Twitter. In the summer of 2017, we gathered the poems together into anthologies and launched them in a celebratory Festival of Poetries.

In 2018, there was an extra book at that Festival. Thanks to a grant from the Royal Society of Literature's Literature Matters scheme, we were able to produce 'The Young Person's International Dictionary of Rare and Precious Words'. We collected students' favourite words and phrases from home and encouraged them to write poems around them, like this example by Anton:

'Это не трамвай!'

This isn't a tram!
My mother cries.
Закрой двери!
My mother says.
Shut the doors!

I imagine a tram. A tram
at the end of the line,
screeching rusty tracks,
a soft wind filtering
its fading interior,
a metallic bulky haul
of emptiness.

This tram only stops
when the doors slam shut.
So this tram never stops.
And this tram has no more tracks.

Now our living room is full
of Russia.
And still, it is not a tram.

Anton Chrapovikiji (aged eighteen)

The finished volume includes a hundred words, and poems about them, from 'Accomplishment', through such rare and precious terms as 'Bahi', 'Cham', 'Dinlo', 'Hijab', 'Lubita', 'Marlet', 'Oguek Szendelorz', 'Pronunciation', 'Raal', 'Trauma', and 'Vsst', to 'Zero'. There is never a shortage of languages. Recently, I ran a workshop with local primary school children and found that in a group of twenty, we had eighteen other languages in the room. I had to remind the only monolingually English-speaking child that everyone has a special language in their home — the one their mother uses, just for home. Her poem was one of the best.

The Prismatic Vision

The different facets of the 'Prismatic Translation' strand combine. Once you see that language is a continuum of variation, and that the relationship between speech and script can be constructed differently, then you can understand why translation is inherently creative. It generates new meanings and can invent new words and fresh ways of putting them together. When you realize that, you can see why multilingualism and creative writing belong together in the classroom. Any speaker or writer of any language is operating in a landscape of prismatic diversity. When you express yourself through language, you find yourself among languages.

Works Cited

Clanchy, Kate (ed.). 2018. *England: Poems from a School* (London: Picador).

Creative Multilingualism. 2020. https://www.creativeml.ox.ac.uk

Finnish Immigration Service Refugee Advice Centre. 2010. *Interpretation in the Asylum Process: Guide for Interpreters* (Helsinki: AT-Julkaisutoimisto Oy), https://migri.fi/documents/5202425/6164491/Interpretation+in+the+asylum+process+-+guide+for+interpreters+%28en%29

Huth, Alexander G., et al. 2016. 'Natural Speech Reveals the Semantic Maps that Tile Human Cortex', *Nature*, 532: 453–58, https://doi.org/10.1038/nature17637, https://www.ncbi.nlm.nih.gov/pmc/articles/PMC4852309

Prismatic Jane Eyre: An Experiment in the Study of Translations, https://prismaticjaneeyre.org/

Ronen, Shahar, et al. 2014. 'Links that Speak: The Global Language Network and Its Association with Global Fame', *PNAS*, 111: E5615–22, https://doi.org/10.1073/pnas.1410931111

Find Out More

Clanchy, Kate (ed.). 2018. *England: Poems from a School* **(London: Picador).**

This anthology of poems written by multilingual schoolchildren at Oxford Spires Academy includes many that were produced during the prismatic workshops.

Park, Sowon S. (ed.). 2016. *The Chinese Scriptworld and World Literature***, a special issue of the** *Journal of World Literature***, 1.**

This ground-breaking collection of essays shows how research on writing systems can change how you think about language.

Prismatic Jane Eyre: An Experiment in the Study of Translations, https://prismaticjaneeyre.org/

Discover the prismatic world of translation through the many versions of *Jane Eyre*. The website includes interactive maps and other illuminating visualizations.

Reynolds, Matthew. 2016. *Translation: A Very Short Introduction* **(Oxford: Oxford University Press),** https://doi.org/10.1093/actrade/9780198712114.001.0001

A popular introduction to translation which ranges across the whole field from conflict zones to poetry, and also lays the foundations of the prismatic view.

Reynolds, Matthew (ed.). 2020. *Prismatic Translation* **(Cambridge: Legenda).**

An in-depth presentation of the prismatic theory of translation, with case studies ranging from ancient Egyptian hieroglyphs to modern digital media.

Reynolds, Matthew, Sowon S. Park, Giovanni Pietro Vitali and Eleni Philippou. 2020. 'Creating New Meanings: Prismatic Translation', Research Strand 6 of Creative Multilingualism, https://www.creativeml.ox.ac.uk/research/prismatic-translation

Research project on prismatic translation conducted as part of the Creative Multilingualism programme between 2016 and 2020. This chapter draws on that research.

Credits

Permission to include their contribution was kindly granted by the following:

Anton Chrapovikiji for the poem 'Это не трамвай!'.

Alexander G. Huth et al. for the 'semantic atlas' of the human brain, in Alexander G. Huth et al. (2016), https://www.ncbi.nlm.nih.gov/pmc/

articles/PMC4852309/. Research by Alexander Huth, Wendy de Heer, Thomas Griffiths, Frederic Theunissen and Jack Gallant. Visualizations created by Alexander Huth using pycortex software (http://pycortex.org) by James Gao, Mark Lescroart and Alexander Huth (Fig. 3).

Mukahang Limbu for the Language Life 'Connecting to People' and his photograph (Fig. 4).

Eleni Philippou for the Language Life 'True to my Linguistic Reality' and her photograph (Fig. 2).

Matthew Reynolds and Giovanni Pietro Vitali for the map showing the global distribution of translations of *Jane Eyre*, from the first one in 1848 to the present day, in *Prismatic Jane Eyre: An Experiment in the Study of Translations*, https://prismaticjaneeyre.org/maps/ (Fig. 1).

7. Getting Creative in the Languages Classroom

Suzanne Graham, Linda Fisher, Julia Hofweber and Heike Krüsemann

> Language learning opens your mind

The following principles are central to the work of 'Linguistic Creativity in Language Learning', a research strand of Creative Multilingualism:

We create language every day.

Language diversity facilitates creative diversity.

Linguistic diversity nurtures diverse expression of feelings, thoughts and identities, and diverse ways of knowing and seeing the world.

In this chapter we outline how they might be considered in relation to classroom language learning.

One of the authors of this chapter recently gave a talk in a school in England to fourteen-year-olds about the benefits of carrying on with language study when they were older. Something that seemed to raise the learners' curiosity in particular was reference to English-speaking celebrities working in a range of music or entertainment fields who had learnt different languages, either at university or independently. In other words, they represented examples of 'Language Lives' these young learners could relate to. And, besides language study, what all the following people have in common is being highly creative:

> *Languages Lives*
>
> ## Can You Guess Which Languages These People Have Learnt?
>
> Chris Martin — singer and songwriter from the band Coldplay
>
> J. K. Rowling — *Harry Potter* author
>
> Natalie Portman — actor
>
> Mark Zuckerberg — Facebook founder[1]

When we learn or teach a foreign language at school, we may not automatically think about how it relates to creativity. For example, when one of us asked young learners what they disliked about learning French, one of them replied 'the endless repetition of it all', referring to lessons covering similar content and to the drills used to help the memorization of vocabulary. In other words, for that learner, language lessons seemed to be the very opposite of 'creative'. Indeed, language syllabuses in schools are often criticized for focusing on what might be seen as the mundane and trivial (such as the language needed to buy a train ticket, to describe what one's bedroom looks like, or even the contents of one's pencil case). In fact, as we hope to show in this chapter, language learning has the potential to develop what one might call *general creativity*, which, for the moment, we will define as the ability to come up with novel, yet appropriate solutions to a given problem, often diverging from conventional thought patterns (Kharkhurin 2009: 60). Additionally, we discuss ways in which the languages classroom can incorporate activities that encourage learners' *linguistic creativity*, namely their ability to use language that goes beyond the production and understanding of a narrow range of pre-fabricated phrases, as well as commanding a range of vocabulary (lexical breadth and diversity) that can be used in different combinations to express their own thoughts rather than just reproducing the perspectives of others.

---

1   Chris Martin learnt Ancient Greek and Latin; J. K. Rowling learnt French, German, Portuguese, Ancient Greek and Latin; Natalie Portman learnt French, Japanese, German and Spanish; Mark Zuckerberg learnt French, Hebrew, Ancient Greek and Latin.

In the final sections, we draw on a study we conducted with nearly 600 adolescent learners of French and German in England during the course of an academic year. We give full details later, but in brief, learners worked with two different types of text — poems, or factual, news-type texts — and experienced two different teaching approaches. The first drew their attention to the personal and emotional aspects of each text type and asked them to respond creatively, personally and emotionally to what they had read. The second, by contrast, focused on the grammar and vocabulary of the text, as well as on a factual understanding of it. We were interested in how learners' general creativity developed in each of these conditions, as well as the impact that might follow on their attitudes towards language learning, their vocabulary breadth and diversity, and on their ability to read and write French or German.

General Creativity and Language Learning

Above, we gave a provisional definition of general creativity, as the ability to come up with novel, yet appropriate solutions to a given problem, and the tendency to diverge from conventional thought patterns. Additional definitions include 'the act of making something new and different from what others are making' (Leikin 2013: 433). Being able to speak more than one language has been found in some studies to enhance that kind of creative ability, arguably because bilingualism improves mental flexibility and agility. For example, Mark Leikin (2013) presented children with a problem to which they needed to suggest a solution (in the problem scenario, a cat is trying to reach a hat on a high shelf. A chair, a stool, a bedside table and a stick are presented as items that could help). Bilingual children attending a bilingual kindergarten were found to offer more creative solutions (for example, 'throw a bag at it, and the cap will fall down' (p. 440)) than monolingual children.

But creativity is hard to 'measure'. For example, if we take as our definition of creativity the ability to generate solutions which are (**1**) **Original and novel**, and (**2**) **Functional and appropriate**, how would you rate the objects in Box 1 for their creativity?

Box 1 How 'Creative' Are These Objects?
Rate them on a 1–5 scale for the following criteria:
1) originality; and 2) functionality

Fig. 1 Photograph by Mykl Roventine (2009), Wikimedia Commons, CC BY 2.0, https://commons.wikimedia.org/w/index.php?curid=8277883

Fig. 2 Photograph by owner of Pet Rock Net (2003), Wikimedia Commons, CC BY-SA 3.0, https://commons.wikimedia.org/w/index.php?curid=7549364#/media/File:Pet_rock.jpg

Fig. 3 Photograph by Sherwin Ilagan Solina (2011), Wikimedia Commons, Public Domain, https://commons.wikimedia.org/w/index.php?curid=17836500

Fig. 4 Photograph by Camlacaze (2013), CC BY-SA 4.0, https://commons.wikimedia.org/w/index.php?curid=42135378

While there are no right or wrong answers, arguably Figures 3 and 4 are more 'creative' in that as well as being 'original', they also have functionality as a pool table and a lorry respectively. The other two images do not really go beyond originality.

A frequently used tool to assess general creativity is the Abbreviated Torrance Test for Adults (ATTA) (Goff and Torrance 2002; see also Scholastic Testing Service, Inc. 2020), which assesses divergent thinking and both the verbal and figurative expression of creative thinking. Those taking the test are asked to carry out three tasks: (1) A verbal, problem identification task, listing all the problems a person would encounter if they could fly, without being in an airplane or similar vehicle; (2) a picture completion task, taking three wiggly lines and combining them to make as many new images as possible; and (3) a picture construction task, turning a row of triangles into different images. Tasks are scored along the following lines, using the verbal, problem identification task as an illustration:-

1. **Fluency**: number of responses that are relevant, i.e. **functional**;

2. **Originality**: number of responses that are **novel**, i.e. not in the ATTA scoring manual list of the 'common responses' recorded when the ATTA was pilot-tested;

3. **Additional criteria** (max. 2 points awardable): colourfulness of imagery — do the descriptions evoke concrete and vivid images?; expression of emotional reactions to the question; future orientation, thinking bigger/taking into consideration

societal problems in the future; humour, conceptual incongruity; provocative questions, raising issues that are original.

Let's look at a response a learner recently gave us to the first task (*list the problems encountered if one could fly*).

> **Box 2 A Learner Lists the Problems Encountered If One Could Fly**
>
> 1) the sky could get very crowded, 2) there would be less space for animals such as birds to fly, 3) the ground could become overgrown with plants, 4) buildings could be destroyed, 5) a new world could build up in the sky, 6) the ground would become unused and forgotten about, 7) new technology to make things more accessible from the sky could arise.
>
> **Using the criteria above, how many points for creativity would you give this response to the ATTA verbal creativity task, and why? (See Appendix 1).**

The ATTA was used in two studies that explored whether learning a foreign language in school — in other words, **learning** to be bilingual or multilingual in a formal educational setting — would also enhance general creativity. Findings suggest that for primary school learners and young adolescents, classroom language learning does indeed contribute to the development of general creativity (Landry 1973; Lasagabaster 2000). It may be, of course, that only certain types of language teaching encourage the development of general creativity. For example, a focus on learning through repetition and memorization within a narrow range of topics, and tasks that rarely go beyond known and predictable language, seems unlikely to foster creative growth. We will return to this argument later.

It is worth emphasizing at this point that the definitions of creativity underpinning the ATTA are not the only ones that are used in academic research. Definitions may, furthermore, be culturally dependent. For example, while Western cultures tend to see creativity in terms of a product or in terms of problem-solving, Eastern cultures may lay more value on emotional and personal aspects of creativity and on further exploration of the self and personal meanings (Lubart 1999). Similarly, others such as Mark Runco (2007) discuss the 'creative personality', focusing on personal attributes and emotional dispositions rather than cognitive abilities. Runco summarizes research findings which suggest that such attributes include: autonomy, flexibility, preference for complexity, openness to a range of experiences and emotions, sensitivity, playfulness, wide interest and curiosity, as well as tolerance of ambiguity. Similarly, other researchers, such as Stephen Dollinger et al. (2007), have explored the values which are more likely to be held by creative individuals, finding that the two dimensions of values that most strongly predicted creativity were 'openness' and 'self-transcendence'. The former includes self-direction, curiosity, openness to change and stimulation; the latter, benevolence, appreciation of natural beauty, broad-mindedness, tolerance and concern with protecting the welfare of all people and the environment. They make the important point that, unlike personality traits, values are not innate, but can be developed. The implication we draw from this is that by developing the values of openness and self-transcendence, we can also develop general creativity. We argue below that the languages classroom has huge potential for fostering these values.

Linguistic Creativity

So far, we have suggested that the simple fact of being able to speak another language might enhance an individual's general creativity, given the right circumstances. We would also hope that during the course of formal language study, learners would develop the ability to use the target language itself creatively, as well as the ability to understand metaphorical and other figurative expressions in the target language (the language being learnt). On the one hand, this means being able to use and understand language in novel linguistic combinations, rather than simply producing or responding to pre-learnt phrases. Using a relatively wide range of vocabulary (lexical diversity) would also be considered to be a feature of linguistic creativity. On the other hand, it also implies being able to carry out the types of activity in the target language that would be considered 'creative' if carried out in a mother tongue. Such activities might include the creative use of language to convey a story with an exciting plot or atmospheric narrative, or the use of language to express emotions and personal views; the ability to appreciate the aesthetic and emotional aspects of language heard or read; and the ability to use language to respond to unfamiliar/unexpected contexts and events.

In England, the context for our own study, learners are expected to be able to do many of these things by the time they reach 16. In the public examination they sit at that age, they are judged on their ability to 'make independent, creative and more complex use of the language' (Department for Education 2015: 7), at least in writing, which includes 'using language to create an effect; using language to express thoughts, ideas, feelings and emotions' (Edexcel 2016: 24).

We will consider some ways in which linguistic creativity might be developed later. But let us turn first to developing general creativity.

Developing General Creativity — a Role for Poetry?

As outlined above, general creativity has been shown to include the following characteristics: original and flexible thinking, openness and tolerance (to ambiguity, to a range of experiences, emotions, perspectives), curiosity, imagination and a liking for stimulation and independent thinking. What sort of activities and materials might allow learners and teachers to develop and exercise these attributes?

For us, first and foremost, the creative languages classroom should allow learners to express a range of opinions and perspectives and offer a learning environment where experimentation and imagination rather than just linguistic accuracy are valued. The creative languages classroom would also provide stimulation, encourage learners to experience a range of emotions, and give them opportunities to consider and empathize with the experiences and perspectives of others as a form of imaginative understanding.

A recent British Council publication (Maley and Peachey 2015) provides a useful overview of ideas for creative approaches to language teaching, including the use of scenario-based tasks, drama, art and open-ended activities. The suggested approaches often introduce an element of unexpectedness and unpredictability, or 'surprise'. Unpredictability can lead to greater stimulation for learners, and hence opportunities for creativity. Unpredictability also leads to learners experiencing emotions and stimulation, with benefits for learners' levels of engagement in the languages classroom. Jean-Marc Dewaele et al. (2017) found a direct relationship between the levels of foreign language enjoyment (FLE) expressed by adolescent language learners in England and the extent to which the teacher/teaching was 'unpredictable', in the sense of varying activities, not always following the same routines and not always expecting the same responses. While this kind of unpredictability might be thought to potentially lead to greater foreign language classroom anxiety (FLCA), Dewaele et al. (2017) found that it did not, and that learners still enjoyed lessons even if they experienced some anxiety. Although this might be surprising, it suggests that experiencing some kind of emotion may be better than feeling nothing at all. They thus suggest that 'teachers should strive to boost FLE rather than worry too much about students' FLCA' (p. 676).

Unpredictability and associated emotions are, however, often missing from the languages classroom, as Dewaele (2015: 13) argues persuasively:

> One of the main problems of foreign language (FL) teaching is that the emotional component is too often ignored, resulting in relatively emotion-free (and therefore often boring) classroom sessions […] that require little emotional investment and therefore little potential for unpredictability, outbursts, surprise, risk-taking, embarrassment, anxiety […] and enjoyment.

One way of increasing 'emotional investment', 'potential for unpredictability' and, we would argue, creativity as a result, is through the use of literature in the languages classroom. Literature is often ambiguous, and thus can be read and discussed from a number of perspectives, it is open to a number of possible interpretations, appeals to the imagination and emotions, and therefore offers possibilities for the development and exercising of creativity (Duff and Malley 1990; Malley 1989). Poetry in particular offers these opportunities, tending to be more ambiguous than prose, to employ novel and unusual linguistic combinations and images, and to focus on the emotions. The philosopher John Stuart Mill, in an essay entitled 'What is Poetry?' (1833: 106), argues that such a focus on emotions, 'the delineation of the deeper and more secret workings of the human heart', is one of poetry's key characteristics. Poetry can also arouse emotions in the reader and speak to those who thus recall 'what they have felt, or whose imagination it stirs up to conceive what they could feel, or what they might have been able to feel, had their outward circumstances been different'. Poets, like other creative individuals, 'experience the world in novel and original ways' (Csikszentmihalyi 1997: 25). Such divergent thinking is then often manifested through imagery and unusual juxtapositions of words, allowing the reader to similarly experience the world in novel and original ways.

Our list of characteristics associated with creativity also included openness and tolerance (to ambiguity, to a range of experiences and perspectives). We might additionally include 'empathy' here, which has links to imagination (and hence to creativity) insofar as both involve the ability to conceive of, see, feel, experience something outside one's immediate self. Again, poetry can be used to foster this openness to other perspectives, as illustrated in an interesting study by Virgina M. Scott and Julie A. Huntington (2002). They worked with university students studying French who were learning about a French-speaking country in West Africa, Côte d'Ivoire (Ivory Coast). One group of students read and discussed a fact sheet about the country, which presented information about its economy, religion and so forth in French. Another group studied the poem 'Raconte-moi' by Véronique Tadjo, which the authors describe as follows:

> the poem mourns the gradual loss of the cultural heritage and traditions of the people of Côte d'Ivoire. Composed in free verse, 'Raconte-moi' evokes a series of symbolic images: 'the griot who sings the Africa of times immemorial', 'the beauty of the ancestors with faded smiles', and 'my past returned from the depths of my memory like a totem snake bound to my ankles'... (Scott and Huntingdon 2002: 625)

After studying the texts and writing about what they now knew about Côte d'Ivoire, both groups were asked to respond to the question: 'If you met a student from Cote d'Ivoire, what would you ask him or her?'. The responses of the group that had studied the poem were not only more varied and showed greater originality, but also displayed what the authors call 'cognitive flexibility', the 'acknowledgment of multiple views, tolerance of ambiguity' (p. 623), which, as we have discussed earlier, can be considered as important aspects of creativity. As Scott and Huntingdon explain, using literature in a specific way can help learners grasp that 'there is no single understanding or "truth"'. This requires a teaching approach that encourages learners to think 'How do I feel about this issue? Why? How might someone else feel about this?' (p. 624).

Nevertheless, some authors, such as Willis Edmondson (1997), are critical of the use of literary texts in general for language teaching, claiming that they encourage a teacher-centred approach and can be highly demotivating for some learners. Indeed, it is important to emphasize that using poetry (or other forms of literature) with language learners will not automatically lead to improved creativity. Nor will using poetry automatically lead to improved enjoyment of language study, a more positive attitude towards language study, or improved linguistic proficiency. As Amos Paran (2008: 42) argues, 'what may well be a determining factor is the way in which the learners are exposed to literature'. Paran's hesitancy here comes from the relatively small body of research that has been conducted on the impact of using literature on language learners, particularly in terms of establishing what are the teaching methods that might predict positive outcomes. The few studies he reviews that have looked at this issue suggest, albeit tentatively, that if learners are asked to give personal responses to literary texts, to engage with them on an emotional level, and give some kind of creative response to them of their own, then better outcomes (linguistic and non-linguistic) will be achieved than if they are just asked comprehension questions on the factual meaning of the text, or asked to identify any grammatical features it exemplifies.

Developing Linguistic Creativity through Poetry

Scott and Huntington did not assess whether learners in the factual text group also differed from learners in the poem group in terms of how many words they retained from those they encountered in the texts. This is an interesting question because the fact that poetry is emotionally as well as cognitively engaging may also have implications for vocabulary learning, according to certain theories of second language vocabulary acquisition. Vocabulary learning through reading is considered to be more effective if learners have a deeper sense of 'involvement' and process the language more deeply (Laufer and Hulstjin 2001). Engagement with figurative language, for example metaphorical language within poetry may increase learners' chance of retaining new vocabulary and structures encountered in texts, although again, few studies have tested this empirically. As we argued earlier, poetry is creative in part because it uses novel combinations of words. This too, from a theoretical perspective, suggests possibilities for vocabulary learning through poems. There is evidence from studies of reading in the mother tongue to suggest that presenting new words in novel contexts leads to better learning (Johns, Dye and Jones 2016), precisely because learners have to work harder to understand a word in a passage that is different from the kind they are used to reading (Nation 2017) and they thus process it more deeply. For example, speakers of English as a first language might have only ever encountered the word *benign* in a medical context (*benign tumour*), but it can also appear in a number of diverse, less familiar contexts (*benign weather*, *benign economy* or *benign ruler*). Similarly, beginner learners of French might only ever meet words such as *frère* (brother) in the context of talking about their family, or the verb *ouvrir* (to open) in the context of classroom commands ('Open your books!'). Students' learning of these words may be enhanced by encountering them in contexts such as the poem 'L'homme qui te ressemble' ('The man like you') by René Philombé, where *frère* is used in the sense of 'fellow human', and *ouvrir* in the sense of opening the door to someone, to welcome and accept them, as in the following line:

Ouvre-moi mon frère ('Open the door to me, my brother')

Thus in addition to prompting learners to reflect on the importance of tolerance and common humanity underlying any surface differences, the poem's figurative juxtaposition of 'ouvrir' and 'mon frère' may lead to better vocabulary development. This chimes with a study conducted by the Creative Multilingualism research strand 'The Creative Power of Metaphor' (see Kohl et al. 2020), which found that language learners at both intermediate and advanced level tended to show weaknesses in understanding metaphorical meanings of verbs, suggesting that more attention should be given to these in language teaching (see Chapter 1 in this volume).

In addition, if we consider linguistic creativity to include being able to use and understand language in novel linguistic combinations, rather than simply producing or responding to pre-learnt phrases, then classroom activities that stimulate learners to express opinions and feelings, and to imagine the perspective of others, provide opportunities for what Merrill Swain (1985) calls 'pushed output'. This means that learners' productive skills improve because as they are forced to express their meanings, they try out a wider range of novel linguistic combinations, and restructure the language they have previously learnt and used as pre-fabricated chunks. Studying how adults responded to literature, Myonghee Kim (2004) found that encouraging personal responses (such as creating dramatic representations of the text) led to greater interaction in the classroom, which we would expect to lead to enhanced language development.

Linguistic Creativity in Language Learning — Our Study

We now turn to how we have explored the impact of using poems in the languages classroom. Our study was motivated by a number of considerations. First, the context in which we work, England, has recently seen a much greater emphasis on literature in language syllabuses. Older learners (sixteen years plus), are required, from 2018, to appreciate literary works for their artistic merit, as well as for their meaning or topical interest. These developments are mirrored in the curriculum for younger learners: learners aged seven to eleven are expected to 'appreciate stories, songs, poems and rhymes in the language'; for learners aged eleven to fourteen, the curriculum states that they should 'read literary texts in the language' which will in turn 'stimulate ideas, develop creative expression' and help learners 'write prose using an increasingly wide range of grammar and vocabulary and write creatively to express their own ideas and opinions' (Department for Education 2013). Finally, at age sixteen, when learners take the school-leaving certificate, the GCSE, they are required not only to respond to extracts from literary texts but, as we outlined earlier, to also demonstrate their ability 'to make independent, creative and more complex use of the language' (Department for Education 2015: 7) in the exam paper that tests writing skills. It is thus implied that exposing learners to literary texts will develop their ability to use language 'creatively'. While this assumption seems intuitive and plausible, there is in fact little empirical evidence about whether literary texts rather than non-literary, factual texts are more effective with teenage language learners, because research to date has paid little if any attention to this issue (Paran 2008). Previous research has not only concentrated on the use of literature with adult learners but has rarely directly compared the use of literary and non-literary texts. Nor has it considered to any great extent the impact of *how* each kind of text is used. To understand what impact the use of literature might have, we needed to compare it to using non-literary texts, with mode of use, or teaching approach, as another moderating variable.

We chose poems as our literary text form. As we have already discussed, we see poems as offering the greatest potential for developing creativity because of their tendency to use novel and unusual combinations of language and imagery, their ambiguity and their frequent focus on emotions. In addition, to evaluate the impact on learners of using literature, we needed to compare its impact with using factual texts. We thus wanted a clear contrast between the literary and non-literary texts we used. We felt that poems offered a greater contrast with non-literary texts than literary prose did.

In terms of teaching approaches, two contrasting ways of using texts emerged from a review of the research literature that we conducted (see Bobkina and Dominguez 2014, for a summary of teaching approaches). The first of these we have already outlined: learners engage primarily with the text on the level of personal, emotional and imaginative response. We called this the 'creative' approach, because, as discussed, we see creativity as being fostered through activities whose goals are the development of original and flexible thinking, curiosity, imagination, stimulation and independent thinking, as well as openness and tolerance (to ambiguity, to a range of experiences, emotions and perspectives). The second approach we term 'functional'. Here the focus is primarily on the text as a vehicle for teaching language, vocabulary and grammar, and for developing the skill of identifying key information in a text on a factual level.

With two teaching approaches and two text types, we needed a study design which combined both elements. In other words, we needed to assess the impact on learners of (1) poems taught 'creatively'; (2) poems taught 'functionally'; (3) factual texts taught 'creatively'; and (4) factual texts taught 'functionally'. The fifteen participant schools with which we worked were therefore grouped initially by text type: one group of students (173 French, 107 German) studied only poems throughout the study, the other group (187 French, 110 German) only factual texts. Each group studied six texts and for three they experienced a creative teaching approach, and for the other three, a functional teaching approach. All teaching was conducted by the learners' usual French or German teacher. On the Common European Framework of Reference for Languages (CEFR), learners' proficiency level would be judged as being around A1.

In order to make more valid comparisons between the two text types, it was important that we kept the linguistic content as equal as possible. We began by selecting six poems (in consultation with teachers) on topics that we felt would be accessible and interesting to fourteen-year-olds but which also addressed certain more difficult and controversial issues (such as grief, migration, animal captivity), as we consider that stimulation, unpredictability and the experience of emotions and curiosity are important elements of fostering creativity. We then selected and adapted **authentic factual texts** so that the vocabulary and grammatical structures they used overlapped with what was in the poems. Both text types were matched in terms of difficulty level, word length, sentence complexity and so forth. An outline of the kinds of activities we developed can be found in Appendix 2.

We have assessed the impact of each text type and teaching approach on learners' general creativity, using the ATTA already outlined. A questionnaire has assessed impact on learners' attitudes towards, and motivation for language learning, while a range of tests have been used to assess impact on vocabulary size, reading skills, general creativity and linguistic creativity in writing. Further details can be found in Julia Hofweber and Suzanne Graham (2018). Space does not permit the reporting of detailed results from the study. We can, however, summarize the most important ones. First, the most positive impact from working with the texts occurred among the learners of French. Over the year their vocabulary size increased significantly, by about 300 words. The largest increase occurred under the the creative approach across both text types, which learners also found more helpful and enjoyable. General creativity also increased significantly, but only for learners of French experiencing the poems under a creative approach. The French poems led to significant increases in the grammatical complexity of learners' writing, across both approaches. By contrast, for the German group, vocabulary and creativity gains were not statistically significant, and they also stated a preference for the functional-type activities. Interestingly, across both languages, learners whose writing improved under the creative approach, improved far less under the functional approach and vice versa. Overall, these mixed results suggest that learners are individuals with varying needs and preferences, which teaching needs to take account of. For the French group however there was encouraging evidence of the greatest benefits coming from the creative approach, which also emerged from interviews conducted at the end of the study. Learners told us that studying literary texts 'was really fun, cos you get like to learn new stuff, learn how to express your feelings' and that they 'quite liked finding the emotions […] through the text'. Teachers liked that the materials of both kinds allowed them to engage with bigger issues, and they enjoyed seeing a different side to their pupils. One teacher commented that the poems 'allowed [learners] to open their minds and express themselves in different ways, dipping into their emotions. Taking part in the project has given me the courage to try out more ambitious things in my classroom in the future'.

Concluding Thoughts

In this chapter, we have presented different dimensions of general creativity, emphasizing its links with original and flexible thinking, and openness to a range of experiences, emotions and perspectives. We have argued for classroom activities that give opportunities for these experiences, introduce an element of unexpectedness and unpredictability and stimulate imagination and its related characteristic, empathy. We have outlined the potential benefits for linguistic creativity that might then flow from this focus on general creativity.

As part of the questionnaire we gave learners, we asked them to complete the sentence 'If French/German were food, it would be…' as a way of gaining insights into more subconscious aspects of their feelings about language learning. Some of their responses showed a resigned attitude towards the more mundane aspects of their language classes they typically experience, as something to be tolerated. Thus for one learner, if German was a food it would be 'a bowl of cereal', 'boring but important-ish'. By overlooking creativity in language learning, we may risk making it very much like the breakfast cereal this learner refers to. We hope that some of the ideas we have presented in this chapter will inspire others to use them, to help learners become aware that language is not only functional, but can be beautiful, moving and, above all, creative.

Works Cited

Bobkina, Jelena, and Elena Dominguez. 2014. 'The Use of Literature and Literary Texts in the EFL Classroom: Between Consensus and Controversy', *International Journal Of Applied Linguistics & English Literature*, 3: 249–60, https://doi.org/10.7575/aiac.ijalel.v.3n.2p.248

Chevalier-Karfis, Camille. 2008. 'Famous French Poem "Demain dès l'aube" by Victor Hugo', *French Today*, 2 January, https://www.frenchtoday.com/french-poetry-reading/poem-demain-des-l-aube-hugo

Creative Multilingualism. 2020. https://www.creativeml.ox.ac.uk

Csikszentmihalyi, Mihaly. 1997. *Creativity: The Psychology of Discovery and Invention* (New York: HarperCollins).

Department for Education. 2013. 'Statutory Guidance. National Curriculum in England: Languages Programmes of Study', *GOV.UK*, https://www.gov.uk/government/publications/national-curriculum-in-england-languages-progammes-of-study/national-curriculum-in-england-languages-progammes-of-study

Department for Education. 2015. *Modern Foreign Languages: GCSE Subject Content* (London: DFE), https://assets.publishing.service.gov.uk/government/uploads/system/uploads/attachment_data/file/485567/GCSE_subject_content_modern_foreign_langs.pdf

Dewaele, Jean-Marc. 2015. 'On Emotions in Foreign Language Learning and Use', *The Language Teacher*, 39: 13–15.

Dewaele, Jean-Marc, John Witney, Kazuya Saito and Livia Dewaele. 2017. 'Foreign Language Enjoyment and Anxiety: The Effect of Teacher and Learner Variables', *Language Teaching Research*, 22: 676–97, https://doi.org/10.1177/1362168817692161

Dollinger, Stephen J., Philip A. Burke and Nathaniel W. Gump. 2007. 'Creativity and Values', *Creativity Research Journal*, 19(2–3): 91–103, https://doi.org/10.1080/10400410701395028

Edexcel. 2016. *GCSE (9–1) French. Specification* (Harlow: Pearson Education Limited), https://qualifications.pearson.com/en/qualifications/edexcel-gcses/french-2016.html

Edmondson, Willis. 1997. 'The Role of Literature in Foreign Language Learning and Teaching: Some Valid Assumptions and Invalid Arguments', in *AILA Review No. 12 – 1995/6, Applied Linguistics Across Disciplines*, ed. by Anna Mauranen and Kari Sajavaara (Milton Keynes: Aztech Creative Print), pp. 42–55.

Goff, Kathy, and Paul E. Torrance. 2002. *The Abbreviated Torrance Test for Adults* (Bensenville, IL: Scholastic Testing Service).

Graham, Suzanne, and Linda Fisher. 2020a. 'Creative Teaching Resources', Creative Multilingualism, https://www.creativeml.ox.ac.uk/creative-teaching-resources

Graham, Suzanne, and Linda Fisher. 2020b. 'Demain, dès l'aube: PowerPoint and Lesson Plan', in 'French Creative Teaching Resources', Creative Multilingualism, https://www.creativeml.ox.ac.uk/french-creative-teaching-resources

Hofweber, Julia, and Suzanne Graham. 2018. 'Linguistic Creativity in Language Learning: Investigating the Impact of Creative Text Materials and Teaching Approaches in the Second Language Classroom', *Scottish Languages Review*, 33: 19–28.

Hoang, Ha. 2014. 'Metaphor and Second Language Learning: The State of the Field', *TESL-EJ*, 18(2).

Hugo, Victor. 1847. 'Demain, dès l'aube'. With an English translation by Camille Chevalier-Karfis (2008), https://www.frenchtoday.com/french-poetry-reading/poem-demain-des-l-aube-hugo

Hugo, Victor. 1973. *Les contemplations* (Paris: Gallimard).

Johns, Brendan T., Melody Dye and Michael N. Jones. 2015. 'The Influence of Contextual Diversity on Word Learning', *Psychonomic Bulletin & Review*, 23: 1214–20, https://doi.org/10.3758/s13423-015-0980-7

Kharkhurin, Anatoliy V. 2009. 'The Role of Bilingualism in Creative Performance on Divergent Thinking and Invented Alien Creatures Tests', *The Journal Of Creative Behavior*, 43: 59–71, https://doi.org/10.1002/j.2162-6057.2009.tb01306.x

Kim, Myonghee. 2004. 'Literature Discussions in Adult L2 Learning', *Language and Education*, 18: 145–66, https://doi.org/10.1080/09500780408666872

Kohl, Katrin, Marianna Bolognesi and Ana Werkmann Horvat. 2020. 'The Creative Power of Metaphor', Research Strand 1 of Creative Multilingualism, https://www.creativeml.ox.ac.uk/research/metaphor

Landry, Richard. G. 1973. 'The Enhancement of Figural Creativity through Second Language Learning at the Elementary School Level', *Foreign Language Annals*, 7: 111–15, https://doi.org/10.1111/j.1944-9720.1973.tb00073.x

Lasagabaster, David. (2000). 'The Effects of Three Bilingual Education Models on Linguistic Creativity', *IRAL-International Review of Applied Linguistics in Language Teaching*, 38(3–4): 213–28, https://doi.org/10.1515/iral.2000.38.3-4.213

Laufer, Batia, and Jan Hulstijn. 2001. 'Incidental Vocabulary Acquisition in a Second Language: The Construct of Task-Induced Involvement', *Applied Linguistics*, 22: 1–26, https://doi.org/10.1093/applin/22.1.1

Leikin, Mark. 2013. 'The Effect of Bilingualism on Creativity: Developmental and Educational Perspectives', *International Journal of Bilingualism*, 17(4): 431–47, https://doi.org/10.1177/1367006912438300

Lubart, Todd I. 1999. 'Creativity Across Cultures', in *Handbook of Creativity*, ed. by Robert J. Sternberg (Cambridge: Cambridge University Press), pp. 339–50, https://doi.org/10.1017/cbo9780511807916.019

Maley, Alan. 1989. 'Down from the Pedestal: Literature as Resource', in *Literature and the Learner: Methodological Approaches*, ed. by Ronald Carter, Richard Walker and Christopher Brumfit (Cambridge: Modern English Publications), pp. 10–23.

Maley, Alan, and Alan Duff. 1990. *Literature* (Oxford: Oxford University Press).

Maley, Alan, and Nik Peachey. 2015. *Creativity in the English Language Classroom* (London: British Council), https://www.teachingenglish.org.uk/sites/teacheng/files/pub_F004_ELT_Creativity_FINAL_v2%20WEB.pdf

Mill, John S. 1833. 'What Is Poetry?', https://www.uni-due.de/lyriktheorie/texte/1833_mill1.html

Nation, Kate. 2017. 'Nurturing a Lexical Legacy: Reading Experience is Critical for the Development of Word Reading Skill', *Science of Learning*, 2(1): 3, https://doi.org/10.1038/s41539-017-0004-7

Paran, Amos. 2008. 'The Role of Literature in Instructed Foreign Language Learning and Teaching: An Evidence-Based Survey', *Language Teaching*, 41: 465–96, https://doi.org/10.1017/s026144480800520x

Philombé, René. 1977. *Petites gouttes de chant pour créer l'homme: Poèmes* (Yaoundé-Messa: Éditions Semences africaines).

Runco, Mark A. 2007. *Creativity. Theories and Themes: Research, Development and Practice* (Amsterdam: Elsevier).

Scholastic Testing Service, Inc. 2020. *The Torrance® Tests of Creative Thinking and Gifted Education Products at STS*, https://www.ststesting.com/gift/

Scott, Virginia. M., and Julie A. Huntington. 2002. 'Reading Culture: Using Literature to Develop C2 Competence', *Foreign Language Annals*, 35: 622–31, https://doi.org/10.1111/j.1944-9720.2002.tb01900.x

Swain, Merrill. 1985. 'Communicative Competence: Some Roles of Comprehensible Input and Comprehensible Output in its Development', in Input in Second Language Acquisition, ed. by Susan M. Gass and Carolyn G. Madden (Rowley, MA: Newbury House), pp. 235–53.

Thériault, Gilles-Claude. 2013. 'HUGO, Victor — Demain dès l'aube (version 2).', 4:12, posted online by Gilles-Claude Thériault, YouTube, 11 September 2013, https://www.youtube.com/watch?v=lvuy4wCSHUA

Find Out More

Cushen, Patrick. J., and Jennifer Wiley. 2011. 'Aha! Voilà! Eureka! Bilingualism and Insightful Problem Solving', *Learning and Individual Differences,* **21(4): 458–62, https://doi.org/10.1016/j.lindif.2011.02.007**

Cushen and Wiley shed light on how bilingualism relates to creativity, in a study which reports that bilinguals can show advantages on creative problem-solving tasks and on those involving cognitive flexibility.

Fisher, Linda. 2013. 'Discerning Change in Young Students' Beliefs about Their Language Learning through the Use of Metaphor Elicitation in the Classroom', *Research Papers in Education,* **28(3): 373–92, https://doi.org/10.1080/02671522.2011.648654**

This article presents insights into how students perceive language learning, in a study that asked 12–13 year olds to express their views in the form of metaphors that described what language learning was like from their perspective.

Graham, Suzanne, Linda Fisher, Julia Hofweber and Heike Krüsemann. 2020. 'Linguistic Creativity in Language Learning', Research Strand 7 of Creative Multilingualism, https://www.creativeml.ox.ac.uk/research/

Research project on language teaching and learning conducted as part of the Creative Multilingualism programme between 2016 and 2020. This chapter draws on that research.

Hanauer, David. I. 2001. 'The Task of Poetry Reading and Second Language Learning', *Applied Linguistics,* **22(3): 295–23, https://doi.org/10.1093/applin/22.3.295**

This study suggests ways in which poetry can draw students' attention to important aspects of the language and so benefit their learning. It also explores how poetry reading can enhance students' cultural awareness.

Müller, Lisa-Maria, et al. 2018. 'Language Learning Motivation at the Transition from Primary to Secondary School', OASIS Summary of Graham, Suzanne, et al. (2016), *British Educational Research Journal,* **https://oasis-database.org/concern/summaries/0g354f20t?locale=en**

Summary of a study of how motivation for language learning changes as students move from primary to secondary school, reporting that young students value learning activities related to culture, communication and creativity.

Owen, Stephen, and Robert Woore. 2019. 'Teaching Reading to Beginner Learners of French in Secondary School', OASIS Summary of Woore, Robert., et al. 2018, https://oasis-database.org/concern/summaries/nc580m68d?locale=en

Summary of a study that used semi-authentic texts with beginner learners of French, showing that learners enjoyed them, responded well to more challenging, culturally-rooted material and increased their French vocabulary as a result.

Appendix 1: Scores for the ATTA Verbal Creativity Task Response Given in Box 2

The verbal, problem identification task is one of three tasks used in the Abbreviated Torrance Test for Adults (ATTA) to assess creativity. The score for this task is added to scores for the other two parts of the test to give a 'creativity score' which is relative rather than absolute.

Creativity is defined as the generation of solutions that are both **novel**/out-of-the-box and **functional**, so both aspects need to be considered when scoring responses. The Abbreviated Torrance Test uses a range of criteria to score creativity. The ATTA is a 'standardized' test, meaning that its authors have tested it with a large number of participants to create a scoring manual with detailed normed criteria.

Verbal creativity task 1 (*Imagine you could fly without the help of an aeroplane — list as many problems as you can think of*):

Example answer:

1) the sky could get very crowded, 2) there would be less space for animals such as birds to fly, 3) the ground could become overgrown with plants, 4) buildings could be destroyed, 5) a new world could build up in the sky, 6) the ground would become unused and forgotten about, 7) new technology to make things more accessible from the sky could arise.

A) Core criteria (count each point)

- **Fluency**: number of responses that are relevant, i.e. **functional**.

Score: the seven problems listed can be considered as sufficiently relevant and different from each other to be counted as **7 points**.

- **Originality**: number of responses that are **novel**. The ATTA manual provides an 'originality' exclusion list of common responses, i.e. problems frequently listed when the ATTA was pilot-tested. Responses only receive points for originality if they are not already on this list.

Score: the example response listed three issues that are not on the originality exclusion list (*less space for birds to fly, ground unused an* *overgrown, new world and technology*). **3 points** are therefore given for originality.

B) Additional criteria (max. 2 points for each category)
- **Richness**: Points of colourfulness of imagery — do the descriptions evoke concrete and vivid images?

Score: the example answer contains at least two instances with detailed descriptions of problem (*less space for birds, ground overgrown with plants*). **2 points** are therefore given for richness.

- **Expression of emotions**: points for expressing emotional reactions to the problems.

Score: In the example answer there is no evidence of emotional reactions. **0 points** are therefore given for expression of emotions.

- **Future orientation**: points for considering societal problems in the future

Score: The example answer scores highly on this criterion (*new world, ground forgotten, sky crowded*). **2 points** are therefore given for future orientation.

- **Humour**: points for conceptual incongruity

Score: In the example answer there is no evidence of humour. **0 points** are therefore given for humour.

- **Provocative questions**: points for raising issues that are original

Score: In the example answer there is no evidence of provocative questions. **0 points** are therefore given for provocative questions.

TOTAL POINTS: 14

Appendix 2: Creative Activities in the Classroom — Practical Ideas

Here we give details of how we have used poems and also factual texts to achieve some of the goals we outlined earlier, namely providing opportunities for original, independent and flexible thinking, openness and tolerance (to ambiguity, to a range of experiences, emotions, perspectives), curiosity, imagination and stimulation. We use the example of the French poem 'Demain, dès l'aube' ('Tomorrow, at dawn') by Victor Hugo (1847). It was written after the tragic death of the poet's nineteen-year-old daughter, Léopoldine, in a boating accident. The poem depicts a journey through the countryside, suggesting that the protagonist (the poet) is on his way to meet a loved one. The destination is ambiguous at the start, and it is not clear who the two protagonists are, nor what their relationship is. It is only at the very end that the reader realizes that the narrator is journeying towards the grave of the loved one, on which he places a sprig of green holly and flowering heather.

The factual text that was used as a match to this poem presented the plight of people from the French-speaking island Saint-Martin, who had lost loved ones in Hurricane Irma. As a parallel to the metaphorical journey depicted in the Hugo poem, the factual text outlined the five stages of grief experienced by the mourners. The activities used with both the poem and the factual text were more or less identical, so, for brevity, we outline only those used with the poem (see Graham and Fisher 2020b).

In 'Demain, dès l'aube', the poet's journey is both a literal one through space, but also a metaphorical journey through different stages of grief: from despair, indifference to everything except reaching the journey's end point, and finally to hope and belief in the immortality of the loved one. The poet's determination to reach his destination is conveyed by the repetition of verbs of movement in the future tense. Indeed, it is the future tense, and a factual comprehension of where the poet goes and what he does, that tend to be emphasized in most other teaching resources that feature the poem, but usually without much consideration of how they contribute to the poem's mood, meaning or symbolism.

What might an alternative approach look like, using the same text? Openness to the poet's perspective, a readiness to engage with the ambiguities of the poem and its symbolism, need to be built up to gradually. As a first step, the activities we used were aimed at helping learners to understand something about the person who wrote the poem and why they wrote it, in order to facilitate comprehension on both a literal and figurative level. Our opening activity gave learners some basic facts about Hugo, outlining briefly the tragic event that prompted him to write the poem. Then, to encourage initial empathy, learners were asked to look at three pictures, one of which depicted Hugo. In order to identify which of the images might be him, learners needed to appreciate that he would be grieving, serious and so forth, thus exercising imaginative understanding of his mental state.

The next stage then offered further possibilities for imagination and potentially divergent thinking. Learners were presented with visual images linked to the boating accident, and then anticipated or predicted what the poem might be about, what its tone and atmosphere might be like, how it might make them feel. Both this and the previous activity could be conducted in the learners' mother tongue, but equally, as demonstrated in the resources for the poem (Graham and Fisher 2020b), they could take place in French, the target language, with support from example words and phrases that learners could use to help them articulate such predictions.

In other words, there is preparation work to be done to help learners be ready to engage emotionally and deeply with the poem and thus stimulate their creativity. This is then followed by the initial presentation of the poem itself. We used music and images to enhance the impact on learners — for example, a reading of the poem from YouTube which combines evocative music by Bruno Garbay with an expressive reading by Gilles-Claude Thériault (2013). Employing a range of media (music, images, the spoken and written word), we would argue, not only heightens learners' engagement with the poem, but also aids their understanding of its theme and mood, stimulating their imagination and potentially leading to deeper processing of the poem's language.

Similarly, rather than focusing on the use of the future tense in the poem from a grammatical perspective, we asked learners to identify lines from the text that convey stages in the poet's 'journey' through his grief, from despair to some sort of acceptance. In the final part of this activity, learners selected what they saw as the most important lines of the poem. Arguably the most important are the last lines, in which the placing of the holly and the heather on the grave symbolizes the poet's sense of immortality and that his daughter will live on; learners however were free to make their own choice, with reasons, in an effort to encourage divergent thinking. A final writing activity (given as homework) focused learners on the metaphorical aspects of the poem, asking them to think of images (either expressed through words or drawings) to convey the different aspects of the poet's journey through grief. Offering them the choice of presentation format we considered important for the development of the autonomy that is central to creativity.

8. Inspiring Language Learners

*Jane Hiddleston, Laura Lonsdale,
Chiara Cappellaro and Daniel Tyler-McTighe*

> Languages hold infinite potential for creativity

Language learning in a child's early life involves lots of language play and nonsense — while literacy teaching involves far too little, as David Crystal has highlighted: 'Reading and writing do not have to be a prison-house. Release is possible. And maybe language play can provide the key' (1998: 217). The teaching of languages in schools similarly tends to be far too constrained, with syllabuses allowing little time for language play, let alone creative experimentation with language diversity. A focus on 'useful' language required for practical transactions and communicating information; 'relevant' topics designed to turn young people into worthy adults; and excessively difficult exams that undermine learners' confidence in their linguistic abilities — these factors are likely to have contributed to the steadily diminishing take-up of languages in schools in the United Kingdom, despite the best efforts of many excellent and committed teachers to make languages appealing. In addition, it's difficult to motivate students when there is a general tendency to assume that monolingualism is the norm and 'global English' is all that's needed for international and intercultural communication.

Creative Multilingualism puts linguistic creativity at the heart of languages and language learning, and builds on the fact that we are all innately multilingual. Languages come from deep inside us and are intimately bound up with our creative potential and its expression. From before we are even born, our languages help to shape who we are, allow us to develop rich and meaningful relationships, and give us infinite possibilities for expressing ourselves creatively. We learn to switch effortlessly between different registers, from grunting to poetic utterances. We acquire the ability to communicate appropriately and effectively in different ways with our family members, best friend and pussycat. In our day-to-day interactions, we may use different accents, one for home and one for school or work; different dialects, depending on the region we come from and where we find ourselves; and for some of us, our cultural environment prompts us to develop that potential into a command of two or more different languages.

Moreover, our knowledge and use of our native language or languages changes in the course of our lives. We are continually expanding our repertoire within the language or languages we know, and potentially learning new languages right through to old age. Research in cognitive neuroscience is increasingly coming up with evidence to suggest that learning languages, and speaking more than one language, is good for the brain, much as exercise is good for the body — this suggests that our brains are designed to be multilingual. Bilingualism has been shown to delay the onset of dementia by some four to five years when compared to monolingualism since it involves enhanced cognitive stimulation. Indeed, a research group based in London and Edinburgh has come up with the concept of a 'Healthy Linguistic Diet' (Mehmedbegovic-Smith and Bak 2020), demonstrating that learning of languages and their regular use improve the health of our brain. There's a lot of evidence to suggest that multilingualism is built into the human DNA.

Looking into the development of languages over time also makes clear that diversification has been busily at work throughout the history of mankind. Natural languages are not generally invented from scratch — they have evolved from other languages as peoples have migrated across territories, seas and continents, a process that is continuing as people from different parts of the world converge on cities, bringing their languages with them while also connecting with new languages. While such processes generate an infinite multitude of dialects and regional variations, joint derivations also leave a multitude of traces in the related languages in the form of 'cognates', for example English 'brother' and German 'Bruder' (see Chapter 3 in this volume for many ways in which this principle can help language learning).

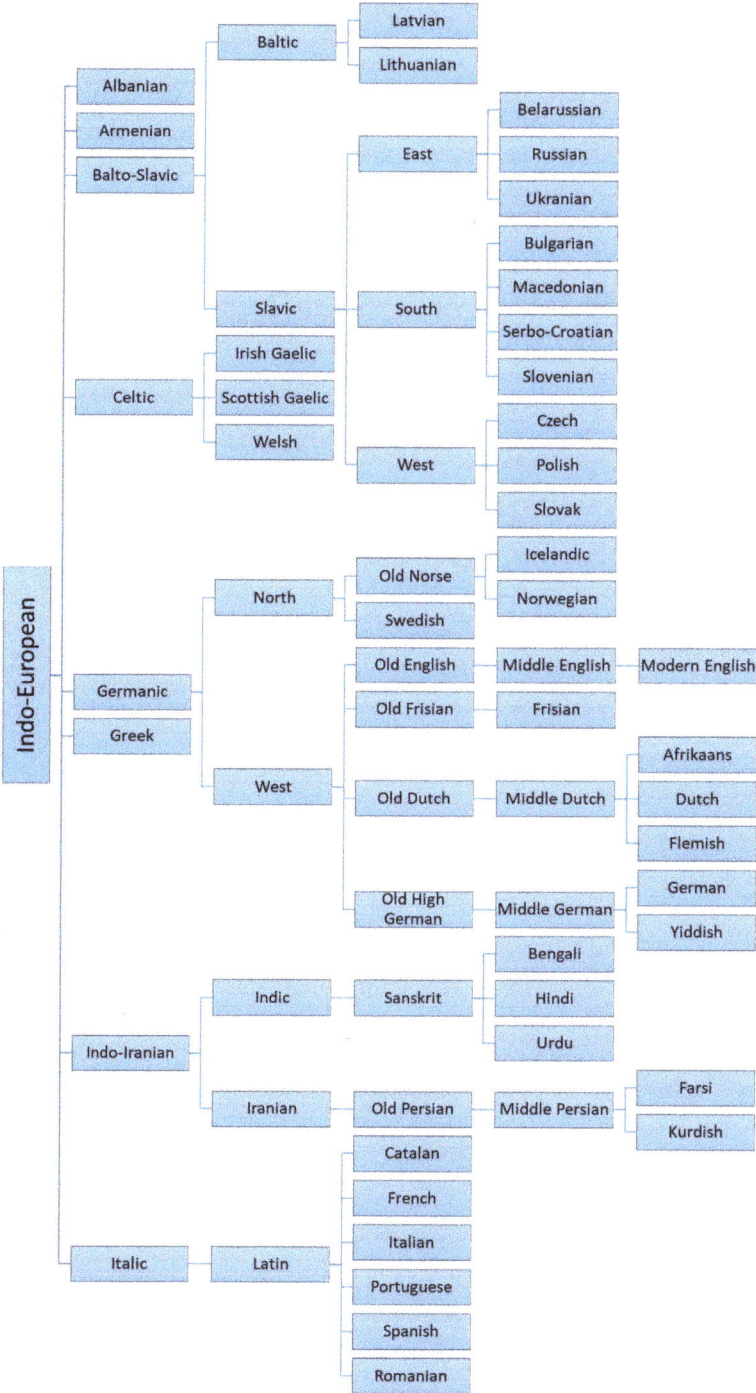

Fig. 1 Family tree diagram depicting relationships between Indo-European languages — assuming a common ancestor that remains elusive (2020). Reproduced by kind permission of Chiara Cappellaro.

Language historians often define language relationships by presenting them in the form of a 'family tree' such as that depicting the relationships between Indo-European languages in Chapter 3 or the more schematic representation given here in Figure 1.

In learning languages, we can also benefit from the many episodes of historical and current contact between languages, such as the intensive contact with Norman French that became so important for the development of modern English, and the extensive influence of English on other languages in the current world. We can draw on the language or languages we know to explore similarities and differences and build bridges to the new one (see, for example, the EuroCom framework: Hufeisen and Marx 2014; McCann et al. 2003). We can also experiment with translation to compare how facts, ideas, emotions and stories are expressed in different languages. While 'immersion' in a new language helps to internalize it, working across languages enhances our understanding of the interplay between the many facets of linguistic and cultural similarity and difference.

In the course of investigating the interaction between language diversity and creativity, Creative Multilingualism has been considering many aspects of language learning, involving teachers and learners. An empirical research project investigated how pupils studying Modern Foreign Languages (MFL) respond to different types of task, focusing on more functional ones and more creative ones (see Graham et al. 2020 and Chapter 7 in this volume on 'Getting Creative in the Languages Classroom' for further insights). A set of workshops with poets writing in languages spoken by students of English as an Additional Language in an Oxford school enabled English as an additional language (EAL) students to engage in creative writing and translation involving their native language (see Reynolds et al. 2020 on 'Prismatic Translation' and the final part of Chapter 6 in this volume). The present chapter is devoted to three further projects conducted in the course of our research on Creative Multilingualism:

- In the section 'Celebrating the Diversity of Languages through Multilingual Poetry', Jane Hiddleston and Laura Lonsdale present multilingual creative writing workshops in which they took their research on 'Creativity and World Literatures' (see the final section of Chapter 5 in this volume) into schools.

- In the section 'Learning from Language Connections', Chiara Cappellaro and Martin Maiden report on the response to workshops they ran in schools that built on the research into 'Creating Intelligibility across Languages and Communites' reported in Chapter 3 in this volume.

- The final section of the chapter is devoted to the 'Multilingual Performance Project' (MPP) directed by Daniel Tyler-McTighe, which is connected to the research into 'Languages in the Creative Economy' presented in Chapter 4 in this volume. The MPP is designed to encourage teachers to exploit the enormous potential of drama for language teaching. Workshops and resources equip them with the skills to try out drama activities in the languages classroom, as reported here by some participants.

All three projects discussed in this chapter are designed to demonstrate how insights gained in the course of Creative Multilingualism research can be put into practice, enabling teachers and learners to experiment with multilingual creativity and experience its benefits for language learning.

Celebrating the Diversity of Languages through Multilingual Poetry

Jane Hiddleston and Laura Lonsdale

We wanted to take our research on 'Multilingualism and Creativity in World Literature' (see Ouyang et al. 2020 and the final part of Chapter 5 in this volume) into schools in order to give teachers and students the opportunity to try out new approaches to language learning that involve a rich diversity of languages. We ran workshops for Year 10 pupils taking French or Spanish GCSE in East and West London schools, where a high proportion of students speak more than one language.

The workshops took place in both London and Oxford, and their objective was to engage and celebrate the linguistic and cultural diversity of these schools and their local communities, encouraging students to think positively and creatively about both the languages they speak at home and the languages they are learning at school. With a multitude of languages ranging from Bengali to Romanian, we had plenty to work with! Sessions focused on linguistic diversity as a source of creativity. They introduced students to poems and prose texts employing more than one language (including either French or Spanish), and gave them the opportunity to try out their own creative, multilingual writing.

An introductory session consisted of a broad and wide-ranging celebration of multilingualism and the many languages spoken by students in the room. We had some lively discussions of the singular and dynamic ways in which they use their languages, while also reading together and discussing some of the poems from the project *Brave New Voices* by our partner organization PEN that specifically reflect on 'my language'.

A highlight was the work we did with the Portuguese poem 'Eu Falo' and its English translation 'I speak', which students were able to translate again into French, Spanish, Italian, Polish, Swedish, Kosovan, Egyptian Arabic, Moroccan Arabic, Thai, Burmese and Japanese. They spoke in lively and thoughtful ways about the challenges of the exercise and the phrases that seemed to resist translation. We were impressed by the students' energetic engagement with the activities we set, by their extraordinary linguistic competence, and the thoughtfulness with which they were able to analyse their language usage.

But it was in the second and third sessions that their creativity really came to light. During the second session, we read translingual poems using French and Spanish, and found the students could cope admirably with challenging poetic material. They had a lot of subtle and intelligent ideas about intercultural creativity and its social and ethical implications. In the final session, they were introduced to various poetic forms before working to produce their own multilingual creations. Students were bold in writing in a range of languages, many using French and Spanish, but we also had whole poems in Urdu and Swedish, and a beautiful poem about friendship alternating between lines in English, Italian and Spanish.

The workshops revealed to us the extraordinary linguistic talent alive in these London schools, a talent students seemed not to recognize in themselves, and which the curriculum at the moment does not valorize.

They showed us how committed the students are to their languages but also to learning new languages — they really demonstrated their passion for discovery, for communication, for learning about new ways of seeing the world. Here is an acrostic poem created by a student in Year 12 at Haggerston School in Hackney in 2017:

Le Monde est à nous

Le role de
La race, de la rEligion

La laicité est-elle la Meilleure chose
Mais qu'en est-il des lOis en France?
Par exemple, la loi coNtre le port du
voile intégral
Répète, que le monDe est à nous
Dans une mEsure, the world is
ours

Le cœur tient des rÊves, l'esprit forme
des plans
Malgré l'abSence de moyens de réalisation
Peut-êTre the world is theirs, not yours

L'argent, les droits, les gens
la puissAnce, la possession.
Un système dans lequel

The world is miNe, and oui
the world is yOurs

The world is for toUt le monde, for personne
La question:
le monde est-il à nouS?

Karishma Kaur

The poems created by the students gave us insight into their enormously diverse and dynamic communities, conveying their respect for one another's differences and willingness to listen and learn.

Feedback from the Participants

Of those who responded ...

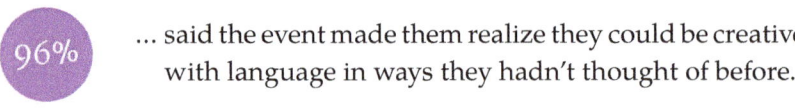
96% ... said the event made them realize they could be creative with language in ways they hadn't thought of before.

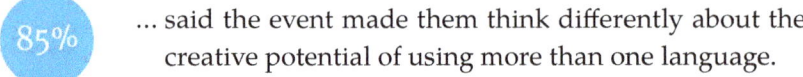
85% ... said the event made them think differently about the creative potential of using more than one language.

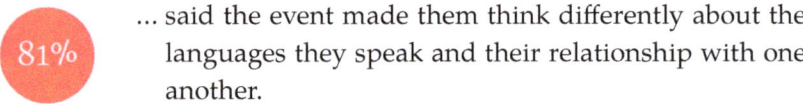
81% ... said the event made them think differently about the languages they speak and their relationship with one another.

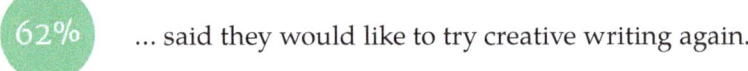
62% ... said they would like to try creative writing again.

And here are some of their comments:
- 'I had never heard of multilingualism!'
- 'The event has made me more creative, I used different languages and learned some as well'
- 'I understand better the importance of languages and that we can have fun with them'
- 'Mixing languages makes things sound interesting and fun'
- 'Poems and mixing languages can help show greater meaning'
- 'This event has brought a lot of people together and made us think about sensitive topics like racism, etc.'

Feedback from Teachers

James Johnson (Haggerston School, Hackney):

> Our students not only got the chance to think about how their own linguistic backgrounds inform their study of French and Spanish, but they also got the sense that their experiences and backgrounds are valuable and valued as a source of creativity and energy that will only help them as they pursue their language studies to A Level and beyond. To see our students make genuinely insightful analysis about poetry in a mixture of other languages and then apply a range of techniques in their own work was a real treat, and broke down barriers between subject areas that certainly linger on in many students. Normally we don't make enough space for this type of work and activity. The engagement of students and the level of challenge was clear for all to see.

Ciara Mulvenna (St Paul's Way Trust School, Tower Hamlets):

> The activities allowed students to think about their relationship with languages in ways they hadn't done before, and has sowed the seed for a lot of valuable discussion around the links between language, culture and identity. The project has given me and my department some real food for thought around how we might celebrate home languages. Indeed, we plan to use some of the activities we saw during the workshops as part of our introduction to Modern Foreign Languages in Year 7, as a way to increase motivation.

As organizers of the workshops, we were privileged to work with highly dedicated and talented teachers. We loved the way the students rose to the occasion, not only displaying some excellent reading skills but writing haikus, cinquains, acrostics and more in several languages. We are convinced that more work needs to be done both to remind school children of their fantastic assets and abilities, and to show them the extent of what they can do both with the languages they speak at home and with those they learn in the classroom.

Learning from Language Connections

Chiara Cappellaro and Martin Maiden

Our research in the Creative Multilingualism strand on 'Creating Intelligibility across Languages and Communities' (see Maiden et al. 2020 and Chapter 3 in this volume) focuses on the nature of comprehension and incomprehension of different, but related languages (e.g. Spanish and Italian, or German and Dutch). Our findings have bearing on how we learn languages — and on how we can make learning both easier and more interesting. We therefore decided to visit a school in Oxford, where we spoke to a large audience of Year 9 students about the empowering fact that *foreign languages are not as 'foreign' as we think*.

In particular, our talk was aimed at increasing awareness of the following issues:

1. **Multilingualism is not unusual**. It is what most speakers experience in their life.

2. **Learning a new language is a bit like climbing a mountain**. Getting to the top (being able to express oneself in a given community as a native speaker of the language would do) is what we should all aim for, but this is not always possible. What is always possible, however, is to get some way up the 'mountain' using one's creativity and deductive powers to learn to identify and exploit similarities between languages.

3. **Similarities among languages can be of (at least) two types: familiar/genetic and contact-induced**. We gave some examples of this as follows:

    a. Showing similarities between words referring to body parts in 'sister' Germanic and Romance languages.

    b. Highlighting similarities in everyday words like 'chocolate', 'tomato' and 'bus stop', which are due to borrowing in languages that are very different from one another, like Japanese and English.

4. **Sometimes 'tricks' can be used to find correspondences between languages** and we explained how these tricks reflect sound changes that can be traced back in time. For example, if we consider how German 'z' (pronounced [ts]) often corresponds to English 't', it is not difficult to guess that the German words *zwei* and *zehn* (numbers) correspond to English *two* and *ten*.

In a post-talk Q & A session, one student asked a sensible but unexpected question: where can I find information on tricks, such as how the German <z> often corresponds to the English <t>? We hesitated in answering. The literature on sound change is very rich, but there is, to our knowledge, no immediate resource for young learners that we could recommend.

Feedback after the event showed that the pupils were most struck by how similar languages are, and how they 'steal' from one another — facts they had not known before attending the session.

 ... of pupils said that languages are more interesting than they previously thought.

 ... of attendees stated that they are now more confident about their ability to understand the meaning of individual words written in a foreign language.

We were delighted to see such positive feedback and hope the presentation inspired and encouraged them to start or continue learning a language.

Multilingual Performance Project

Daniel Tyler-McTighe

The Multilingual Performance Project (MPP) draws on research Creative Multilingualism has been conducting on 'Languages in the Creative Economy' (see Dudrah et al. 2020 and Chapter 4 in this volume), working with members of the performing arts scene in Birmingham. It builds on the fact that languages have an important performative dimension. Just watch how politicians use gesture to get their message across. Theatrical acting takes this further, involving the whole body. It doesn't have to be Shakespeare, Racine or Calderón — for all of us, acting is in our blood, as we can see when we imitate someone else's speech, or take on a particular persona in public that's rather different from the way we are at home.

As the MPP Director, I was initially based at the Birmingham Repertory Theatre but worked with schools across England and Wales, connecting them with local theatres — these included Prime Theatre in Swindon, Hull Truck Theatre, Hampstead Theatre and Wales Millennium Centre. They supported these multilingual performances and workshops with staff expertise, performance spaces and/or props. I ran workshops for teachers while also creating resources for use in the classroom.

The project involved many different forms, from short sketches, play readings and news broadcasts through to full theatre productions. The aim was to give learners opportunities to discover their 'Multilingual Me' and experience language learning as fun and exciting. We wanted students to explore languages in a setting which allowed them to do the best they could with simple words, and where they could make up for something they were unable to say in other ways, for example by using mime. This can be particularly helpful for building up confidence in speaking skills, which are otherwise hard to practise since we all get embarrassed when we forget vital words, realize we're making basic grammatical mistakes, and can't even begin to feel fluent. In a fun acting game, such issues become irrelevant if they are not critical to winning.

An important dimension of the MPP was to showcase and celebrate the multilingual nature of schools and demonstrate how students' home languages can interact productively with language teaching in the classroom. We also discovered the natural connection between sign language and gesture, which is such a fundamental part of performance. Moreover, performance turned out to have tremendous potential for engaging students with learning disabilities.

For teachers not used to acting or staging plays, involving performance in their teaching can seem intimidating. A key aim of MPP was therefore to encourage teachers to appreciate that drama work is doable even if you are a novice, and rewarding as a means of engaging even lower-attaining students and building a sense of common endeavour. We encouraged language teachers to join forces with teachers in their school's Drama or English department, and we ran a number of workshops to give teachers hands-on experience (see Fig. 2).

Fig. 2 Multilingual Performance Project workshop, 2019. Photograph by Ben Gregory-Ring (2019).

A project like this needs to be highly flexible so that each performance and the participants involved can be geared to the teacher's experience and interests, the age and interests of the students, and the school's resources and needs. In order to avoid putting pressure on teachers, we ensured that commitment to the MPP could be low, and performances small-scale.

Here are some accounts about MPP projects. Holly Bateman, a theatre practitioner from the Birmingham REP, directed an interactive performance project with actors, teachers and students entitled *The Birds*. Teacher Sarah Williams tried out a number of performance games she learned at MPP workshops, and Ann Poole gives a glimpse of the stress and satisfaction of creating a performance with primary school children.

Dramatic Ways of Realizing that Multilingualism Can Be Beneficial

Holly Bateman,
Royal Birmingham Conservatoire / Birmingham Repertory Theatre

Did you know that corvids, the crow family, are native to every single continent, and found everywhere except the polar ice caps? Consider how many languages they must encounter throughout the world, how many different names they must have! Now imagine five nests, all belonging to different species of birds, all with their own unique language skill set, and primary school children being encouraged to meet them, join them, learn their language and teach the birds elements of their own home language.

This was our starting point when developing this project. We wanted children to be encouraged to embrace many different forms of communication, and see that a wealth of languages can boost their creativity and ability to communicate. Each nest has a puzzle to solve, be it through sign language, music notation with a non-verbal Robin, multiple spoken languages or using an emoji dictionary. If the children can help the Birds realize that their multilingualism can be beneficial, maybe the bird flu outbreak can be averted!

The Birds was created by Applied Theatre students at the Royal Birmingham Conservatoire in association with the Multilingual Performance Project. The interactive performance project toured Birmingham schools in November 2018, with the final performance taking place at the Birmingham REP.

The initial stimulus for the piece came from a brief introduction to some of the research being undertaken by the Creative Multilingualism research strand 'Creating a Meaningful World: Nature in Name, Metaphor and Myth' (see Gosler et al. 2020 and Chapter 2 in this volume). In one of their projects, they're looking into the different names and myths associated with the same bird as it migrates across countries and cultures. This gave our creative team the initial spark to look at birds speaking different languages and facing the challenge of needing to communicate to build bridges.

The Birds was a great success, and both actors and the participating schools commented on how much they enjoyed the project.

Katie Hoare (actor):

> After weeks of rehearsals and a long intensive week of polishing scenes, organizing props, gathering costumes and face paint, we are all extremely proud to say we have a full-blown show. As it is drawing to a close, it's a perfect time to start reflecting on what has been learned during the process, especially thinking about how the concept of language is being used.
>
> Throughout the performance, a wide range of different communication skills are being used. However, after polishing the scenes, I noticed a lot can be said physically with body language. Then questions started popping up — *I am portraying a crow, how do crows move?* How can crow characters show emotion through physicality? After the exploration of crows, I figured they are quite crooked. So, when exploring emotions through physicality we created this crooked body language. For example, when we laugh, our shoulders shake up and down, in a tense manner.
>
> Personally, I have learned an incredible amount of useful information throughout the entire process, especially how language is vital in everyday life. Not only have I learned aspects of sign language and how you can teach through song, I have also learned skills that I can take on and use in my own practice. From performing to devising the show, I have been enlightened on this whole new adventure by language and how it can be used as a tool. Not only can our show *The Birds* encourage children to learn different ways of communication, and learn from their fellow peers, I believe there are ways it could be adapted for adults. There are lessons to be learned from the performance about how important it is to understand the concept of multilingualism and the different ways of communicating and using languages.

Sophie Fleming (teacher at Colmore Infant and Nursery School):

> Our children are so used to coming into the hall and sitting in lines for assembly or to watch a show, so it was a really different experience

for them to walk in and become part of the performance straightaway. They came away from the performance full of joy; they had experienced something new, they loved the 'story', it was interactive and fun, and they also understood the overall message. When we got back to the classroom I could hear things like 'this is the best day ever!' and one girl said 'If I could give it a number for how much I liked it out of 10, I would give it 10!' I thought the actors were brilliant with the children, and they spotted children who were a little nervous or needed some support.

Using Drama Activities in Modern Foreign Language Lessons with Secondary School Pupils

Sarah Williams, Greenford High School, Ealing

Two eager, intrepid Modern Foreign Language teachers, Maddie Fisher and I, had the pleasure of attending a workshop on using the Multilingual Performance Project's exercises and skills in language teaching. Both of us have some drama background and we were very open to bringing drama skills into our teaching of French, German and Spanish. The MPP practitioner led us through various 'games' focused on a 'whole body' approach to teaching languages that we both warmed to. Much laughter resulted and several participants quickly suggested how they might use or adapt these ideas back in the classroom.

The following week, I tried out two games with my Year 10 German class and Year 9 French class, both lower-attaining groups. I used the games of Sevens (see below), first using numbers, as it was introduced, and then playing the same game using a phrase I wanted the class to really get the hang of. In my experience, German students perennially struggle to get the perfect tense right, so we played the game using the sentence 'Letzte Woche bin ich nach Stuttgart gefahren', a sentence of exactly seven words. In French we played 'je ne m'entends pas bien avec mon père'. In both cases, this appealed to classes which were often restless and struggled to maintain focus on a task for long. They liked the game and were keen to stay 'in'. But what to do with those who are 'out'? More on this later.

As Year 10 had just learned parts of the body, I also used the Illnesses and Injuries game (see below), giving each student a 'breakage' (such as 'Ich habe mir das Bein gebrochen') that they had to embody, repeat and exchange with their peers. This also drilled the perfect tense structure again. To my delight and astonishment, this produced lots of spontaneous language, such as 'Oh, das ist schlecht', 'Ich kann nicht sehen', 'Ich kann nicht Fußball spielen', 'Das tut mir leid', etc.

We shared our learning with colleagues later that month, and chose to teach them the same two games. We deliberately put everyone slightly out of their comfort zone by trying the games in the languages they are least familiar with, to emulate the students' experience. Again, much laughter ensued, which I think is a great tool, as laughter relaxes us all — if learning is fun, it is likely to be more effective.

All colleagues were tasked with trying one of the games in their teaching in the following week. Follow-up reports were largely positive. One colleague shared a useful solution for managing those who are 'out': she keeps them in the game, but they gain a 'point', with the idea being to gain none, so with more points, you 'lose'. Notably colleagues said that it had animated and engaged their classes, the 'physical' aspect of the work had had a positive effect on engagement, and students wanted to learn, though because they get excited, behaviour can be harder to manage.

Like so many new ideas, one tries many, and it's probably down to the individual character or preferences of the teacher which ones actually 'stick'. Personally, I plan to keep using Sevens and variations on the Illnesses and Injuries game throughout the year, to see whether this might have a long-term effect on students' confidence in speaking and their ability to speak spontaneously.

How I Produced My First Ever (Multilingual) School Play

Ann Poole, SS Philip and James' CE Primary School, Oxford

In 2016, I took part in the Pilot project for the Multilingual Performance Project (MPP). I attended a workshop for teachers focusing on drama games and then tried the ideas with my primary school classes and ran an after-school drama/MFL club. Children responded well to the activities, and I enjoyed the ways in which the activities improved my teaching. In March 2018, I attended the MPP launch led by MPP Director Daniel Tyler-McTighe at the Birmingham REP and took away more ideas and the confidence to try them out.

In mid-March, an opportunity arose in school to produce a play to be shown to parents at The North Wall theatre in Oxford at the end of May. I impulsively volunteered myself — and now I had to come up with a plan! Here's how we went from idea to production. Remembering Daniel's offer of assistance, and being unsure of where to start, I emailed him for advice. I had previously led only a handful of performances in assemblies and wondered whether to adapt one of those into a longer piece. After discussing performing rights with Daniel, I came to the conclusion that an 'off-the-peg' play would be easiest to work with.

A quick search led me to a play which incorporated both songs and limited use of several languages. It was called 'The Great Globetrotting Game' (Easy Peasy Plays) and with its message about global unity it seemed to fit my needs perfectly. I also had support from a colleague who agreed to work with me, and had some experience of producing plays at university. Both of us were relative novices but keen to give it a go. By the end of March, I had found a play and a co-producer, though no idea of who would be our performers as yet! In fact, this would not be decided until late April once children signed up for the different activities on offer.

In April, we set a date for Daniel to visit us during rehearsals. He advised me on many aspects of production that I hadn't even considered, including more games, stage geography and how to run sessions. Daniel offered to liaise with the theatre to design our stage projections using QLab (an audio playback software designed for theatre and live entertainment), and to help supply us with costumes, both from his own store and from Birmingham REP's. Needless to say, I felt much more confident that I could actually produce something worth watching!

Children who had signed up for the play were given a script and auditions took place. Most of the roles were easy to allocate — children just seemed to fit the characters in the play. We arranged for song rehearsals to take place during one lunchtime per week — not ideal, but the songs were catchy and available on the website in karaoke form.

In mid-May, Daniel paid a visit to school with a suitcase full of costumes and props, a Powerpoint showing the background projections he had prepared, and more top tips.

Soon afterwards, rehearsals could finally begin! We had our group of performers who had (mostly) learnt their lines as requested and could sing along to the songs. We followed advice from Daniel on how to energize or calm things down with games and activities. We soon realized what a lot of work still needed to be done and how quickly time goes when you're having fun...

Rehearsals went pretty well — children enjoyed all the games alongside practising their parts and we discovered hidden talents amongst our group. We were able to make use of the linguistic talents of our pupils and learning a few phrases in Japanese, French and Spanish was not a problem for them. Having a pupil who knew how to perform the Sand Dance (a graceful one, not the comedy version) was really special! At the same time, panic started to set in when we realized how many props and costumes we still needed to make: Japanese cherry blossom, Egyptian robes and collars, yeti outfits, to name but a few.

On the day before the performance, Daniel arrived to watch rehearsals. Daniel was very impressed with what he saw, and gave children advice on making everything bigger for a theatre audience. He taught the children a 'theatre bow' to take applause from the audience. Children were able to ask Daniel for advice on voice projection and calming their nerves — useful for us teachers too!

The Big Day finally arrived. Not everything was finished and perfect but we all felt excited. We had a final dress rehearsal with projections and lighting, and we played a few games and activities to calm the nerves before the audience arrived for the afternoon performance... The afternoon performance went almost to plan (one song went a bit awry and children rushed their lines somewhat) but the audience were very kind and applauded them heartily as they took their bows. The evening performance was as good as we could have wished — nerves had gone and the children remembered advice from Daniel about using their bodies as well as their voices. It was super for them to hear the audience laugh, clap and sing along at the appropriate times. As children were reunited with their parents it was clear from their comments that they were very impressed by the performance. Colleagues who had attended the show were equally enthusiastic — some had tears in their eyes during one particular solo song and the finale about saying 'hello' around the world.

The post-show reunion with the cast was delayed because of half-term holidays but eventually we were able to award certificates and get some feedback from the children. Their comments were overwhelmingly positive: 'I loved it all [...] thank you for boosting my confidence because I was very scared'; 'I really liked the atmosphere'; 'I really liked that we got loads of help'; 'I learnt [...] that you have to really live the character to be convincing'; 'The warm-up games were fun [...] everything was fun!'; 'I enjoyed going behind the scenes at the North Wall Theatre and Dr Dan visiting us.'

All of the comments were feelings shared by my co-producer and myself with perhaps the most accurate being 'It was sooo fun!'; 'I learnt that it's good to do what you are not good at'; and 'It was an amazing experience for all of us!'

Thank you very much Daniel and the MPP Project! Merci! Gracias! Arigato!

Energizing the Learners: Resources for Teachers

The MPP is not just for teachers who were able to participate in our workshops. Below, we have outlined some great activities that can be implemented in the classroom. You might want to join up with another teacher or even a drama teacher to try them out — or just take the plunge with the help of your students! See 'Find Out More' below for further resources.

> **Buzzy Bees (aka Busy Bees)**
>
> This is a great way to energize the room, as well as being a really interesting way to test students' vocabulary and quick thinking! Played in another language, it's a brilliant vocabulary test for students. You need a bit of space for this one, but a classroom with space between desks can do.
>
> The game leader stands at the head of the room and shouts 'Buzzy Bees BUZZ!' Students begin to 'buzz' around the room. The game leader (GL) then calls 'Buzzy Bees make something beginning with...' and chooses a letter of the alphabet; the GL begins counting down from 5. Each student must then freeze in a statue of something beginning with that letter. (For example, the letter 'L' might yield statues of lions, lemons, legs, leaves, luscious lips, ladders...).

The GL then proceeds to ask each student what they are representing. Any student who has the same as someone else is out; likewise, any student who hasn't managed to think of something is out. The game continues, with fewer and fewer people in each round, until a winner (or winners) are declared. Extra praise may be given for any exemplary statues created.

Sevens

Sevens is an exciting warm-up game which can help bring energy and focus into the room. It's very simple; participants only need to be able to count to 7 in the chosen language. It can also be adapted for more advanced groups if needed.

Get your group to stand in a circle and count, one at a time, to 7 and continue round the circle, starting again from 1 every time you've reached 7. The direction of the count is indicated by a handslap to the shoulder, so you pass it round the circle.

Once everyone's confident with that, you can start adding in the other rules.

The first one is that you can change direction by changing the direction of the handslap, i.e. you slap the other shoulder.

Next, number 7 has to take their hand over their head, i.e. the hand movement changes. And you can change direction with number 7 too.

Once everyone's got those rules, you can start to get people out. If they hesitate, if they get it wrong, if they haven't got enough energy...

Illnesses and Injuries

This drama activity can be used in many different ways and at lots of different levels and abilities. It's always popular as people seem to love sharing stories of their illnesses and injuries. From basic vocabulary about body parts and visits to the doctor, to complicated sentence structure and the use of past/present tense, all skill levels can take part in this activity.

Each person first has to think of an illness or injury they have suffered (and are willing to share with the class!) and the story that surrounds it (e.g. 'When I was on holiday with my Dad I fell off my bike and broke my collar bone.') Participants then show, physically, how they would look

> with that illness or injury (i.e. holding collar bone and grimacing). The game leader scans the room, and when everyone has a clear statue they can begin.
>
> Each person must walk (or limp!) around the room with their illness/injury. When they meet another person they must swap stories, and then absorb the other person's injury/illness with their own. (Broken collar bone meets someone with food poisoning from a wedding. They swap stories and walk away both with a broken collar bone AND food poisoning.)
>
> Depending on group size/ability, set a limit on how many interactions each person should have. When they reach the limit (i.e. two interactions/four injuries) they should again freeze, showing the GL what they now look like. Once everyone is frozen, the GL can choose particularly interesting looking statues to share their stories. (e.g. 'I was on holiday with my Dad and I fell off my bike and broke my collarbone, and the next day I went to a wedding and got food poisoning. Then I decided to play football to make myself feel better and broke my ankle. I thought making a sandwich would be the easiest thing to settle my stomach and I cut my finger…')
>
> (Adapted from Chris Johnston's game 'Ailments' (2010: 15))

Works Cited

Creative Multilingualism. 2020. https://www.creativeml.ox.ac.uk

Creative Multilingualism (MPP). 2018a. 'MFL teaching activity: Buzzy Bees', 2:18, posted online by Creative Multilingualism, YouTube, 18 September 2018, https://www.youtube.com/watch?v=WVZgJWuQMt0

Creative Multilingualism (MPP). 2018b. 'MFL teaching activity: Illnesses & Injuries', 2:55, posted online by Creative Multilingualism, YouTube, 18 September 2018, https://www.youtube.com/watch?v=VmEBiKdRfEs

Creative Multilingualism (MPP). 2018c. 'MFL teaching activity: Sevens', 1:39, posted online by Creative Multilingualism, YouTube, 18 September 2018, https://www.youtube.com/watch?v=MEfakN_QXC4

Creative Multilingualism (MPP). 2020b. 'Multilingual Performance Project (MPP)', www.creativeml.ox.ac.uk/projects/multilingual-performance-project

Crystal, David. 1998. *Language Play* (London: Penguin).

Dudrah, Rajinder, Philip Bullock, Julie Curtis and Noah Birksted-Breen. 2020. 'Languages in the Creative Economy', Research Strand 4 of

Creative Multilingualism, https://www.creativeml.ox.ac.uk/research/creative-economy

English PEN. 2013. *Brave New Voices — Learning Resources and Animations*, https://www.englishpen.org/outreach/young-people/brave-new-voices-translation-animations/

Gosler, Andrew, Karen Park and Felice S. Wyndham. 2020. 'Creating a Meaningful World: Nature in Name, Metaphor and Myth', Research Strand 2 of Creative Multilingualism, https://www.creativeml.ox.ac.uk/research/naming

Graham, Suzanne, Linda Fisher, Julia Hofweber and Heike Krüsemann. 2020. 'Linguistic Creativity in Language Learning', Research Strand 7 of Creative Multilingualism, https://www.creativeml.ox.ac.uk/research/

Hufeisen, Britta, and Nicole Marx (eds). 2014. *EuroComGerm — Die sieben Siebe: Germanische Sprachen lesen lernen*, 2nd edn (Aachen: Shaker Verlag).

Johnston, Chris. 2010. *Drama Games for Those Who Like to Say No* (London: Nick Hern Books).

Maiden, Martin, Aditi Lahiri and Chiara Cappellaro. 2020. 'Creating Intelligibility across Languages and Communities', Research Strand 3 of Creative Multilingualism, https://www.creativeml.ox.ac.uk/research/intelligibility

McCann, William J., Horst G. Klein et al. 2003. *EuroComRom — The Seven Sieves: How to Read All the Romance Languages Right Away*, 2nd edn (Aachen: Shaker).

Mehmedbegovic-Smith, Dina, and Thomas H. Bak. 2020. *Healthy Linguistic Diet*, http://healthylinguisticdiet.com/

Ouyang, Wen-chin, Jane Hiddleston, Laura Lonsdale and Nora Parr. 2020. 'Creativity and World Literatures: Languages in Dialogue', Research Strand 5 of Creative Multilingualism, https://www.creativeml.ox.ac.uk/research/world-literatures

Reynolds, Matthew, Sowon S. Park, Giovanni Pietro Vitali and Eleni Philippou. 2020. 'Creating New Meanings: Prismatic Translation', Research Strand 6 of Creative Multilingualism, https://www.creativeml.ox.ac.uk/research/prismatic-translation

Find Out More

Creative Multilingualism. 2020c. 'Resources', https://www.creativeml.ox.ac.uk/resources

This collection of resources offers a wide range of creative activities for the classroom, including how to stage a multilingual concert, how to teach the creation of short films in any language, and suggestions for enabling students to experience the joys of translation.

Creative Multilingualism (MPP). 2020a. 'Multilingual Drama Teaching Activities', https://www.creativeml.ox.ac.uk/resources/multilingual-drama-teaching-activities

Short videos explain and demonstrate a variety of games including (and in addition to) 'Buzzy Bees', 'Sevens' and 'Illnesses and Injuries', and provide ideas for adapting them for different purposes.

Creative Multilingualism (MPP). 2020b. 'Multilingual Performance Project', https://www.creativeml.ox.ac.uk/mpp

This web page gives an outline of the Multilingual Performance Project and provides links to resources for schools including the MPP Starter Pack for teachers.

Farmer, David. 2019. 'Drama Resource: Books on Drama for Language Teaching and Learning', *Drama Resource*, **https://dramaresource.com/books-on-drama-for-language-teaching-and-learning/**

A webpage reviewing resources for using drama in the classroom.

Credits

Permission to include their contribution was kindly granted by the following:

Holly Bateman for her contribution.

Chiara Cappellaro for the 'Family tree diagram' (2020) (Fig. 1).

Sophie Fleming (Colmore Infant and Nursery School) for her comment on performing *The Birds*.

Katie Hoare for her comment on performing *The Birds*.

James Johnson (Haggerston School, Hackney) for his poetry workshop feedback.

Karishma Kaur for the poem 'Le Monde est à nous' (2017).

Ciara Mulvenna (St Paul's Way Trust School, Tower Hamlets) for her poetry workshop feedback.

Ann Poole (SS Philip and James' CE Primary School, Oxford) for her contribution.

Sarah Williams (Greenford High School, Ealing) for her contribution.

9. Languages at Work

Katrin Kohl and Jonathan Black

> Languages create connections with people

We can't do work without languages — and they come in many forms.

We negotiate linguistic diversity every day in our own language. Building on this creatively forms an ideal starting point for developing the 'transferable' communication skills needed in any job, using any language. Moreover, it develops sensitivity towards linguistic expression, providing fertile ground for learning other languages and integrating language knowledge actively in one's skills profile.

One secret for developing a career is to *have choices* so you can make the most of opportunities; that means never assuming a particular talent, skill or type of knowledge will not be useful, perhaps at a much later point. It might turn out to be the seed of exceptional expertise on which to build qualifications and the basis for career options. Or the unique factor that makes an application stand out from a crowd of competitors.

Wherever you work, the chances are that in the course of the day, you'll need to use many different ways of speaking and writing. From 'Good morning!' to 'Hi!', from formal to informal, the day will involve continual adjustments as you talk and write to different people. Email greetings and sign-offs will vary, and you may imperceptibly evolve distinctive styles for different individuals. The language we use defines our functional, hierarchical and empathetic relationship with each person slightly differently — in ways that can really matter.

Ever been in a situation where someone else makes you feel inhibited, tense and a bit smaller than them? They may actually believe they're more important than you, or they may be deploying strategies to make you think they're more important. The effect will be made up of what they say, their tone, how loudly they speak, their facial expression and their body language. All these factors are worth analyzing. Recognizing other people's strategies of self-promotion firstly makes you less susceptible to feeling intimidated, and secondly allows you to extend your understanding of how communication works and all the different aspects of ourselves on which it draws.

The reason we refer to 'body language' is because it can be at least as powerful communicatively as verbal language. The Internet is packed with advice on body language in the workplace — why it's important, how it's used, how to read it, mistakes people make and body language tips for career success. Communication is a complex process that involves not just our speech organs but our whole being. Even without specific training on body language, you can see how gestures can gain linguistic significance in a wide variety of ways. We all use paralinguistics to support what we say, for example when we point in a particular direction, or show the size or shape of an object with our hands. In professional contexts, people may be trained in how to use gesture effectively. If you're a politician, it will be a strategy used to help persuade people. If you're an actor, it will be a key part of every speech and of silent responses as well. And the hands take on a central communicative role if you're deaf, forming the medium through which your distinctive language is expressed, e.g. British Sign Language or Chinese Sign Language.

Beyond the words and body language involved in communication, everyone has soaked up a distinctive cultural heritage in the course of their lives. And as workplaces become more diverse in an increasingly globalized world, the cultural dynamics that play out in day-to-day work relations become more varied and multi-faceted. While diversity brings a wider range of ideas and approaches, it can also cause misunderstandings, distrust and overt or subliminal conflict. Workplaces and schools can be like microcosms of the political world. Whether in school, work or politics, the world needs people who are curious about others, open to embracing cultural difference and interested in making communication work for all the people involved in the conversation.

Learning languages is uniquely valuable in sensitizing you to cultural difference, different ways of thinking and different ways of doing things. If you gain expertise in a language other than your own, it can give you useful insights when mediating between cultures, and understanding how people in another part of the world tick. There are other, more specific benefits too: knowledge of another language can enrich personal relationships, open up job opportunities, allow you to trade more effectively in another country and fulfil important roles in international relations, cross-cultural conflict and global challenges.

This chapter explores the opportunities and benefits languages offer for our personal development, with specific information for school and university students thinking about careers and more generally for anyone who has an interest in the valuable and rewarding role of languages in the workplace.

Exploiting the Potential of Your Existing Language Life

Our knowledge and use of language are tied up with the way we think, what we do and how we relate to each other. Throughout our lives, language is intrinsically connected with our creativity, which itself offers immense potential for further development in ways that are highly relevant to jobs and careers. Fortunately, you can train your language learning skills by connecting consciously and creatively with the process of language learning you have been engaged in throughout your life.

Our knowledge of words is inseparable from the people and things that make up the world around us. Even abstract ideas tend to be metaphorical extensions of physical things or processes — consider 'glass ceilings', 'networks' or economic 'growth'. It's a useful life skill to develop a passion for dictionaries — big dictionaries of your native language, and bilingual dictionaries — and the creation of new words within your own language (see Chapter 10). Depending on your preferences, they can be online or hard copies — both lend themselves to browsing, which is never wasted time. Big monolingual dictionaries will give you a feeling for the extraordinarily nuanced meanings of day-to-day words — and it's useful to get into the habit of checking every word you're not a hundred percent sure of, including its spelling. This area of language learning is sometimes neglected or even discouraged in communication-oriented language teaching, on the grounds that words should always be learned within sentences and meaningful contexts. However, this ignores the fact that individual words evolve in meaningful contexts and relationships and form part of a continuously evolving, living lexical system. Contexts come in many forms, and exploring the history and use of a single word can open up a fascinating world in which it gained its literal and metaphorical meanings. Finding out about that world can be a highly effective way of remembering them.

For English, the history or 'etymology' of words is given in the *Oxford English Dictionary* (*OED*) and some of its smaller versions. A word's etymology encompasses time and place: it tells you how far back it goes and where it has come from. Take 'club' (the kind you hit people over the head with) — did you know this comes from Old Norse *klubba*, which migrated to the British Isles with the Vikings? Or consider 'pyjamas' — imported from Urdu and Persian *pāy-jāma* and recorded in English from 1801, with the plural '-s' added in alignment with 'breeches' and 'trousers' when Asian and Middle Eastern trousers were adapted by Europeans for nightwear (the jacket being included in the meaning only later). An interest in the origin of words, the relationship between their various meanings and the bonds they create to form intriguing idioms will go a long way in sustaining an interest in foreign languages.

The words of your own language also introduce you to translation. For example, English often has two words with similar meanings but differing linguistic and cultural provenance, such as the words 'beginning' and 'end' with a Germanic origin, and their equivalents 'commencement' and 'termination' deriving from Latin and Old French. They're synonyms, but we wouldn't normally use them in the same context. We're aware that the words with Germanic origin tend to sound more ordinary, so we would normally choose these in normal conversation; however, we would 'translate' them into the more formal equivalents in certain formal or administrative contexts. Moreover, it's not rocket science for English speakers to work out what the German words 'der Beginn' and 'das Ende' mean, or how to translate the French words 'le commencement' and 'la termination'. This gets you off to a good start if you're learning one of those languages (see Chapter 3 in this volume for further tips).

Moreover, we know from our own language that words don't necessarily have one-to-one synonyms. If asked to find a 'plain English' equivalent for 'my provenance', one might come up with 'where I come from'. To get a sense of the many different ways phrases can be translated into another language, the online dictionary and translation concordance Linguee is useful. Linguee provides access to a large 'corpus' of material — a collection of real-life text — and gives you pairs of sentences for a word or expression you type in, in two languages. It covers a wide range of European languages as well as Japanese and Chinese, and translators use it when looking for solutions to translating tricky phrases that have no obvious equivalent. For a research project that explores the multitude of ways in which a literary text may be translated, see the section on 'Prismatic Jane Eyre' in Chapter 6 in this volume (see also Reynolds et al. 2020).

Translation is an immensely rich resource for language learning. Indeed, you may have grown up translating and interpreting in the home — for a relative who doesn't speak the official language of the country, or for a family member who is deaf. Certainly, though, forms of translation are part of all our daily lives. We translate whenever we talk to someone who doesn't know as much as we do about something — we spell out acronyms as full terms, choose 'plain English' rather than the jargon we might use at work or school, translate dialect or slang into standard language and polite words when talking in formal contexts. You can build on all these skills when using translation in your language learning.

Making the Most of the Many Languages Around You

The United Kingdom has the largest number of community languages in Europe, and more than 300 languages are now spoken in UK schools (BBC 2014). Some people may see them as a hindrance to integration and an impediment for the development of English language skills. Yet in many schools they are recognized and embraced as a tremendous personal opportunity and career benefit both for their speakers and for other students in the classroom. There are formal qualifications available for languages beyond the French, Spanish and German 'mainstream' qualifications, and many community schools do outstanding work supporting learners who speak a language beyond English at home.

The figure of over 300 gives an inkling of the linguistic riches out there in an Anglophone country that often sees itself as 'monoglot'.

Moreover, this number is increasing as globalization changes the languages landscape, bringing forth new varieties, and fusions between different languages. Take Hinglish — while not recognized as an official language in India or the UK, it's nevertheless being taken seriously enough for Portsmouth College (UK) to have included it among their Modern Business Language and Culture courses.

Individuals who know a language other than English have access to an immensely valuable resource — one that deserves to be nurtured, developed and shared with others. It is a skill in its own right that opens up special communication channels to other people who speak the same language, and pathways to other parts of the world. Moreover, knowing a second language makes it easier to learn a third because linguistic difference becomes easier to appreciate, so it can set you on a path to becoming a highly competent linguist.

It's never too late to start learning a language, whether you know one or more. And it's never too early to expand your repertoire. An example is Mukahang Limbu (see Language Lives, 'Connecting to People', in Chapter 6 in this volume), who came to England from Nepal when he was six, made the most of his contact with Hindi and Urdu to learn to converse in them, taught himself basic Korean, Japanese and Mandarin, learned German at school, improved his English to the point of winning creative-writing prizes, and is now studying English and Modern Languages. Another example is George Hodgson (see Language Lives, 'The Careers Potential of Swear Words', below), who started out as an English monoglot in a London school but joined in when his classmates spoke Bengali, took GCSE exams in French, German and Latin, and went on to be British Ambassador in Senegal, using his French daily.

Keeping our ears and minds open to the languages spoken around us pays dividends, all the more so if we take the trouble to learn one or more of them. It's not predictable how or when it might bring a particular career benefit, but it will certainly stimulate your neural networks since cognition and language are interconnected. Studies of bilingual children indicate that they have enhanced creative abilities by comparison with monolingual children (see Cushen & Wiley 2011; Leikin 2013). A research project based on the concept of a 'Healthy Linguistic Diet' (see also Chapter 8 in this volume) has demonstrated that multilingualism is cognitively advantageous across the lifespan. It is associated with slower cognitive ageing, delayed onset of dementia and better recovery from stroke. Moreover, cognitive benefits are observable among language learners of all ages, and evident also among learners who have not yet reached proficiency (Bak and Mehmedbegovic 2017).

Taking an interest in other languages stimulates curiosity about how languages, communication and other cultures work, and fosters willingness to take on something new. Moreover, learning a language enhances your openness to language learning and strengthens the skills it takes to do so. Every bit of another language you learn increases your confidence that it's possible to learn more. This means it becomes less daunting to go to places where the native language is different to your own, making it seem more feasible to learn some of that language. It can enable you to develop a career in a field such as business or intelligence in which the employer will give you training in an unusual language where there is a shortage of expertise. And it's likely to make you more willing to take the plunge if a job opportunity abroad offers itself, while also equipping you to demonstrate that you're the right person for the job.

Language Lives
The Careers Potential of Swear Words

George Hodgson

The first foreign language I really engaged with was Bengali. Most of the kids at my primary school in Tower Hamlets in East London were of Bangladeshi heritage. In the classroom, we sang Bengali songs. In the playground, we delighted in Bengali swear words. I'd be too embarrassed to own up to recalling the lyrics of a song about a frog, let alone the insults, but I will admit to still remembering how to count from one to ten.

At secondary school, I studied French, German and Latin up to GCSE. There was neither singing nor swearing. But we had great teachers, with a passion for languages and for sharing them — even with under-appreciative teenagers. I became more appreciative when, some years later, my rusty French was enough to strike up a conversation with an attractive French girl, now my wife.

As British Ambassador in Dakar, I speak more French on any given day than I do English. Without it, I just wouldn't be as effective in my job. That, quite simply, is why language skills are a priority for the Foreign and

Commonwealth Office (FCO). A blog by my colleague Danny Pruce in Manila on 'Learning Languages' (2017) offers a nice insight into studying Tagalog full-time at the FCO's in-house language centre... a far more serious undertaking than French.

Here in Senegal, I've been impressed by the language skills of the young British volunteers that I've met, working with great organizations like the International Citizen Service or Project Trust in local communities, and living with host families. Many of them learn Wolof: it's far more widely spoken than French, and Senegal's real lingua franca.

Equally impressive are the language skills of ordinary Senegalese people. For a majority in Senegal, multilingualism is a way of life. The same is not quite true in the United Kingdom. That said, there are of course millions of people in the UK who are multilingual — speakers of recognized minority languages like Welsh or Gaelic, or of languages that have come to the UK more recently, like Polish or Punjabi... or indeed Bengali. There are over a million bilingual pupils at school in Britain.

The British Council's paper *Languages for the Future* (2017) is well worth a read. As the British Council argues in its summary, 'in a new era of cooperation with Europe and with the rest of the world, investment in upgrading the UK's ability to understand and engage with people internationally is critical'. I couldn't agree more.

George Hodgson was British Ambassador to Senegal and non-resident Ambassador to Cabo Verde and Guinea-Bissau from 2015 to 2019. He previously served in Washington, Kabul, Islamabad, Brussels and London, and was Head of the Ebola Taskforce, Africa Directorate, in 2014 to 2015.

Fig. 1 George Hodgson. Reproduced with his kind permission. Photograph by Maimouna Dembele (2018).

Getting into a New Language — and Its Cultural World

Every language we learn takes us into an exciting new world — if we let it. The difficulty for English native speakers who live in an Anglophone country is that English has become like an invisible bubble that makes it seem as if there really is no other language that is necessary or useful. This can be demoralizing for learners because it removes a wide range of incentives which learners in other countries have when they learn English, keeping them motivated along the way, and providing them with well-polished skills to learn further languages.

Equipping yourself with the ability to learn languages isn't easy if you didn't learn them at school, or if language learning at school left you feeling that you were no good at them. Often that will be because of unrealistic expectations, and under-estimation of the awesome complexity of language. Did you know that a child will on average have spent some 9000 hours learning its native language by the age of five (Klein 1986: 9) — a learning process which generally carries on in ideal 'immersive' conditions that can't normally be replicated in a country where the language isn't routinely spoken.

The most effective way to learn a foreign language will mostly be to enrol on a good 'live' course. But there are also other ways of dipping your toe in the water, and in any case it's worth reflecting on some basic principles. We've come up with some tips below.

Proceed from what you know. To get a real sense of the complexity of learning a language, think of your own language and look at it through the eyes of a foreigner — its grammar, its immense vocabulary, its wonderfully illogical idioms, its pronunciation, its spelling, its idiosyncratic stylistic conventions. This will also help you with learning a foreign language because you will be able to compare it with the language you already know. How many hours do you think you've spent learning your native language, in ideal conditions? What does that mean for learning another language, later in life and alongside many other commitments? It's essential to be realistic, but also good to set yourself a challenge.

Research the challenge. As with climbing a mountain, you need to familiarize yourself with the terrain, the climate and the pitfalls (both obvious and hidden). It's also wise to consider how challenging the language of your choice is likely to be. Generally speaking, a language that is historically relatively close to your own will be easier than one from a completely different language family. And a language with an unfamiliar script, or use of different tones, will be even more taxing. That's not a reason to avoid it — but it will take much longer to progress to speaking it, and it will almost certainly require support from a teacher. Try out the language of your choice — climb up a foothill and see whether you still fancy that mountain. It won't be wasted time.

Assess the necessary resources. If you just want to learn the basics in a language and get some words, phrases and a bit of rudimentary grammar under your belt, a free app-based course like those offered by Duolingo can do a good job — so long as you set aside regular time for learning, which is essential for making progress however you approach the task. But don't expect to progress far on your own — it's generally more effective to learn with a teacher, and difficult to sustain the momentum without one. Assuming you can quickly learn to speak a language on your own with an off-the-peg course is rather like setting off up that mountain in shorts and trainers.

Don't set the bar too high. This can be the biggest problem of all in learning a language. In fact, if you see yourself as untalented in language learning because you didn't get very far at school, a key factor may be that the demands were too high and the exams too difficult, or perhaps you expected too much of yourself in the available conditions. There's often an expectation that you'll zoom ahead, and if you're good at languages, you'll be fluent in a few years' time and able to converse like a native speaker. The reality is that unless you speak the language in the home or live in a country where it's spoken, you'll probably never reach full fluency or native-speaker competence. Does that mean it's not worth doing? Of course not. We don't think it's only worth learning the violin, IT skills or playing football if we can expect to become like Yehudi Menuhin, Bill Gates or Lionel Messi. Start out with straightforward goals, see how you get on, and value the modest achievements alongside all those transferable skills. Try out a free app or a subscription course to see what works for you. If you fall in love with the language, you can really devote yourself to learning it thoroughly and live and work in the country. You'll then get really good at it — and together with your native language skills, you'll become an awesome linguist.

Spend time on words. They're a lot more straightforward to learn on your own than the grammar of a language, and they will get you a long way in understanding the gist of even difficult texts. Find out how they're formed in the language you're learning. If you're learning a noun, see if there's a related verb and adjective and learn them as well. Spend time on studying how they're translated in a bilingual dictionary, in a range of sample contexts. Put them individually on cards with the translation on the back — writing them out neatly helps with remembering them, and you can then keep testing yourself and saying them out loud. Try using an app such as those offered by Memrise.

Make sure you devote plenty of time to the fun stuff. Unless you're doing an intensive taught course, which provides a strong motivational framework for learning, it's unlikely that a diet of just learning grammar, vocabulary and practical uses of them will keep you going for the time it takes to learn a language well. Give the language a rich cultural context right from the start. Connect the nuts and bolts with the things that really interest you. The Internet can provide virtually infinite material that you can read in translation as well as in the original. It's the people who make the language interesting — their customs, history, films, theatre, politics, sport, food. Whatever turns you on.

Learn with materials that interest you — but above all materials that aren't too difficult . Watch films in the language with subtitles — first in English, then in the other language. But start easy. The material in course books may be rather dull in terms of content, but it will be graded so it's suitable for the stage you're at. Read really simple children's books with a strong plot, or watch a dubbed Disney film in the language you're learning. Read a translation of a book you already know. See if you can't get chatting to someone in the language you're learning who shares your personal interest in a sport or cultural activity, stamps or spiders. Spend time surfing the net, reading the news both in your native language and in the language you're learning. Read about something that interests you in both languages and draw out relevant vocabulary in the foreign language so you can gradually build on it.

Allow scope for your creativity. Some of the greatest poems are short and simple. Creative writing doesn't depend on knowing complex language. It can be a wonderful project to write a diary in the language you're learning — if you write it only for your own eyes, you don't need

Language Lives
Transferably Creative

Jessica Benhamou

I've been working in film and TV journalism since graduating in 2012 with a BA in Modern Languages. Highlights include working on Netflix's *The Crown* and BBC's *Panorama*. In 2017, a short film I produced, *Juliet Remembered*, screened at the Oxford International Film Festival.

My ability to speak and write in French has allowed me to travel and opened doors to more opportunities — I've worked in Paris at France24, in Tel Aviv for i24news on their French channel and as a live-translator for Sky News. But beyond being able to work in French, other linguistic and analytical skills have been highly transferable for my creative work as a writer and producer.

Translation requires a precision and attention to language that I use all the time as a writer. Translation is a precarious balancing act where the writer tries to faithfully preserve the sense, style, tone and message of an original sentence in the most succinct way. Writing requires a person to be a wordsmith, and a screenwriter has to be particularly economical like a translator.

Studying a foreign language teaches you how to listen. A linguist knows how to detect subtle intonations, rhythm, irony and comic timing in a foreign language. This has helped me in post-production where the film comes together layer by layer. First you have the visual edit, followed by the sound design, music, colour grade and special effects.

Fig. 2 Jessica Benhamou. Reproduced with her kind permission. Photograph by Brittany Ashworth, CC BY.

> Beyond the linguistic component, a Modern Languages student learns about other cultures and other ways of thinking. Studying foreign works has allowed me to diversify my pool of resources. And reading widely and critically for my degree has prepared me for the volume of script reading I have to do now. I can quickly assess the potential of a story or why a script is not working. Writing essays as part of my course taught me about the importance of structure and momentum. Both the script and the edit in post-production have to be tightly reigned in, but also keep moving resolutely towards a conclusion.
>
> Finally, a Modern Languages degree teaches you about the power of imagination — to empathize with the lives of others. The desire to learn about other cultures surely attracts individuals with a curious, adventurous nature, who are looking to engage meaningfully with the world around them.
>
> *Jessica Benhamou is a British-Israeli producer and writer who works in film and journalism.*

to worry about making mistakes. Above all, though, try your hand at translation. This will immeasurably help your language learning, your understanding of how the language works, and how it differs from your own language. This can keep you going for a long time and run along any other learning you do. Any story, book or other text that exists in your native language and the language you're learning can be used to develop your translation skills, in both directions. You can translate the one and use the other to compare with what you have produced — even just ten minutes a day is worth doing. You may not always be able to figure out why you didn't get it right — you either have to decide that the value is in the doing rather than achieving perfection, or you will need to ask a teacher. You can also compare the original, the published translation and your translation with Google Translate... And you can get to know great works of literature, reading the original alongside a translation, or perhaps getting two different translations that will allow you to experience how translation is always a creative activity.

Get together with other learners. Organize regular get-togethers where you only speak in the language. Meet up to discuss a film, do cooking in the language, or just chat. If there's no-one close-by, talk by skype and social media. Or find a native speaker of the language who would like to learn your language so you can spend half your time teaching and half your time learning.

Go to the country. Go to a country where the language is spoken, especially if you're beginning to lose motivation. Immerse yourself in the culture. There's nothing like it to make learning the language seem worthwhile. Don't feel offended if people talk back in English — just keep going, trying out your knowledge of their language. Go beyond the tourist centres, ideally on your own — you'll find that speaking English isn't nearly as global as it's made out to be.

All the above is highly relevant for personal development and for career purposes. The language itself may prove useful, and you can look out for jobs that will give you an opportunity to use it; learning a language trains many intellectual skills you need for purposes of work; extending your cultural range and knowledge of people will enrich your working relationships; and opening yourself up to another culture, way of doing things and way of thinking is a habit that will be invaluable for any career and new job.

Creating a Career out of Languages

Careers sometimes seem rather like a set of ready-made pigeonholes that offer clearly defined and delineated options. An alternative way of looking at a career is as a highly individual pathway, created from personal interests, strengths and values in response to career options and opportunities. There is no right or wrong pathway, and given the rapid speed with which careers are changing, the most important skills of all are likely to be flexibility, a willingness to move outside your comfort zone, enthusiasm for thinking outside the box — and the resilience to carry on learning.

Learning languages is an ideal training ground, whatever career you end up with. It makes sense to integrate languages in your career vision from the start, because they will always expand your options, whether you realize your original vision or end up doing something quite different. The skill of knowing the language may or may not make you more employable for the job you want to do, but even if it makes little difference in itself, the transferable skills you will have acquired can enhance your overall profile and interview performance.

A study commissioned by the British Academy with the title *Born Global* established that employers particularly value the following 'transferable skills' developed by graduates in languages (2016: 3–4):

- 'rigorous thinking, problem-solving and resilience',
- 'analytical, inter-cultural communication skills and global mindset'.

The study further established the following:

- Seven out of ten companies surveyed believe that future executives will need foreign language skills and international experience,
- 71% of mainly senior business people in UK companies said their language skills had given them a competitive edge in applying for jobs, and 67% said that language skills enabled them to apply for a wider range of jobs than would have been open to them otherwise.

Careers built specifically on language skills include those of translator, interpreter and teacher. For all of these, a knowledge of languages needs to be coupled with other skills, and choices need to be made about the specific work environment that is typical for jobs in these areas.

Translators work with written texts, translating them from one language into another. A professional translator will translate into their native language, normally from one or perhaps two other languages. They will specialize in certain types of text and certain fields — for example business documentation, legal texts, medical material or literature. Within those, they may specialize further, since you can't translate a text properly unless you understand what it's saying, and the more technical the text, the more important specialist knowledge becomes. Training will normally consist of a degree — generally in languages — and a further professional qualification.

Translators need to be highly attuned to the changing needs of a job in which machine translation is increasingly being used to deal with more routine texts. The translator's work is more and more about editing, and gearing the text to the target market. The higher the proportion of work that is done by translation software tools, the more the work carried out by human translators will demand problem-solving skills and a creative ability to find appropriate equivalents where automatically generated solutions are unsuitable. There will always be a need for translators, and literary translation will remain a job for human beings. But few people can make a living from translating literature, and the competition for other work can be fierce, with employment by agencies often being poorly paid. Freelance work needs an excellent business sense, willingness to spend long hours at a computer working to tight deadlines, and an imaginative approach to customer relations. Options include setting up your own agency, or working for the United Nations or the European Union, both of which require an excellent knowledge of at least two relevant languages beyond the translator's native language.

Interpreters transpose the spoken word from one language into another either in *consecutive* interpreting (when the interpreter waits until the speaker has delivered a segment of speech and then renders the message in the target language) or *simultaneous* interpreting (in which the interpreter provides the target-language version continuously alongside the speaker's version). It demands intense concentration and extensive training. Interpreters need an outstanding command of their native language and at least one other language, they need an excellent memory, they need to be good at thinking on their feet, and they need to enjoy performing under high pressure.

By contrast with translation, where you can consult dictionaries and other sources as you work, interpreting involves preparing the vocabulary and relevant knowledge of the subject for each assignment in advance of the event. While conference interpreters generally work in booths and take it in turns, smaller-scale assignments might consist of interpreting in meetings between politicians, between patients and doctors or health officials, or between parties in a legal dispute or immigration tribunal. The work here consists in creating understanding between the parties. As with translation, artificial intelligence is changing the landscape, so adaptability is key. Many interpreters work for organizations such as the EU, the UN and government agencies, while others are freelance, usually specializing in a particular field or range of fields.

Foreign language teachers need a deep knowledge of the language they're teaching, including the ability to explain its grammar, and ideally a good knowledge of the learner's first language. The nature of the work will depend on the age group of the learners and the setting and purpose of the instruction — primary or secondary school? Higher

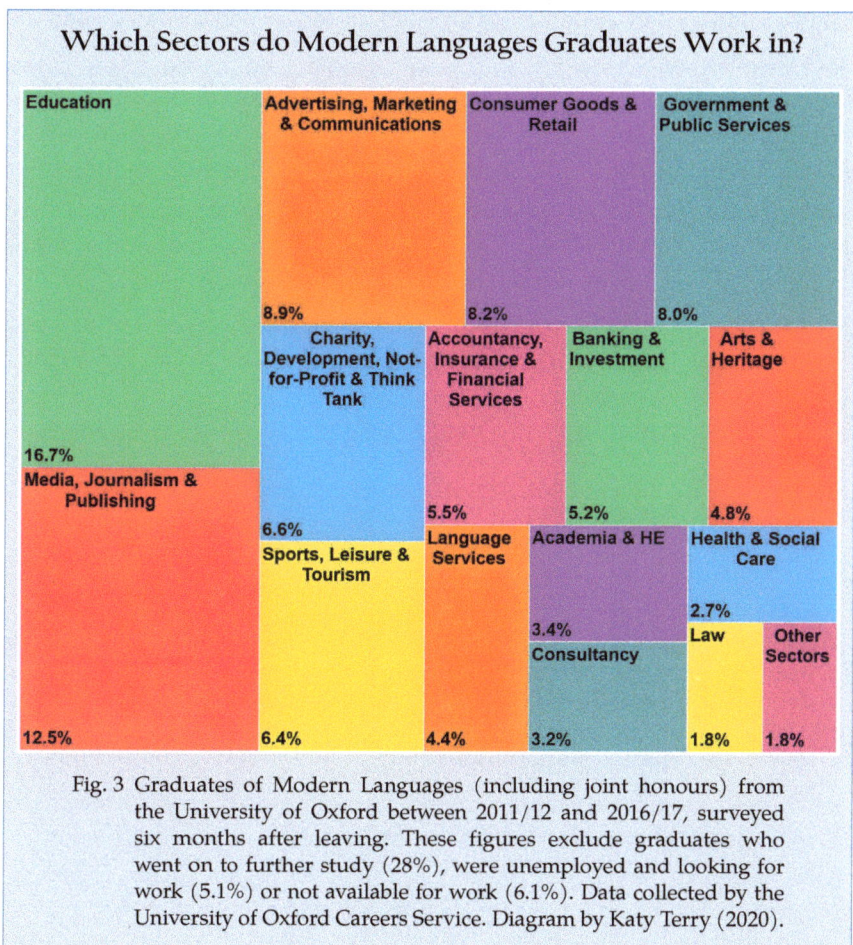

Fig. 3 Graduates of Modern Languages (including joint honours) from the University of Oxford between 2011/12 and 2016/17, surveyed six months after leaving. These figures exclude graduates who went on to further study (28%), were unemployed and looking for work (5.1%) or not available for work (6.1%). Data collected by the University of Oxford Careers Service. Diagram by Katy Terry (2020).

education? A language school? A company? This will affect the type of syllabus, the level of learner motivation, and the nature of the job.

The received wisdom is often that native speakers of the target language are the best teachers, or even the only truly valuable teachers. This isn't necessarily the case, especially at school level, where first-hand appreciation of the learners' main difficulties can be even more important than a knowledge of all the nuances of the target language. A key role — perhaps *the* key role — of a teacher is to keep the learner motivated and encouraged. Enthusiasm, imagination, creativity and empathy are therefore invaluable attributes of a language teacher — and teachers who generate a lasting love of languages in their students fulfil an invaluable job.

Beyond the above career options, the opportunities opened up by a degree in languages are infinite, as is evident from the huge variety of employment areas university graduates in Modern Languages go into. The range also gives an inkling of what you can do with a high level of competence in languages that you've learned in other ways. The infographic (Fig. 3) shows the distribution of employment sectors.

Taking a creative approach to developing a career involving languages can help you draw confidently on your very own experience. Choosing a career is a living process. Learning a language can help with creating a personal vision, injecting a spirit of adventure — and trusting in serendipity.

Works Cited

Bak, Thomas, and Dina Mehmedbegovic. 2017. 'Healthy Linguistic Diet: The Value of Linguistic Diversity and Language Learning Across the Lifespan', *Languages, Society & Policy*, https://doi.org/10.17863/CAM.9854 [See also Mehmedbegovic-Smith, Dina, and Thomas H. Bak. 2020. *Healthy Linguistic Diet*, https://healthylinguisticdiet.com]

BBC. 2014. 'Languages across Europe', 14 October, http://www.bbc.co.uk/languages/european_languages/definitions.shtml

British Academy. 2016. *Born Global: Implications for Higher Education*, https://www.thebritishacademy.ac.uk/sites/default/files/Born%20Global%20-%20Implications%20for%20Higher%20Education_1.pdf]

British Council. 2017. *Languages for the Future*, https://www.britishcouncil.org/sites/default/files/languages_for_the_future_2017.pdf [See also the summary of the report's findings at https://www.britishcouncil.org/research-policy-insight/policy-reports/languages-future-2017

Creative Multilingualism. 2020. https://www.creativeml.ox.ac.uk

Cushen, Patrick J., and Jennifer Wiley. 2011. 'Aha! Voila! Eureka! Bilingualism and Insightful Problem Solving', *Learning and Individual Differences*, 21(4): 458–62, https://doi.org/10.1016/j.lindif.2011.02.007

Duolingo. 2020. https://www.duolingo.com/

International Citizen Service. 2020. https://www.volunteerics.org/

Klein, Wolfgang. 1986. *Second Language Acquisition*, Cambridge Textbooks in Linguistics (Cambridge: Cambridge University Press).

Leikin, Mark. 2013. 'The Effect of Bilingualism on Creativity: Developmental and Educational Perspectives', *International Journal of Bilingualism*, 17(4): 431–47, https://doi.org/10.1177/1367006912438300

Linguee. 2020. https://www.linguee.com

Memrise. 2020. https://www.memrise.com

OED. 2020. www.oed.com

Project Trust. 2020. https://projecttrust.org.uk/

Pruce, Daniel. 2017. 'Learning Languages', *Foreign Office Blogs*, 1 June, https://blogs.fco.gov.uk/danielpruce/2017/06/01/learning-languages/

Reynolds, Matthew, Sowon S. Park, Giovanni Pietro Vitali and Eleni Philippou. 2020. 'Creating New Meanings: Prismatic Translation', Research Strand 6 of Creative Multilingualism, https://www.creativeml.ox.ac.uk/research/prismatic-translation

Tinsley, Teresa, and Kathryn Board. 2017. *Languages for the Future. The Foreign Languages the United Kingdom Needs to Become a Truly Global Nation* (London: British Council), https://www.britishcouncil.org/research-policy-insight/policy-reports/languages-future-2017

Find Out More

AGCAS. 2019. 'What Can I Do with a Modern Languages Degree?', *Prospects*, https://www.prospects.ac.uk/careers-advice/what-can-i-do-with-my-degree/modern-languages

Information provided by The Association of Graduate Careers Advisory Services on different types of career requiring a high level of languages competence and also other types of career where languages are an important adjunct.

Black, Jonathan. 2019. *How to Find the Career You've Always Wanted* (London: Robinson).

This book offers advice on career planning and choices, writing a CV and preparing for an interview. See also the author's fortnightly column 'Dear Jonathan' in the *Financial Times* (https://www.ft.com/dear-jonathan), and the FT Career Starters videos: https://www.youtube.com/watch?v=yjdvCHWVtE4&list=PLqIpf04KBv61XrP8rtadMl5YpVxZt7Wkc

Creative Multilingualism (Careers). 2016. 'What do Modern Languages Students Do after Graduating?', https://www.creativeml.ox.ac.uk/blog/working-languages/what-do-modern-languages-students-do-after-graduating

Responses from Oxford graduates in Modern Languages about the varied paths their careers have taken, from teaching, interpreting and food writing to producing TV commercials and running a venture capital fund. The responses were compiled by the Russian department but the variety of career paths is typical for other languages, too.

Creative Multilingualism (Careers). 2020. 'How Languages Help in Your Career', https://www.creativeml.ox.ac.uk/careers

A short film consisting of comments from people in a variety of careers on the ways in which languages play a — sometimes surprising — part. More extended videos of the interviews give a deeper insight into the role languages have played in their careers.

Credits

Permission for Creative Multilingualism to publish their contribution was kindly granted by the following:

Jessica Benhamou for the Language Life 'Transferably Creative' and the photograph of herself (Fig. 2)

George Hodgson for the Language Life 'The Careers Potential of Swear Words' and the photograph of himself (Fig. 1).

10. Creating Languages
Katrin Kohl

> We create language every day

Languages are so fundamental to our experience of the world from before we are even born that it is difficult for most of us to imagine what life would be like without them — and hard not to take for granted what they enable us to do. None of the scientific and technological inventions that make our modern lives what they are would have happened without language — the inventor will always be working with what has been passed on via linguistic communication, will often collaborate through speech or writing with other people, and will invariably be using cognitive abilities that involve linguistic processes. Moreover, that inventor will not be operating with 'language' in general, but with one, or perhaps two or more, particular languages in a particular era and cultural space. The concept of 'language' is an abstraction. What human beings actually listen to, speak, read and write is a richly varied panoply of languages that have been created by their speakers in the course of a long history that reaches back into the mists of time — a collective linguistic repertoire that continues to evolve as we speak.

Creative Multilingualism is about the creative processes that are at work in our use of languages, in the many ways in which languages connect, meld and bring forth new varieties, and in the living interaction between languages. This chapter initially considers some fundamental questions that have bearing on our understanding of the relationship between language, linguistic diversity and creativity, and goes on to look at the relevance of creativity to marginalized languages, at invented languages or 'conlangs' (constructed languages), and at the role of language play and language humour in relation to linguistic creativity.

Where Does Linguistic Creativity Happen?

A key moment in researching the role of creativity with respect to language was Noam Chomsky's rejection of behaviourist approaches that assume we learn languages primarily by imitating others, and his observation that we could not possibly generate the infinite range of utterances of which we are easily capable without an innate capacity for generating language independently.

> **An Experiment in Linguistic Creativity**
>
> As we speak and write, we're continually creating language sequences that have never been used by anyone else before. This is not about a special talent of the few, but something we can all do at any time.
>
> You can conduct your own experiment by taking a short chunk of an ordinary email or other piece of text you have written (say, around ten to twelve words) and typing it into Google with double quotation marks round it (this ensures that it searches for exactly that string). See whether it finds the same string of words somewhere else on the Internet, and shorten or lengthen the chunk until you find it replicated elsewhere. You're likely to find that your own day-to-day language is more original than you thought.
>
> What we create in this way in the course of an ordinary day may be new, but it still consists of familiar elements. Yet it holds infinite potential for development, surprise, beauty, humour, a new twist. Using language is like engaging in a continual creativity workout. Meanwhile eloquent speakers, advertising wizards, imaginative poets and inventive performers are the language world's Olympic sprinters.
>
> Just imagine the mind-blowing potential for collective and collaborative creativity embodied by the continually evolving languages in the world!

The objective of the hugely ambitious research project that emerged from this observation is to identify a mental 'universal grammar' as the basis for every individual's linguistic knowledge and processing. In Chomsky's theory, rejection of behaviourist approaches entails separating 'internalized language' from 'externalized language': 'the shift of focus from E-language to I-language, from the study of behavior and its products to the study of systems of mental representations and computation'. Restricting 'language' to its cognitive aspect, he declares that 'the central task is to find the basic elements of I-language — henceforth, language' (Chomsky 1986: 51):

> We should [...] think of knowledge of language as a certain state of the mind/brain, a relatively stable element in transitory mental states once it is attained; furthermore, as a state of some distinguishable faculty of the mind — the language faculty — with its specific properties, structure, and organization, one 'module' of the mind. (Chomsky 1986: 12-13)

Chomsky's purpose was to give language philosophical and scientific legitimacy by defining it as a discrete and stable form of knowledge that is specific to the human species and quite distinct from communicative processes and effects. A key premise of research in the Chomskyan tradition is that stable, discrete 'language' underlies, precedes and is separable from the diversity of languages that is observable in the developed and actively deployed language competence of human beings. And an influential consequence has been an excessively narrow understanding of linguistic creativity, summarized in the definition of 'creativity' given in David Crystal's standard *Dictionary of Linguistics and Phonetics*. This focuses exclusively on Chomsky's 'species-specific' concept, highlighting that it is distinct from the 'sense of "creative" [...] found in artistic or literary contexts, where notions such as imagination and originality are central' (Crystal 2008: 122).

The research conducted in the context of Creative Multilingualism by contrast takes a holistic approach to the concept of 'creativity' and considers linguistic creativity in the mind to be intrinsically connected both with the creative imagination and with creative originality as it manifests itself in artistic expression. Our premise accords with the view prevalent in cognitive linguistics that language is integrated with other cognitive and physical abilities:

> The organization and retrieval of linguistic knowledge is not significantly different from the organization and retrieval of other knowledge in the mind, and the cognitive abilities that we apply to speaking and understanding language are not significantly different from those applied to other cognitive tasks, such as visual perception, reasoning or motor activity. (Croft and Cruse 2004: 2)

Understood like this, there is no division between language in the mind and the language we use in social intercourse and cultural expression. There is also no necessary separation between human language and animal communication, allowing for the possibility that the latter can inform our understanding of human communication.

We assume that linguistic creativity plays a potential part at every stage of the linguistic process, from thought through articulation to social intercourse. The field is wide open for exploring how linguistic creativity connects with other cognitive processes, with our perception of our environment, our active lives in society and our formation and expression of cultural identity.

What Light Does Linguistic Diversity Shed on Linguistic Creativity?

Linguistic diversity can help us to appreciate the creativity we bring to bear when we engage with our environment. For example, the different metaphorical ways of talking about time across cultures and languages (see Kohl et al. 2020 and Chapter 1 in this volume) indicate that language is inextricably connected with thought and the way we interpret the world. Similarly, there is considerable cultural diversity and corresponding linguistic diversity in the ways people across the world categorize colour and talk about it.

Human eyes are capable of perceiving thousands of different colours, but interdisciplinary research spanning psycholinguistics, cognitive science and neuroscience at the University of Lancaster has highlighted significant differences in their categorization and naming. Findings include the following (Casaponsa and Athanosopoulos 2018):

- Different languages and cultural groups carve up the colour spectrum differently. Some languages like Dani, spoken in Papua New Guinea, and Bassa, spoken in Liberia and Sierra Leone, only have two terms, dark and light. Dark roughly translates as 'cool' and includes black, blue and green. Light roughly translates as 'warm' and includes white, red, orange and yellow.
- The Warlpiri people in northern Australia have no term for 'colour' and instead use a rich vocabulary referring to texture, physical sensation and functional purpose.

- Most of the world's languages have five basic colour terms: dark, light, red, yellow, blue/green. Historically, Welsh — like Japanese and Chinese — had a single term covering blue and green (*glas*). In all three languages, the term originally covering both has now been restricted to blue, while a separate term is used for green. Welsh introduced *gwyrdd*, a borrowing from Latin *viridis*.

- There exists evidence that the way we perceive colours can change. A study conducted with speakers of Greek as their first language, which has two terms for light blue and dark blue, found that they tend to perceive these two colours as more similar after living for long periods of time in the United Kingdom, where people refer in English to the one fundamental colour term blue (Athanasopoulos 2009).

The research indicates that our perception of our environment, and the ways we process conceptually and linguistically what we see, are interactive and influence each other. In conjunction with our conceptual creativity, our linguistic creativity contributes vitally to our ability to make the environment we inhabit meaningful, in interaction with the human beings in our social group.

What Can Animal Communication Tell Us about Linguistic Creativity?

Communicative diversification is not restricted to human beings. Distinct dialects have been found in species of mammal including sperm whales (Antunes et al. 2011) and goats (Briefer and McElligott 2012) and in birds including the yellowhammer (Pipek et al. 2018). So why is this significant — beyond suggesting that human beings are part of the animal world rather than separate from it?

Looking at species other than humans allows us to see some basic patterns which illuminate both the role of linguistic diversity and its interaction with creativity. Key findings emerging from studies in animal behaviour confirm that the development of distinctive 'dialects' and 'accents' is intrinsic to socialization and the formation of group identities.

Much as with human language, communication systems in animals involve both homogenization and diversification, continuity and change as groups constitute themselves, creating commonality within the group while distinguishing themselves from other groups. The above-mentioned study of goats involved twenty-three sibling and half-sibling kids who stayed close to their mothers for one week and were then split randomly into four separate 'gangs'. At five weeks, 'each kid gang had developed its own distinctive patois', which 'probably helps with group cohesion' (Coghlan 2012). The study of yellowhammers focused on a community that originated in Brighton in the UK and was introduced to New Zealand in the nineteenth century (Pipek et al. 2018: 247). Drawing in part on historical data, the study concludes that dialects which have become extinct in the UK are preserved in communities in New Zealand: 'We suggest that the yellowhammer dialect system is an avian equivalent of a phenomenon already noted in human languages, in which ancient words or structures are retained in expatriate communities' (Pipek et al. 2018: 245). The similarities between the group formation and diversification processes in mammals and humans and the value these processes have for shaping societies suggest that we use language both instinctively and creatively as we construct our social identities.

Steven Pinker has argued in *The Language Instinct* that language is 'a biological adaptation to communicate information' and that 'knowing a language [...] is knowing how to translate mentalese into strings of words and vice versa' (Pinker 1994: 19, 82). While it is convincing to conceive language as instinctive and adaptive, communication systems evidently have roles that go far beyond the purpose of transmitting information, even in the animal world. And the concept of 'mentalese' — based on the premise that thought is fully separable from language — is inadequate to account for the richly creative ways in which not just human beings, but animals too, modify their identities in the course of forging culturally diverse social relationships.

What is a Language?

While the concept of 'language' is an abstraction in that it manifests itself only in the form of particular languages, the plural concept of 'languages' consists of a multitude of entities which may be distinct where neighbouring languages are mutually unintelligible, but which are often fluidly connected in ways that elude easy classification. To take the example of Alpine communities in Austrian Tyrol: here, inhabitants of a particular village are generally aware of differences between their language and that of people in the next village, though they have no difficulty understanding each other. Do we define the language of such a village as 'German', 'Austrian', 'Tyrolean', 'North Tyrolean', as the language of the valley in which the village is situated or as the language of the particular village? And what about language change as new media influence language use, or language blends as people migrate and meet? Distinctions and fusions between languages and language varieties are influenced by the circumstances of the relevant speech communities and may be continually in flux.

> A language is a dialect with an army and a navy.
>
> *Popularized by sociolinguist and Yiddish scholar Max Weinreich, who allegedly heard it from an audience member at one of his lectures.*

Whether a variety is considered to be a '(standard) language', a 'dialect' or a 'regional variety' depends on a multitude of factors, not least the language spoken by those who rule the territory, and the institutions this group puts in place to control language definition and language change. The people participating in the identity of a language create its 'boundaries' and negotiate its permeability towards 'external' influences, building and controlling its traditions and literary models, and curating the scope given to the inventiveness of its speakers as they respond to the new linguistic demands of an ever-changing world — see, for example, the continually evolving vocabulary for IT and online communication.

Taking account of multilingualism and interaction between languages in the course of power shifts and migration renders the question of 'what is a language' more complex still. To take the example of English, there is now a huge range of Englishes that extend from Manchester to Mumbai, New York to Nairobi. And that's before we have taken account of the many creoles and forms of patois, sector-specific jargon and varieties that have emerged in the context of social media. Are they all part of one language, or are British, American, Indian and Kenyan English distinct languages? The concept of 'global English' can be a useful generalization, and it comes with certain homogenizing tendencies, but the use of a language as a lingua franca also drives its diversification.

The most extreme form of diversification happens at the level of individuals: for example, twins will sometimes develop a private language that cannot be understood by others. And linguistic theory even allows for an individual dialect or 'idiolect' — 'the speech habits of a person as displayed in a particular variety at a given time' (Crystal 2008: 235). Our linguistic creativity is always hard at work, in each one of us.

Creative Empowerment of Marginalized Languages

The world of languages is structured by powerful hierarchies that tend to mirror political power structures and financial muscle. This is evident in the continuing dominant role of the languages exported by the European colonial nations from the fifteenth century onwards, and it is currently evident in the expansion of Chinese as China experiences unprecedented global economic growth and increasing international power. The rise of English as the current main global lingua franca was strengthened by its colonial expansion and establishment as predominant language of the United States, fuelled by the Industrial Revolution and given global reach by the Internet. So what are the implications for languages that do not gain high status and support from such political, economic and technological benefits?

From the perspective of monoglot English speakers, it can seem as if the whole world now speaks English and other languages are dying out. But that ignores the majority of people who do not speak English. It also entails misunderstanding the roles played by lingua francas. A lingua franca facilitates effective communication across language groups — but it does so as part of a multilingual ecosystem that is characterized by complex interactions between more and less local languages. Often it is these local languages, spoken in the home, that are perceived by their speakers as most emotionally expressive and culturally rich.

Human societies typically use many varieties alongside each other. In India and many parts of Africa, people may converse in four or five languages in the course of a day. Many workplaces and schools in the UK, too, are now multilingual spaces which benefit from a diversity of cultures and languages that have come into the country through immigration and continue to be nurtured in homes and local communities. This collective multilingual competence is an asset that should be supported not least educationally since it gives young people career opportunities and the cultural intelligence and linguistic flexibility to connect the UK effectively with other parts of the world.

Languages with distinctive lexical and grammatical systems are dying in many places of the world where Indigenous people have come under territorial, economic and political pressure, climate change is destroying their ecosystem, their habitat has become more connected to the outside world, and/or members have left the community. This loss can justifiably be considered equivalent to the extinction of biological species. Moreover, biological diversity goes hand in hand with linguistic diversity, with loss of linguistic diversity exerting a negative impact on the environment (see Gosler et al. 2020 and Chapter 2 on 'Creating a Meaningful World: Nature in Name, Metaphor and Myth' in this volume). Many communities are responding to the threat of language extinction with proactive measures to preserve their language, in interaction with other forms of cultural expression such as dance, clothing and crafts, and, in some cases, connection with modern technologies and modern forms imported from elsewhere. Anthropologists, linguists and, in some cases, governments have long also contributed to finding ways of preserving linguistic diversity.

Meanwhile cities are bringing forth new linguistic varieties all the time as people from different parts of the world converge and create new ways of expressing themselves within and beyond their groups. In this process, as with regional and national varieties, identity formation plays a crucial part as a creative impetus, as does the need to negotiate status tensions. For example, the linguistic varieties found in Birmingham and researched in the project Slanguages as part of Creative Multilingualism's research on 'Languages in the Creative Economy' (see Dudrah et al. 2020 and Chapter 4 in this volume) gain energy from groups of people who grew up feeling marginalized not least because of their 'nonstandard British' accent but who then discovered rich performative potential in that language difference — a

www.punch-records.co.uk

BRITISH SIGN LANGUAGE
Eight Examples

LIE
A false statement made with deliberate intent to deceive.

Hand up against chin with forefinger outstretched. Mouths the word "lie" while moving hand away.

BRILLIANT
Satisfactory in quality, quantity, or degree.

Hand with raised thumb on open hand moves upwards.

DRIVE
To convey in a vehicle.

Both hands grasp an imaginary driving wheel and move in a circular motion.

JEWELLERY
Articles of gold, silver, precious stones, etc., for personal adornment.

Hand moves across top of body to denote wearing of jewellery.

DRUNK
State in which one's physical and mental faculties are impaired by excess of alcohol.

Fingers extended to make 'V' shape. Make backward and forward movements.

GREAT
Wonderful, first-rate, very good.

Same as BRILLIANT, showing the limitation of conveying slightly different meanings in sign language.

RELAX
To release or bring relief from the effects of tension, anxiety.

Hands make repeated backward and forward movements with fingers outstretched.

COMPLETE
The act of achieving attainment or accomplishment.

Both hands raised with thumb outstretched move downwards.

Fig. 1 Sign languages build on visible cues such as facial expression and gesture. Unlike British Sign Language (BSL), 'Urban Sign Language' (USL) has no official status. It reflects shared usage in parts of the Birmingham deaf community. Posters created for the *Slanguages* exhibition 2017, Wolfson College, Oxford, reproduced by kind permission of Rinkoo Barpaga (Artist), Nick Drew (Design), Rajinder Dudrah (Birmingham City University) and Simon Redgrave (Punch Records).

creative opportunity identified and developed by Slanguages partner Punch Records.

The complexity of what we understand by 'language' is evident in sign language, as is the huge creative potential that lies in embracing language difference. For the Creative Multilingualism team, engaging with the sign-language performances — and provocations — of stand-up comedian Rinkoo Barpaga in the context of Slanguages brought new questions and insights into issues around the nature of human communication: the role of gesture in relation to speech on the one hand and sign language on the other; the productive tensions between innovation and standardization; the processes at work in marginalization and recognition of languages; and not least the political implications of language difference for educational access — with Barpaga having turned disadvantagement in the Birmingham school system into the basis for a career in the performing arts.

Barpaga's concept of 'Urban Sign Language' (USL) draws on the experience of acquiring a group-specific form of signing in an inner-city school context where no access to sign-language education was provided, and later being taught to adopt British Sign Language (BSL) as the only 'proper' form of deaf communication. Urban Sign Language doesn't purport to offer a competing standard. Rather, it poses a challenge to the devaluation of non-standard forms by recognizing the importance of a language created by a group for its own communicative purposes and as an expression of its particular social identity. The provocation is showcased in a pair of posters depicting USL and BSL (see Barpaga et al. 2017 and Fig. 1). At first sight it offers straightforward word-for-word translations between the two forms. Closer comparison makes the viewer aware of the complex interplay between different aspects of language that yield changes of concept in the course of translation: territory and political status (urban versus national); ownership and control of a standard (national institution versus individual/group); class (middle/upper versus lower); cultural control (educated and powerful versus socially and educationally disadvantaged); register (formal versus slang). What the pair of posters shows even beyond the issues concerning different forms of sign language is the creative charge that is generated in the interstices between the categories. The multiple tensions that arise from the clash of unequal varieties provide a rich matrix for linguistic creativity.

Embracing linguistic diversity provides an important catalyst for questioning the enduring legacy of colonialism, addressing inequalities that threaten social stability, and engaging with the current challenges of globalization and environmental exploitation.

Inventing Languages

It has been claimed — on the basis of an ambitious research project published in 1957–1963 — that 'the story of the confusion of tongues, and of the attempt to redeem its loss through the rediscovery or invention of a language common to all humanity, can be found in every culture' (Eco 1997: 1). Whether or not such myths are indeed universal, it's clear that human beings have not been content with the imperfections of 'natural' languages and the impediments to cross-cultural communication that come with their diversity. They have wanted to go beyond the use of a natural language as a lingua franca, for example Latin in the administrative and military classes of the Roman Empire. The Babel myth exemplifies the vision of a 'perfect' language common to all peoples — and conversely the frustration, framed as a divine curse, that linguistic diversity impedes effective cooperation not least on a practical task such as that of building a tower. Yet alongside the invention of perfect languages to be shared by all human beings, there is also a fascination with inventing languages that are culturally specific or group-specific and that may be designed to restrict communication to a closely defined group. In short, people across time and across cultures have been immensely resourceful in generating new languages by exploiting their linguistic creativity.

'Perfect' languages have not just remained general concepts in the world of myth, and language invention has taken many forms. David J. Peterson — creator of the Dothraki language for the *Game of Thrones* television franchise (2011–2019) — surmises that 'the conscious construction of language is probably as old as language itself' (2015: 7). In the Western world, the earliest records are from the Middle Ages, with Hildegard of Bingen's 'Lingua Ignota' ('unknown language') as one of the earliest instances (twelfth century) — perhaps even the earliest. By contrast with this language 'received' via divine inspiration, the early modern era brought forth a rich array of languages designed to satisfy the needs of philosophers and scientists for a medium that would be free of the ambiguities and metaphorical imprecisions of natural languages. An ambitious example is John Wilkins' universal 'Philosophical Language' (1668) — amusingly critiqued by the Argentinian author Jorge Luis Borges in an influential essay (1937–1952) on the grounds that the underlying categorization attempts the impossible.

One of the most successful projects designed to overcome the problems of linguistic diversity was the creation of Esperanto, invented in the late nineteenth century by the Polish ophthalmologist Ludwik Lejzer Zamenhof, who also produced the first grammar of Yiddish. Coming from a multilingual family, he presented his 'International Language' in 1889 under the pseudonym of 'Dr. Esperanto' — meaning 'one who hopes' in the invented language. This was then adopted as the name of the language itself. His purpose was to create a language that would be grammatically and morphologically simple, easy to learn and serve as an internationally shared auxiliary language. While being compatible with linguistic diversity, it would facilitate straightforward international communication and promote peace, an objective Zamenhof articulates with reference to the tensions caused by linguistic difference:

> Indeed, the difference of languages is one of the most fruitful sources of the dissensions and differences among nations, for, of all things that impress a stranger in a foreign land, the language is at once the first and the greatest mark of distinction between him and them; not being able to understand or be understood, we naturally shun the contact of aliens. (Zamenhof 1889: 6)

Rather than constructing his language from scratch, Zamenhof aimed to use existing roots and structures, focusing on Indo-European languages. For the vocabulary, he looked mainly to European and especially Latinate words, given that these had already spread their roots widely through the languages of Europe by means of lexical borrowing (see Fig. 2).

While numbers of speakers have fluctuated, some enthusiasts have brought up their children as native speakers of Esperanto (Bergen 2001) and it continues to attract learners, recently also as one of the languages supported by Duolingo.

Inventiveness and ingenuity have also driven creative projects of a very different kind: constructed languages — or 'conlangs' — designed

Fig. 2. Some common words in Esperanto. Picture compilation by Sharlene Matharu (2020).

to give imagined peoples a distinctive medium capable of expressing their cultural identity. The protagonist in Jonathan Swift's satire *Gulliver's Travels* (1726) has at least a smattering of several languages and is able to learn other languages he encounters as he visits communities such as those of the Yahoos and the Houyhnhnms. But the reader's imagination must fill in the detail. J. R. R. Tolkien went much further. Building on an early interest in Esperanto and experimentation with language invention, he created a whole family of languages as part of the project that has

---

1   *Answer*: Nouns end in –o, plural nouns in –j and adjectives in –a.

given us *The Lord of the Rings* (1954–1955). The best-known languages spoken by the Elves in Tolkien's legendarium are Quenya and Sindarin, which share a common ancestor, primitive Quendian. As a professor of Anglo-Saxon, Tolkien drew on a deep knowledge of etymology, evolving grammatical systems and scripts as well as the mythologies that formed their cultural context to create a world of languages that continues to inspire conlang experts today.

Tolkien's most far-reaching achievement for conlangs was to establish an archetype for fictional languages that defined their scope and potential for the era of television, the Internet and computer games. As conlang professional Peterson acknowledges, Tolkien 'set the bar very high' (2015: 10). In *The Art of Language Invention* (2015), Peterson explains how he developed the languages created for *The Game of Thrones* from snippets given in the novels on which the adaptation is based, George R. R. Martin's *A Song of Ice and Fire* (1996). He also sets out the principles he followed in creating languages for peoples such as the Dothraki warriors of *Game of Thrones* and the alien Irathients and Castithans of the television series *Defiance* (2013–2015), showcasing the considerable sophistication of conlangs and the inspiring force of a fan community that looks forward with excitement to hearing a fictional people gain a new voice. Peterson has even satisfied the growing desire among fans to learn High Valyrian by writing and voicing a Duolingo course in the language.

Experimenting with Our Linguistic Creativity

Our linguistic creativity is at work whenever we think linguistically, speak, write or respond to the language of others. It is a flexible talent that enables us to use, and respond to, different modes of communicating and — depending on our cultural context — more than one language. Most of the time, we're not aware of our linguistic creativity. But it comes to the fore in poetry, advertising, verbal humour and all kinds of play with language. These forms in turn allow us to appreciate the fact that linguistic creativity is continually part of our receptive and productive use of language.

In his study *Language Play* (1998), Crystal engages critically with the view that the chief purpose of language is communicative usefulness:

'The whole point of language, it is assumed, is to foster the transmission of knowledge, however this is defined — as concepts, facts, opinions, emotions, or any other kind of "information"' (pp. 1–2). He posits rather that the neglected 'playful (or "ludic") function of language [...] should be at the heart of any thinking we do about linguistic issues' (p. 1). His book is a tour de force of linguistic play in practice, showing how important language play is in our day-to-day lives and how fundamental it is for our social interactions.

Crystal's argument concerning the crucial importance of language play is persuasive. His book however begs the question whether it should not be linguistic creativity that is regarded as primary, with language play being an exuberantly inventive expression of it. In summarizing what happens in language play, Crystal in actual fact comments on what we routinely control and manipulate creatively when producing language: 'Any aspect of linguistic structure is available to become the focus of language play. We can alter the pronunciation, the writing system, the grammar, the vocabulary, the patterns of spoken or written discourse, or any combination of these' (pp. 9–10). While he identifies such 'bending and breaking' of the rules of the language with an absence of communicative purpose — 'if someone were to ask why we do it, the answer is simply: for fun' (p. 1) — he offers a substantial chapter on the work of 'professionals' including advertisers, headline writers, comedians, collectors, comic writers, authors, artists and theologians (pp. 93–158). The common denominator here would seem to be not so much language play as a creative use of language for a variety of purposes, including commercially motivated persuasion.

Focusing on creativity also brings poetry more fully into view as a mode of expression which has stimulated people down the ages and across cultures to work with the stuff of their language and its special traditions while also discovering new possibilities in other languages. The result is an infinite wealth of forms and types of poem, with every type of language 'rule' being 'broken' — or, to put this in a way that foregrounds the infinite scope for creativity, every opportunity for linguistic innovation in a given language being exploited: seriously, playfully, satirically, experimentally.

Crystal argues that 'language play is natural, spontaneous and universal' (p. 93). Yet his first example, designed to illustrate that 'everyone plays with language or responds to language play' (p. 1), in fact also indicates that language play and linguistic creativity respond to characteristics of a specific language, and evolve in a particular cultural context. Introduced with the title 'ping-pong punning' (pp. 2–3), the example is embedded in the cultural tradition of the UK and influenced at least in part by the nature of the English language. It consists of a humorous conversation between two couples in a sitting room about a 'confrontation' between their respective cats, which gives rise to the creative modification 'catfrontation' and unleashes a pun exchange involving the syllable 'cat': catastrophe, categorical, catalogue, catalyst, catarrh, catechism, with a cartoon adding in 'catatonic'. The puns in turn generate laughter, groans and comments such as 'Oh, that's Christmas-cracker standard' (p. 3) — an allusion to the British Christmas dinner custom of each person having a colourful paper tube that pops when it is pulled apart with the person sitting next to you and contains a paper crown, small gift and slip of paper with a joke — normally involving a pun. The situation is recognizable as characteristic of English domestic life, tending towards middle-class social intercourse.

While punning is a popular social activity across cultures and languages — for example in Japanese, Spanish, and many languages of Indigenous peoples in South America — and might indeed turn out to be practised with every language, Crystal's example is not transferable even to a relatively closely related linguistic culture. To take just one context, it is inconceivable that the conversation cited by him would take place in this form in a German sitting room — and not just because the equivalent of the trigger word, 'Katze', is morphologically more complex and semantically less flexible when forming part of a longer word. Reasons supporting the hypothesis of non-transferability are: German vocabulary, with many words formed by derivation and compounding, has far fewer monosyllables than English and far fewer homophones (words with the same pronunciation but different meanings), lending itself less readily than English to richly varied punning; there is no influential literary tradition of punning akin to that associated especially with Shakespeare; newspapers make far less use of puns and word play than English ones do across the spectrum of the press; punning is less prevalent among children; and Germans — for whom Christmas is traditionally associated with festiveness rather than fun — don't have Christmas crackers, which annually give rise to groans, laughter and punning across British dining tables. One may glean from this comparison that word play draws on the specific features of a language and is deeply rooted in the cultural practices of the society in which the language is used. We cannot therefore generalize about universal forms of linguistic humour on the basis of a single language let alone a single society.

If, on the other hand, we place ordinary linguistic creativity at the centre of inquiry, we don't need to make presuppositions concerning its purpose, or generalize about the ways in which it manifests itself. We can still focus on exceptional or particularly complex forms, investigate the role of linguistic humour and take account of (non) purposes such as play and fun. Word play and indeed punning can have many functions depending on context — political, religious, competitive, sexual, poetic. In his book *The Pun Also Rises*, John Pollack (a Pun-Off World Champion and also speechwriter for Bill Clinton) recounts this ancient Hawaiian custom:

> rivals often settled disputes by means of a riddling contest, challenging each other with conundrums built upon deep local knowledge and intricate wordplay. Making and catching sophisticated puns was often critical to victory, and such punning exchanges weren't intended to be funny. In extreme cases, losers even paid with their lives. (Pollack 2012: 120; source: Beckwith 1970: 455)

Punning, then, may be deadly serious. What we can take from the immense range of language activities Crystal and Pollack discuss is that people love the creative potential of their languages and will exploit it in the entire range of activities that make up their lives.

People's fascination with manipulating similarities and differences between words in language games and contests is just one manifestation of a talent that underpins our capacity to recognize similarities between our own language and related languages (see Maiden et al. 2020 and Chapter 3 in this volume). We have the potential for acute sensitivity towards subtle linguistic differences — in pronunciation, word choice, grammar, tone. But to what extent we train that sensitivity, what we focus it on, and the extent to which we think that a particular difference matters, will vary from language to language, from one speech community and cultural context to another, and indeed between individuals.

We can see this principle at work in the response different speech communities adopt towards new words coming into their language. The processes by which new words enter a language are infinite. A fascinating insight into the variety can be gained from following the quarterly 'Updates to the OED' provided roughly on a quarterly basis by the editorial team of the *Oxford English Dictionary* (*OED*). They range from adoption of words incorporated from a wide variety of other languages to new formations created by abbreviating words, adding new prefixes, creating compounds, or establishing a combination of words as a fixed collocation that is listed as a lexical item. And they may have arisen for a host of different reasons, for example in response to a political development, as a result of the dissemination of a fictional work such as *Star Wars* that has appealed to the popular imagination or because a distinctive word by a particular group in society has gained wider currency.

Words that have been adopted for the *OED*'s online Third Edition include *peoplekind* (*OED* 2019c), *omnishambles* (*OED* 2019b), *whatevs* (*OED* 2019d) and *mama put* (*OED* 2019a). *Peoplekind* was formed from substituting an inclusive noun for the gender-specific prefix *man*, reflecting a linguistically creative response to changing social attitudes. *Omnishambles*, formed by humorously prefixing the (elevated) Latin word for 'all, everything' to an existing informal word for disorder, was adopted from a political satire for use in public discourse. *Whatevs*, formed from abbreviating e.g. 'whatever [you say/want]', was taken over from slang. *Mama put* was formed by joining the noun *mama* with the verb *put*, probably in the sense of 'asking for food to be put for (i.e. given to) the customer'. It is classified as 'Nigerian English' and given with subtly different British, US and West African pronunciations. The compound noun is defined as 'a street vendor, typically a woman, selling cooked food at low prices from a handcart or stall' with the metonymic derivations of a restaurant serving such food, and the food sold by such vendors. The word reflects usage on the basis of distinctive cultural practices by English speakers in, or from, a country with UK links forged by colonialism. The designation of the word as 'Nigerian English' both highlights its origin and indicates the porousness and transience of 'boundaries' between different varieties. Its incorporation in 'the definitive record of the English language' (*OED* website slogan) forms just one episode in the story of the word's creation and creative integration in different Englishes.

In non-Anglophone countries, the expansion of English and widespread adoption of neologisms based on English has given rise to a wide range of different responses, often within the country. Some groups — for example technical innovators and frequently young people — respond readily to new imports from English, and this can give rise to word formations such as the German verbs 'googeln' and 'relaunchen' with derived forms such as 'gegoogelt' and 'gerelauncht', and pseudo-English formations such as 'das Handy' ('mobile phone'). Meanwhile, more conservatively minded groups are concerned to preserve and protect the cultural and linguistic distinctiveness of the language that has been shaped by tradition. Such controversies can be followed, for example, in the debates generated in France and the French-speaking world by the pronouncements of the Académie Française.

Our languages are rule-governed, but we don't just adopt the rules passively in order to reproduce them, and we don't just 'break' them. Implementing them is a creative act in which individuals and groups, communities and institutions interact. We are continually interpreting the rules to fit the context, developing our speech habits, responding to new stimuli, and adapting our language to new people, situations and individual expressive needs and desires. Creativity is intrinsic to language and a driving force in generating linguistic diversity and language change, in interaction with the diversity and changing lives of people.

Works Cited

Antunes, Ricardo, et al. 2011. 'Individually Distinctive Acoustic Features in Sperm Whale Codas', *Animal Behaviour*, 81(4): 723–30, https://doi.org/10.1016/j.anbehav.2010.12.019

Athanasopoulos, Panos. 2009. 'Cognitive Representation of Colour in Bilinguals: The Case of Greek Blues', *Bilingualism: Language and Cognition*, 12(1): 83–95, https://doi.org/10.1017/s136672890800388x

Barpaga, Rinkoo, Nick Drew, Rajinder Dudrah and Simon Redgrave. 2017. 'British Sign Language (BSL): Eight Examples' and 'Urban Sign Language (USL): Eight Equivalents', posters created for the *Slanguages* exhibition 2017, Wolfson College, Oxford.

Beckwith, Martha. 1970. *Hawaiian Mythology* (Honolulu: University of Hawaii Press).

Bergen, Benjamin. 2001. 'Nativization Processes in L1 Esperanto', *Journal of Child Language*, 28: 575–95, https://doi.org/10.1017/S0305000901004779

Borges, Jorge Luis. 1937–1952. 'El idioma analítico de John Wilkins', with English translation: [The Analytical Language of John Wilkins], http://languagelog.ldc.upenn.edu/myl/ldc/wilkins.html

Briefer, Elodie F., and Alan G. McElligott. 2012. 'Social Effects on Vocal Ontogeny in an Ungulate, the Goat, *Capra hircus*', *Animal Behaviour*, 83(4): 991–1000, https://doi.org/10.1016/j.anbehav.2012.01.020

Casaponsa, Aina, and Panas Athanosopoulos. 2018. 'The Way You See Colour Depends on What Language You Speak', *The Conversation*, 16 April, https://theconversation.com/the-way-you-see-colour-depends-on-what-language-you-speak-94833

Chomsky, Noam. 1986. *Knowledge of Language: Its Nature, Origin and Use* (New York: Praeger).

Coghlan, Andy. 2012. 'Young Goats Can Develop Distinct Accents', *New Scientist*, 16 February, https://www.newscientist.com/article/dn21481-young-goats-can-develop-distinct-accents

Creative Multilingualism. 2020. https://www.creativeml.ox.ac.uk

Croft, William, and D. Alan Cruse 2004. *Cognitive Linguistics* (Cambridge: Cambridge University Press), https://doi.org/10.1017/cbo9780511803864

Crystal, David. 2008. *A Dictionary of Linguistics and Phonetics*, 6th edn (Malden, MA: Blackwell).

Crystal, David. 1998. *Language Play* (London: Penguin).

Dudrah, Rajinder, Philip Bullock, Julie Curtis and Noah Birksted-Breen. 2020. 'Languages in the Creative Economy', Research Strand 4 of Creative Multilingualism, https://www.creativeml.ox.ac.uk/research/creative-economy

Duolingo. 2020. https://www.duolingo.com/

Eco, Umberto. 1997. *The Search for the Perfect Language*, trans. by James Fentress (London: Fontana).

Gosler, Andrew, Karen Park and Felice S. Wyndham. 2020. 'Creating a Meaningful World: Nature in Name, Metaphor and Myth', Research Strand 2 of Creative Multilingualism, https://www.creativeml.ox.ac.uk/research/naming

Kohl, Katrin, Marianna Bolognesi and Ana Werkmann Horvat. 2020. 'The Creative Power of Metaphor', Research Strand 1 of Creative Multilingualism, https://www.creativeml.ox.ac.uk/research/metaphor

OED. 2019a. 'mama put, *n.*', *OED*, https://www.oed.com/view/Entry/82854804?redirectedFrom=mama+put#eid

OED. 2019b. 'omnishambles, *n.*', *OED*, https://www.oed.com/view/Entry/83178718?redirectedFrom=omnishambles#eid

OED. 2019c. 'peoplekind, *n.*', *OED*, https://www.oed.com/view/Entry/78879462?redirectedFrom=peoplekind#eid

OED. 2019d. 'whatevs, *int.* and *pron.*', *OED*, https://www.oed.com/view/Entry/79334939?redirectedFrom=whatevs#eid

OED. 'Updates to the OED'. Published approximately quarterly, https://public.oed.com/updates/

Peterson, David J. 2015. *The Art of Language Invention: From Horse-Lords to Dark Elves, the Words Behind World-Building* (New York: Penguin).

Pinker, Steven. 1994. *The Language Instinct: The New Science of Language and Mind* (London: Penguin).

Pipek, Pavel, et al. 2018. 'Dialects of an Invasive Songbird Are Preserved in Its Invaded but Not Native Source Range', *Ecography*, 41: 245–54, https://doi.org/10.1111/ecog.02779

Pollack, John. 2012. *The Pun Also Rises: How the Humble Pun Revolutionized Language, Changed History, and Made Wordplay More Than Some Antics* (New York: Avery).

Punch Records. 2020. https://www.wearepunch.co.uk/ [See also Creative Multilingualism. 2020b. 'Punch Records', https://www.creativeml.ox.ac.uk/about/partners/punch-records]

Swift, Jonathan. 1726. *Gulliver's Travels* (London: Benj. Motte).

Slanguages. 2020. A project under the aegis of 'Languages in the Creative Economy', Research Strand 4 of Creative Multilingualism, https://www.creativeml.ox.ac.uk/projects/slanguages

Wilkins, John. 1668. *An Essay Towards a Real Character and a Philosophical Language* (London: S. Gellibrand), BCCtZjBtiEYC&pg=RA1-PR2&hl=it&source=gbs_selected_pages&cad=2#v=onepage&q&f=false

[Zamenhof, L. L.] Dr. Esperanto. 1889. *An Attempt Towards an International Language*, trans. by Henry Phillips, Jr. (New York: Holt).

Find Out More

Crystal, David. 1998. *Language Play* (London: Penguin).

Many types of language play are explained and illustrated with rich examples. While the book is focused on English, it offers an excellent foundation for investigating language play in other languages.

Duncan, Dennis, et al. 2019. *Babel: Adventures in Translation* (Oxford: Bodleian Library).

A series of illustrated essays offers snapshots of linguistic creativity over a timespan of some 3500 years. The artefacts and texts show how translation has enabled ideas and stories to travel across a rich multitude of cultures and traditions.

Eco, Umberto. 1997. *The Search for the Perfect Language*, **trans. by James Fentress (London: Fontana). Italian version: 1993.** *La ricerca della lingua perfetta nelle cultura europea* **(Rome: Laterza).**

Eco traces the search for the perfect language that would be common to all human beings, elucidating the fascinatingly diverse theories put forward by a host of philosophers and philologists across multilingual Europe.

Peterson, David J. 2015. *The Art of Language Invention: From Horse-Lords to Dark Elves, the Words Behind World-Building* **(New York: Penguin).**

A toolkit for constructing languages that shape sci-fi worlds. Along the way, the inventor of Dothraki for *Game of Thrones* looks in detail at sounds, words and orthography.

Pinker, Steven. 1994. *The Language Instinct: The New Science of Language and Mind* **(London: Penguin).**

Pinker argues that language is innate to human beings, and separate from thought. He looks at issues such as the biological origin of language, language acquisition and the evolution of languages and dialects.

Sacks, Oliver. 2012 (1989). *Seeing Voices: A Journey into the World of the Deaf* **(London: Picador).**

A history of total deafness and analysis of the expressive power of sign language. Sacks also offers an engaging account of the different ways deaf and hearing people learn to categorize their respective world views.

Silverfish Films. 2019. 'Do We Think Differently in Different Languages?', 4:10, *BBC Ideas***, 24 October, https://www.bbc.com/ideas/videos/do-we-think-differently-in-different-languages/p07ry35k**

An engaging short video exploring the interaction between thought and language, involving speakers of different languages.

Credits

Permission to include their contribution was kindly granted by the following:

Rinkoo Barpaga (Artist), Nick Drew (Design), Rajinder Dudrah (Birmingham City University) and Simon Redgrave (Punch Records) for two posters created for the *Slanguages* exhibition 2017, Wolfson College, Oxford (Fig. 1).

Why Learn a Language?

Languages are fundamental to our lives, and they're all valuable — in different ways, different places, with different people, for different purposes. You may already know a little or quite a lot of a language other than your own — it will always be worth exploring it further. And whether or not you have ever learned a language, it will certainly be rewarding to start one from scratch.

The Creative Multilingualism team has come up with the following reasons for language learning, building on the ten Manifesto Statements we presented at the beginning of the book and explored in its ten chapters. Here, we offer some concrete suggestions why it's worth embarking — or continuing — on your own personal language learning journey.

1. Language diversity nurtures diversity of identity, thought and expression

Learning a language …

- … makes you more sensitive to cultural difference.
- … can enable a foreign culture to touch you and move you in new ways.
- … helps you to appreciate what is special about your own culture.
- … allows you to empathize with what it must feel like to be a dog listening to humans talking.

2. Language diversity protects biodiversity

Learning a language …

- … gives you an understanding of humanity's multilingualism as part of the diversity of life.

- ... allows you to explore a new natural environment through indigenous names for plants and animals, created by the people who understand their beauty, complexity and value.
- ... reveals that even scientific facts look different if you approach them through another language and its scientific tradition.
- ... enables you to appreciate birdsong and animal communication in a new way.

3. We're more multilingual than we think

Learning a language ...

- ... makes you notice another language in your own, such as Arabic (*magazine*), Chinese (*tea*), French (*cabbage*), German (*zeitgeist*), Greek (*music*), Hindi (*thug*), Indonesian (*gong*), Italian (*umbrella*), Japanese (*tycoon*), Latin (*corona virus*), Nahuatl (*tomato*), Portuguese (*marmalade*), Russian (*disinformation*), Spanish (*cafeteria*), Swahili (*safari*), Turkish (*yogurt*), Urdu (*cushy*).
- ... allows you to identify lots of words in the other language that you already know or can work out because they have the same origin or are borrowed from English, for example in French (*weekend, parking, brainstorming, interview*), German (*Computer, Job, Meeting, trainieren*) or Spanish (*hobby, running, feedback, email*) (though beware of 'false friends'...).
- ... encourages you to 'read' body language and discover the world of sign languages.
- ... gives you lots of Eureka moments as bits of the language puzzle fit together.

4. Language diversity inspires creativity in performance

Learning a language ...

- ... encourages you to try out a different voice and self-projection.
- ... enables you to imagine yourself in a different culture.

- ... transforms your experience of quotidian interactions — if you visit a country where the language is spoken, even buying a loaf of bread can feel like a theatrical scenario.
- ... allows you to immerse yourself in a whole new world through the performative arts, films and other media, and appreciate how much the original language contributes to the experience.

5. Languages travel and migrate

Learning a language ...

- ... allows you to follow the journeys another language has taken with its people — in battles won and lost, scientific discoveries, art, music, literature.
- ... encourages you to visit countries where the language is at home.
- ... makes life in a global society easier and more enriching.
- ... could give your life a whole new trajectory.

6. Translation is inherently creative

Learning a language ...

- ... allows you to explore language difference through the art of translation.
- ... helps you to mediate between your own culture and the culture in which the language is spoken.
- ... gives you the opportunity to find out how your hobby translates into another culture — cookery, martial arts, gardening, dance, archaeology, castles, diving, bird-watching.
- ... enables you to use translation and interpreting apps more intelligently and effectively.

7. Language learning opens your mind

Learning a language ...

- ... is an adventure in mental travel.

- ... enables you to watch the news from the point of view of another part of the world.
- ... could allow you to enter a part of your heritage that was previously a closed door.
- ... makes you more confident about learning further languages.

8. Languages hold infinite potential for creativity

Learning a language ...

- ... allows you to discover the creative richness of your own language as well as the one you're learning (a single word can inspire a poem!).
- ... provides opportunities for discovering lots of new word play.
- ... enables you to understand poetry, song, musicals, opera in the medium where the language truly harmonises with the sound and rhythm.
- ... gives you access to a new imaginative world of myths and stories in the language in which they were created and transmitted.

9. Languages create connections with people

Learning a language ...

- ... gets you thinking about how language works, and how vital it is for our social lives.
- ... enables you to empathize with people from another country for whom your language is foreign, and show respect for people whose language you are learning.
- ... allows you to feel you belong in a culture that started off feeling foreign.
- ... permits you to help people — in the street, in a hospital, in your school, in your workplace.

10. We create language every day

Learning a language ...

- … gives you a new toolkit for creative thinking.
- … opens up more ways to be linguistically creative.
- … encourages you to explore the differences between your own language and the one you're learning — and makes you aware of how much human creativity has gone into developing such different ways of saying (almost) the same thing.
- … keeps your brain so active that it could help stave off dementia for four to five years.

Not enough?

Then have a look at this study — it gives over 700 reasons grouped in 70 key areas in which languages make a difference: https://www.llas.ac.uk/700reasons.html

The study provides links to relevant research and reaches the following conclusion (http://www.idiomas.idph.com.br/textos/700_reasons.pdf, p. 2):

The strongest of these reasons are the personal benefits and enjoyment people gain from learning a language.

Fig. 1 Communication network. Image by Gordon Johnson, from Pixabay, https://pixabay.com/vectors/social-media-connections-networking-3846597/

Find Out More

The works given in this section include all those which are recommended for further exploration of the topics addressed in the individual chapters of the volume.

AGCAS. 2019. 'What Can I Do with a Modern Languages Degree?', *Prospects*, https://www.prospects.ac.uk/careers-advice/what-can-i-do-with-my-degree/modern-languages

Information provided by The Association of Graduate Careers Advisory Services on different types of career requiring a high level of languages competence and also other types of career where languages are an important adjunct.

Bilingualism Matters. 2020. http://www.bilingualism-matters.ppls.ed.ac.uk

Founded by Antonella Sorace, Bilingualism Matters is a research and information centre on bilingualism based at the University of Edinburgh. The initiative has spread across the world, and its mission is to work with a wide range of partners to research, support and promote bilingualism.

Birksted-Breen, Noah. 2020. 'Vassily Sigarev and the Presnyakov Brothers: Staging the New Russia', in *Contemporary European Playwrights*, **ed. by Maria Delgado, Bryce Lease and Dan Rebellato (London: Routledge), pp. 168–84.**

A chapter about the plays of two iconic Russian playwrights, whose work was critically acclaimed in Russia and the UK in the early 2000s.

Birksted-Breen, Noah, and Rajinder Dudrah. 2018. 'Translating a Russian Play into Hip-hop Theatre: A Conversation', Creative Multilingualism, 28 November, https://www.creativeml.ox.ac.uk/

blog/exploring-multilingualism/translating-russian-play-hip-hop-theatre-conversation

A discussion of the dilemmas faced by the director and the curator of *Oxygen*, from Russian page to British stage.

Black, Jonathan. 2019. *How to Find the Career You've Always Wanted* **(London: Robinson).**

This book offers advice on career planning and choices, writing a CV and preparing for an interview. See also the author's fortnightly column 'Dear Jonathan' in the *Financial Times* (https://www.ft.com/dear-jonathan), and the FT Career Starters videos: https://www.youtube.com/watch?v=yjdvCHWVtE4&list=PLqIpf04KBv61XrP8rtadMl5YpVxZt7Wkc

Casasanto, Daniel. 2013. 'Development of Metaphorical Thinking: The Role of Language', in *Language and the Creative Mind,* **ed. by M. Borkent, J. Hinnell et al. (Stanford: CSLI Publications), pp. 3–18,** http://casasanto.com/papers/Casasanto_Development_of_Metaphorical_Thinking_2013.pdf

This article considers fundamental questions about the interplay between different types of cognitive metaphor and language.

Clanchy, Kate (ed.). 2018. *England: Poems from a School* **(London: Picador).**

This anthology of poems written by multilingual schoolchildren at Oxford Spires Academy includes many that were produced during the prismatic workshops.

Creative Multilingualism. 2020. https://www.creativeml.ox.ac.uk

This website represents the research that underpins the content of this volume. The research was conducted by the authors between 2016 and 2020 and funded by the Arts and Humanities Research Council (AHRC, part of UK Research and Innovation) in the context of its Open World Research Initiative (OWRI). The website includes the projects conducted by the seven research strands (see Chapters 1 to 7) and further sections with blogs, resources and reports on conferences and public engagement work, some of which is presented in Chapters 8 and 9.

Creative Multilingualism. 2020a. LinguaMania: The Podcast, https://podcasts.ox.ac.uk/series/linguamania

This series of eight podcasts was made by the Creative Multilingualism team. It explores connections between languages and creativity, and opens up a wide range of perspectives on language learning.

Creative Multilingualism. 2020c. 'Resources', https://www.creativeml.ox.ac.uk/resources

This collection of resources offers a wide range of creative activities for the classroom, including how to stage a multilingual concert, how to teach the creation of short films in any language, and suggestions for enabling students to experience the joys of translation.

Creative Multilingualism (Careers). 2016. 'What do Modern Languages Students Do after Graduating?', https://www.creativeml.ox.ac.uk/blog/working-languages/what-do-modern-languages-students-do-after-graduating

Responses from Oxford graduates in Modern Languages about the varied paths their careers have taken, from teaching, interpreting and food writing to producing TV commercials and running a venture capital fund. The responses were compiled by the Russian department but the variety of career paths is typical for other languages, too.

Creative Multilingualism (Careers). 2020. 'How Languages Help in Your Career', https://www.creativeml.ox.ac.uk/careers

A short film consisting of comments from people in a variety of careers on the ways in which languages play a – sometimes surprising – part. More extended videos of the interviews give a deeper insight into the role languages have played in their careers.

Creative Multilingualism (MPP). 2020a. 'Multilingual Drama Teaching Activities', https://www.creativeml.ox.ac.uk/resources/multilingual-drama-teaching-activities

Short videos explain and demonstrate a variety of games including (and in addition to) 'Buzzy Bees', 'Sevens' and 'Illnesses and Injuries', and provide ideas for adapting them for different purposes.

Creative Multilingualism (MPP). 2020b. 'Multilingual Performance Project (MPP)', https://www.creativeml.ox.ac.uk/mpp

This web page gives an outline of the Multilingual Performance Project and provides links to resources for schools including the MPP Starter Pack for teachers.

Creative Multilingualism (Slanguages: Oxygen). 2018a. 'Oxygen: A Hip-hop Translation', web page with films and other materials relating to the event on 11 October, Creative Multilingualism, https://www.creativeml.ox.ac.uk/oxygen-hip-hop-translation

This web page brings together a film about the adaptation of *Oxygen*, the recording of the performance, and related material by the participants.

Creative Multilingualism (Slanguages: Oxygen). 2018b. '*Oxygen* Translated into Hip-hop Theatre: The Full Performance', 1:03:38, posted online by Creative Multilingualism, YouTube, 10 December 2018, https://www.youtube.com/watch?v=bozjOgLLR-U

A video showing the workshop performance of *Oxygen*, including a post-performance discussion with the adaptors, director and curator.

Crystal, David. 1998. *Language Play* (London: Penguin).

Many types of language play are explained and illustrated with rich examples. While the book is focused on English, it offers an excellent foundation for investigating language play in other languages.

Crystal, David. 2010. *The Cambridge Encyclopedia of Language*, 3rd edn (Cambridge: Cambridge University Press).

David Crystal's depth of insight into everything to do with language and languages is unsurpassed, as is his talent for making complex research accessible. This book offers an invaluable point of entry on fundamental questions concerning languages.

Curtis, Julie. 2018. 'Collaboration and Ownership in Cross-Cultural Creativity', Creative Multilingualism, 28 November, https://www.creativeml.ox.ac.uk/blog/exploring-multilingualism/collaboration-and-ownership-cross-cultural-creativity

This blog post gives an academic perspective on the process of adapting *Oxygen* for a UK audience.

Cushen, Patrick. J., and Jennifer Wiley. 2011. 'Aha! Voilà! Eureka! Bilingualism and Insightful Problem Solving', *Learning and Individual Differences,* **21: 458–62, https://doi.org/10.1016/j.lindif.2011.02.007**

Cushen and Wiley shed light on how bilingualism relates to creativity, in a study which reports that bilinguals can show advantages on creative problem-solving tasks and on those involving cognitive flexibility.

Damrosch, David. 2003. *What Is World Literature?* **(Princeton: Princeton University Press).**

A very accessible introduction to the idea of world literature as literature that travels and how to read it.

Dudrah, Rajinder, Philip Bullock, Julie Curtis and Noah Birksted-Breen. 2020. 'Languages in the Creative Economy', Research Strand 4 of Creative Multilingualism, https://www.creativeml.ox.ac.uk/research/creative-economy

Research project on language diversity in the creative arts conducted as part of the Creative Multilingualism programme between 2016 and 2020. This chapter draws on that research.

Duncan, Dennis, et al. 2019. *Babel: Adventures in Translation* **(Oxford: Bodleian Library).**

A series of illustrated essays offers snapshots of linguistic creativity over a timespan of some 3500 years. The artefacts and texts show how translation has enabled ideas and stories to travel across a rich multitude of cultures and traditions.

Eco, Umberto. 1997. *The Search for the Perfect Language,* **trans. by James Fentress (London: Fontana). Italian version: 1993.** *La ricerca della lingua perfetta nelle cultura europea* **(Rome: Laterza).**

Eco traces the search for the perfect language that would be common to all human beings, elucidating the fascinatingly diverse theories put forward by a host of philosophers and philologists across multilingual Europe.

Edwards, John. 2012. *Multilingualism: Understanding Linguistic Diversity* **(London: Continuum).**

An excellent short introduction to the diversity of languages, and to the emergence and consequences of multilingualism.

Ethno-ornithology World Atlas. 2020. https://ewatlas.net

EWA is an online space that promotes nature and language conservation: a place where communities can record and share their knowledge, language traditions and understandings of nature. EWA is about building relationships between Indigenous and local communities, conservationists, academics and their institutions, to promote bird and language conservation through the engagement with, respect for and celebration of diverse cultural traditions of knowledge.

Evans, Nicholas. 2010. *Dying Words: Endangered Languages and What They Have to Tell Us* **(Oxford: Wiley-Blackwell).**

Nicholas Evans writes with eloquence and insight on language diversity, bringing into stark focus what we stand to lose in a time of massive language extinction.

Farmer, David. 2019. 'Drama Resource: Books on Drama for Language Teaching and Learning', *Drama Resource,* **https://dramaresource.com/books-on-drama-for-language-teaching-and-learning/**

A webpage reviewing resources for using drama in the classroom.

Fisher, Linda. 2013. 'Discerning Change in Young Students' Beliefs about Their Language Learning through the Use of Metaphor Elicitation in the Classroom', *Research Papers in Education,* **28(3): 373–92, https://doi.org/10.1080/02671522.2011.648654**

This article presents insights into how students perceive language learning, in a study that asked 12-13 year olds to express their views in the form of metaphors that described what language learning was like from their perspective.

Gibbs, Raymond W. 1994. *The Poetics of Mind: Figurative Thought, Language and Understanding* **(Cambridge: Cambridge University Press).**

The author shows how figurative language reveals the poetic structure of the mind, drawing on psychology, linguistics, philosophy, anthropology and literary theory.

Glucksberg, Sam. 2003. 'The Psycholinguistics of Metaphor', *Trends in Cognitive Sciences*, 7(2): 92–96, https://doi.org/10.1016/s1364-6613(02)00040-2

An examination of how people create and understand metaphors such as 'lawyers are sharks', demonstrating that we process these as easily as literal meanings.

Gosler, Andrew, Karen Park and Felice S. Wyndham. 2020. 'Creating a Meaningful World: Nature in Name, Metaphor and Myth', Research Strand 2 of Creative Multilingualism, https://www.creativeml.ox.ac.uk/research/naming

Research project on naming conducted as part of the Creative Multilingualism programme between 2016 and 2020. This chapter draws on that research.

Graham, Suzanne, Linda Fisher, Julia Hofweber and Heike Krüsemann. 2020. 'Linguistic Creativity in Language Learning', Research Strand 7 of Creative Multilingualism, https://www.creativeml.ox.ac.uk/research/

Research project on language teaching and learning conducted as part of the Creative Multilingualism programme between 2016 and 2020. This chapter draws on that research.

Gramling, David. 2016. *The Invention of Monolingualism* **(London: Bloomsbury Academics),** https://doi.org/10.5040/9781501318078

A cogent account of the process through which our multilingualism has been reduced to monolingualism.

Hanauer, David. I. 2001. 'The Task of Poetry Reading and Second Language Learning', *Applied Linguistics*, 22(3): 295–23, https://doi.org/10.1093/applin/22.3.295

This study suggests ways in which poetry can draw students' attention to important aspects of the language and so benefit their learning. It also explores how poetry reading can enhance students' cultural awareness.

Helgesson, Stefan, and Pieter Vermeulen (eds). 2016. *Institutions of World Literature: Writing, Translation, Markets* **(New York and Abingdon: Routledge).**

This volume explores the creative, cultural and financial forces that go into the translation and circulation of national literatures, and the making of world literature.

Hiddleston, Jane, and Wen-chin Ouyang (eds). [Forthcoming: 2021.] *Multilingual Literature as World Literature* (London: Bloomsbury).

The essays in this volume display ways in which literatures that juxtapose and blend what are usually considered to be sovereign linguistic systems contest the very category of 'national literature', while raising questions about the concept and definition of language.

Irwin, Robert. 1994. *The Arabian Nights: A Companion* (London: Penguin).

A comprehensive account of the history of *The Arabian Nights* in Arabic and European translations.

Janson, Tore. 2012. *The History of Languages: An Introduction* (Oxford: Oxford University Press).

This book offers an approachable and attractive introduction to how languages may be related historically, and to the nature and history of linguistic diversity.

Jones, Rodney H. (ed.). 2016. *The Routledge Handbook of Language and Creativity* (Abingdon: Routledge), https://doi.org/10.4324/9781315694566

A volume that presents current research on the relationship between language and creativity in various disciplines, including sections on literary creativity, multimodal and multimedia creativity, and creativity in language teaching and learning.

Kharkhurin, Anatoliy V. 2012. *Multilingualism and Creativity* (Bristol: Multilingual Matters).

This valuable study examines theoretical approaches to the connection between multilingualism and creativity, offering useful discussions of relevant research on both areas as a basis for presenting empirical evidence and educational applications.

Kohl, Katrin, Marianna Bolognesi and Ana Werkmann Horvat. 2019. 'The Creative Power of Metaphor: Multimedia Output', Creative

Multilingualism, https://www.creativeml.ox.ac.uk/creative-power-metaphor-multimedia-output

These videos look at different aspects of metaphor, focusing on linguistic diversity, emotion, communication and creativity. The videos draw on interviews with researchers who attended an international conference organized by the Creative Multilingualism research strand 'The Creative Power of Metaphor' in 2019.

Kohl, Katrin, Marianna Bolognesi and Ana Werkmann Horvat. 2020. 'The Creative Power of Metaphor', Research Strand 1 of Creative Multilingualism, https://www.creativeml.ox.ac.uk/research/metaphor

Research project on metaphor conducted as part of the Creative Multilingualism programme between 2016 and 2020. This chapter draws on that research.

Lennon, Brian. 2010. *In Babel's Shadow* **(Minnesota: University of Minnesota Press),** https://doi.org/10.5749/minnesota/9780816665013.001.0001

Lennon exposes the problems globalization generates with regards to translation and publication of multilingual literature.

Lewis, M. Paul. 2009. *Ethnologue: Languages of the World* **(Dallas: SIL International),** http://www.ethnologue.com

A comprehensive and regularly updated catalogue of all the known living languages in the world.

Littlemore, Jeannette, and Graham Low. 2006. *Figurative Thinking and Foreign Language Learning* **(Basingstoke, UK: Palgrave Macmillan),** https://doi.org/10.1057/9780230627567

The authors look at the role of figurative speech and figurative thinking in language teaching and learning and discuss the need to attend to figurative extensions of meaning when teaching vocabulary.

Loh, Jonathan, and David Harmon. 2014. *Biocultural Diversity: Threatened Species, Endangered Languages* **(Zeist: WWF-Netherlands).**

A clear and concise overview of biocultural diversity, engaging with the topic on the themes of evolution, decline and status.

Macfarlane, Robert, and Jackie Morris. 2017. *The Lost Words* (London: Hamish Hamilton).

In response to the 2007 decision by the editorial team of the *Oxford Junior Dictionary* to replace several words for the natural world with words for the Internet age, author Robert Macfarlane and illustrator Jackie Morris created *The Lost Words*. The book is both a work of art and a compelling reminder of the magic and power of language.

Maffi, Luisa (ed.). 2001. *On Biocultural Diversity: Linking Language Knowledge and the Environment* (Washington, DC: Smithsonian Institution Press).

This compilation of papers from an interdisciplinary group of leaders working in academia, advocacy and Indigenous communities provides a compelling discussion of connections across biological, linguistic and cultural diversity.

Maher, John C. 2017. *Multilingualism: A Very Short Introduction* (Oxford: Oxford University Press), https://doi.org/10.1093/actrade/9780198724995.001.0001

An excellent overview of the topic with a wealth of interesting facts and thought-provoking comments on multilingualism as a feature of the human condition. The final section on revitalization concludes with the view that 'indigenous is the new cool'.

Maiden, Martin, Aditi Lahiri and Chiara Cappellaro. 2020. 'Creating Intelligibility across Languages and Communities', Research Strand 3 of Creative Multilingualism, https://www.creativeml.ox.ac.uk/research/intelligibility

Research project on intelligibility conducted as part of the Creative Multilingualism programme between 2016 and 2020. This chapter draws on that research.

Marsh, David, and Richard Hill. 2009. *Study on the Contribution of Multilingualism to Creativity: Final Report*, Public Services Contract no EACEA/2007/3995/2, http://www.dylan-project.org/Dylan_en/news/assets/StudyMultilingualism_report_en.pdf

A European Commission study which sets out to establish the scientific basis for the claim that multilingualism – understood as the ability to engage with more than one language in everyday life – contributes to individual and collective creativity.

Martin-Jones, Marylin, Adrian Blackledge and Angela Creese (eds). 2012. *The Routledge Handbook of Multilingualism* **(Abingdon: Routledge), https://doi.org/10.4324/9780203154427**

This collection of essays provides a stimulating insight into a complex field of research, taking account of social, cultural and political angles and contexts. It is aimed at postgraduates and many of the essays are specialized in focus, but it also offers good scope for browsing.

McCann, William J., Horst G. Klein and Tilbert D. Stegmann. 2003. *EuroComRom – The Seven Sieves: How to Read All the Romance Languages Right Away***, 2nd edn (Aachen: Shaker).**

This project offers a detailed and thought-provoking model of how 'family resemblances' can be used as a means of creating bridges across languages.

Mehmedbegovic-Smith, Dina, and Thomas H. Bak. 2020. *Healthy Linguistic Diet***, http://healthylinguisticdiet.com/**

An engaging project based on an analogy between physical and mental health, showcasing evidence that using two or more languages has lifelong benefits for cognitive development and well-being.

Moretti, Franco. 2005. *Graphs, Maps, Trees: Abstract Modes for Literary History* **(London: Verso).**

World literary history is presented in this volume in the form of maps, graphs and trees.

Müller, Lisa-Maria, et al. 2018. 'Language Learning Motivation at the Transition from Primary to Secondary School', OASIS Summary of Graham, Suzanne, et al. (2016), *British Educational Research Journal***, https://oasis-database.org/concern/summaries/0g354f20t?locale=en**

Summary of a study of how motivation for language learning changes as students move from primary to secondary school, reporting that young students value learning activities related to culture, communication and creativity.

Ouyang, Wen-chin. 2005. 'Whose Story Is It? Sindbad the Sailor in Literature and Film', in *New Perspectives on [the] Arabian Nights: Ideological Variations and Narrative Horizons*, ed. by Wen-chin Ouyang and Geert Jan van Gelder (London and New York: Routledge), pp. 1–16.

This essay relates *The Arabian Nights* to classical Arabic literature and provides an account of the globalization of 'Sindbad the Sailor'.

Ouyang, Wen-chin, Jane Hiddleston, Laura Lonsdale and Nora Parr. 2020. 'Creativity and World Literatures: Languages in Dialogue', Research Strand 5 of Creative Multilingualism, https://www.creativeml.ox.ac.uk/research/world-literatures

Research project on world literatures conducted as part of the Creative Multilingualism programme between 2016 and 2020. This chapter draws on that research.

Owen, Stephen, and Robert Woore. 2019. 'Teaching Reading to Beginner Learners of French in Secondary School', OASIS Summary of Woore, Robert., et al. 2018, https://oasis-database.org/concern/summaries/nc580m68d?locale=en

Summary of a study that used semi-authentic texts with beginner learners of French, showing that learners enjoyed them, responded well to more challenging, culturally-rooted material and increased their French vocabulary as a result.

Park, Sowon S. (ed.). 2016. *The Chinese Scriptworld and World Literature*, a special issue of the *Journal of World Literature*, 1.

This groundbreaking collection of essays shows how research on writing systems can change how you think about language.

Peterson, David J. 2015. *The Art of Language Invention: From Horse-Lords to Dark Elves, the Words Behind World-Building* (New York: Penguin).

A toolkit for constructing languages that shape sci-fi worlds. Along the way, the inventor of Dothraki for *The Game of Thrones* looks in detail at sounds, words and orthography.

Pinker, Steven. 1994. *The Language Instinct: The New Science of Language and Mind* (**London: Penguin**).

Pinker argues that language is innate to human beings, and separate from thought. He looks at issues such as the biological origin of language, language acquisition and the evolution of languages and dialects.

Prismatic Jane Eyre: An Experiment in the Study of Translations, https://prismaticjaneeyre.org/

Discover the prismatic world of translation through the many versions of *Jane Eyre*. The website includes interactive maps and other illuminating visualizations.

Project MEITS, Heather Martin and Wendy Ayres-Bennett (eds). 2019. *How Languages Changed My Life* (**[n.p.]: Archway**).

Stories that illuminate how languages have shaped the careers of individuals from many walks of life, including writers and musicians, politicians and activists, teachers and students, scientists and sportspeople.

Reynolds, Matthew. 2016. *Translation: A Very Short Introduction* (**Oxford: Oxford University Press**), https://doi.org/10.1093/actrade/9780198712114.001.0001

A popular introduction to translation which ranges across the whole field from conflict zones to poetry, and also lays the foundations of the prismatic view.

Reynolds, Matthew (ed.). 2020. *Prismatic Translation* (**Cambridge: Legenda**).

An in-depth presentation of the prismatic theory of translation, with case studies ranging from ancient Egyptian hieroglyphs to modern digital media.

Reynolds, Matthew, Sowon S. Park, Giovanni Pietro Vitali and Eleni Philippou. 2020. 'Creating New Meanings : Prismatic Translation', Research Strand 6 of Creative Multilingualism, https://www.creativeml.ox.ac.uk/research/prismatic-translation

Research project on prismatic translation conducted as part of the Creative Multilingualism programme between 2016 and 2020. This chapter draws on that research.

Robinson, Andrew. 2009. *Writing and Script: A Very Short Introduction* **(Oxford: Oxford University Press), https://doi.org/10.1093/actrade/9780199567782.001.0001**

A fascinating introduction to the origins of writing systems and their development across millennia.

Sacks, Oliver. 2012 (1989). *Seeing Voices: A Journey into the World of the Deaf* **(London: Picador).**

A history of total deafness and analysis of the expressive power of sign language. Sacks also offers an engaging account of the different ways deaf and hearing people learn to categorize their respective world views.

Saussure, Fernand de. 1983. *Course in General Linguistics*, **ed. by Charles Bally and Albert Sechehaye, trans. and annotated by Roy Harris (London: Duckworth).**

Cours de linguistique générale (1916) was foundational to modern linguistic theory, introducing a 'scientific' approach to language study and establishing both the study of semiotics and structural linguistics. Though introduced over a hundred years ago, Saussure's general principles remain widely accepted as fundamental to linguistic research, including naming.

Silverfish Films. 2019. 'Do We Think Differently in Different Languages?', 4:10, *BBC Ideas***, 24 October, https://www.bbc.com/ideas/videos/do-we-think-differently-in-different-languages/p07ry35k**

An engaging short video exploring the interaction between thought and language, involving speakers of different languages.

Singleton, David, and Larissa Aronin (eds.). 2018. *Twelve Lectures on Multilingualism* **(Bristol: Multilingual Matters), https://doi.org/10.21832/9781788922074**

A collection of thought-provoking essays on key topics currently being pursued in research on multilingualism, aimed at undergraduates and postgraduates.

Slanguages. 2020. A project under the aegis of 'Languages in the Creative Economy', Research Strand 4 of Creative Multilingualism, https://www.creativeml.ox.ac.uk/projects/slanguages

The process of adapting *Oxygen* into a hip-hop drama was carried out in the framework of Slanguages, which is both a project and a way of conceptualizing creativity through the prism of diverse ethnic-minority languages.

Thomason, Sarah Grey. 2001. *Language Contact: An Introduction* **(Edinburgh: Edinburgh University Press).**

This useful and informative account of the nature and effects of language contact includes coverage of how unrelated languages in contact can come to converge over time.

Warner, Marina. 2011. *Stranger Magic: Charmed States & the Arabian Nights* **(London: Chatto & Windus).**

Warner analyzes the impact of *The Arabian Nights* in European literature and culture.

Weinreich, Max. 1963. *Languages in Contact: Findings and Problems* **(The Hague: Mouton).**

A fundamental and classic work on language contact and its effects on the structure of languages.

Bibliography

The Bibliography includes all items given under Works Cited in the individual chapters, and the items given in Find Out More.

The Adventures of Amir Hamza. 2007. Trans. by Musharraf Ali Farooqi (New York: The Modern Library).

AGCAS. 2019. 'What Can I Do with a Modern Languages Degree?', *Prospects*, https://www.prospects.ac.uk/careers-advice/what-can-i-do-with-my-degree/modern-languages

Allen-Kinross, Pippa. 2018. 'A-level Results 2018: Chinese A-level overtakes German for first time', *Schools Week*, 16 August, https://schoolsweek.co.uk/a-level-results-2018-chinese-a-level-overtakes-german-for-first-time/

Al-Māwardī, Abū al-Ḥasan ʿAlī ibn Muḥammad ibn Ḥabīb. 1983. *Kitāb Naṣīḥat al-mulūk* (Kuwait: Maktabat al-Falāḥ).

Antunes, Ricardo, et al. 2011. 'Individually Distinctive Acoustic Features in Sperm Whale Codas', *Animal Behaviour*, 81(4): 723–30, https://doi.org/10.1016/j.anbehav.2010.12.019

The Arabian Nights. 1990. Trans. by Husain Haddawy (New York: Norton).

The Arabian Nights II: Sinbad and Other Popular Stories. 1995. Trans. by Husain Haddawy (New York: Norton).

Arabian Nights: Sinbad's Adventures. 1975. Dir. by Fumio Kurokawa (Nippon Animation).

Athanasopoulos, Panos. 2009. 'Cognitive Representation of Colour in Bilinguals: The Case of Greek Blues', *Bilingualism: Language and Cognition*, 12(1): 83–95, https://doi.org/10.1017/s136672890800388x

Atwood, Margaret et al. 2015. 'Reconnecting Kids with Nature is Vital, and Needs Cultural Leadership', Letter to the Oxford University Press., http://www.naturemusicpoetry.com/uploads/2/9/3/8/29384149/letter_to_oup_final.pdf

Babalolá, Lékan, et al. 2019a. 'Odu Eji Ogbe. Performance Text [for *Yòrùbá Sonnets*]'.

Babalolá, Lékan, et al. 2019b. *Yòrùbá Sonnets*. Performance of music from Lékan Babalolá's Sakred Funk Quartet with spoken word poetry and mime from Dr Olu Taiwo, organized by Creative Multilingualism under the aegis of Slanguages at Wolfson College, Oxford, on 15 February 2019.

Babalolá, Lékan, et al. 2019c. '*Yòrùbá Sonnets*: Tour 2019'. Flyer.

Bak, Thomas, and Dina Mehmedbegovic. 2017. 'Healthy Linguistic Diet: The Value of Linguistic Diversity and Language Learning Across the Lifespan', *Languages, Society & Policy*, https://doi.org/10.17863/CAM.9854

Barnes, Julian. 1998. *England, England* (London: Jonathan Cape).

Barpaga, Rinkoo, Nick Drew, Rajinder Dudrah and Simon Redgrave. 2017. 'British Sign Language (BSL): Eight Examples' and 'Urban Sign Language (USL): Eight Equivalents', posters created for the *Slanguages* exhibition 2017, Wolfson College, Oxford.

Barth, John. 1991. *The Last Voyage of Somebody the Sailor* (Boston: Little, Brown and Company).

Baudelaire, Charles. 1961. *Œuvres complètes*, ed. by Y.-G. Le Dantec and rev. by Claude Pichois (Paris: Gallimard).

BBC. 2014. 'Languages across Europe', 14 October, http://www.bbc.co.uk/languages/european_languages/definitions.shtml

Beckett, Samuel. 1977. *Ends and Odds: Plays and Sketches* (London: Faber and Faber).

Beckwith, Martha. 1970. *Hawaiian Mythology* (Honolulu: University of Hawaii Press).

Bergen, Benjamin. 2001. 'Nativization Processes in L1 Esperanto', *Journal of Child Language*, 28: 575–95, https://doi.org/10.1017/S0305000901004779

Berlin, Brent. 2006. 'The First Congress of Ethnozoological Nomenclature', *Journal of the Royal Anthropological Institute*, 12(s1): S23–S44, https://doi.org/10.1111/j.1467-9655.2006.00271.x

Bilingualism Matters. 2020. http://www.bilingualism-matters.ppls.ed.ac.uk

Birksted-Breen, Noah. 2020. 'Vassily Sigarev and the Presnyakov Brothers: Staging the New Russia', in *Contemporary European Playwrights*, ed. by Maria Delgado, Bryce Lease and Dan Rebellato (London: Routledge), pp. 168–84.

Birksted-Breen, Noah, and Rajinder Dudrah. 2018. 'Translating a Russian Play into Hip-hop Theatre: A Conversation', Creative Multilingualism, 28 November, https://www.creativeml.ox.ac.uk/blog/exploring-multilingualism/translating-russian-play-hip-hop-theatre-conversation

Black, Jonathan. 'Dear Jonathan'. Fortnightly column in the *Financial Times*, https://www.ft.com/dear-jonathan

Black, Jonathan. 2019. *How to Find the Career You've Always Wanted* (London: Robinson).

Bobkina, Jelena, and Elena Dominguez. 2014. 'The Use of Literature and Literary Texts in the EFL Classroom: Between Consensus and Controversy', *International Journal of Applied Linguistics & English Literature*, 3: 249–60, https://doi.org/10.7575/aiac.ijalel.v.3n.2p.248

Boivin, N., et al. 2016. 'Ecological Consequences of Human Niche Construction: Examining Long-Term Anthropogenic Shaping of Global Species Distributions', *Proceedings of the National Academy of Sciences of the United States of America*, 113(23): 6388–96, https://doi.org/10.1073/pnas.1525200113

Borges, Jorge Luis. 1937–52. 'El idioma analítico de John Wilkins', with English translation: [The Analytical Language of John Wilkins], http://languagelog.ldc.upenn.edu/myl/ldc/wilkins.html

Boroditsky, Lera. 2011. 'How Languages Construct Time', in *Space, Time and Number in the Brain. Searching for the Foundations of Mathematical Thought*, ed. by Stanislas Dehaene and Elizabeth Brannon (London: Elsevier), pp. 333–41.

Boroditsky, Lera, and Alice Gaby. 2010. 'Remembrances of Times East: Absolute Spatial Representations of Time in an Australian Aboriginal Community', *Psychological Science*, 21(11): 1635–39, https://doi.org/10.1177/0956797610386621

Briefer, Elodie F., and Alan G. McElligott. 2012. 'Social Effects on Vocal Ontogeny in an Ungulate, the Goat, *Capra hircus*', *Animal Behaviour*, 83(4): 991–1000, https://doi.org/10.1016/j.anbehav.2012.01.020

British Academy. 2016. *Born Global: Implications for Higher Education*, https://www.thebritishacademy.ac.uk/sites/default/files/Born%20Global%20-%20Implications%20for%20Higher%20Education_1.pdf

British Council. 2017. *Languages for the Future*, https://www.britishcouncil.org/sites/default/files/languages_for_the_future_2017.pdf [see also the summary of the report's findings at https://www.britishcouncil.org/research-policy-insight/policy-reports/languages-future-2017]

Brown, Theodore L. 2003. *Making Truth: Metaphor in Science* (Urbana: University of Illinois Press).

Bulletproof Monk. 2003. Dir. by Paul Hunter (MGM).

Carroll, Sean. 2019. 'Woven from Weirdness', *New Scientist*, 14 September, 34–38.

Casaponsa, Aina, and Panas Athanosopoulos. 2018. 'The Way You See Colour Depends on What Language You Speak', *The Conversation*, 16 April, https://theconversation.com/the-way-you-see-colour-depends-on-what-language-you-speak-94833

Casasanto, Daniel. 2008. 'Who's Afraid of the Big Bad Whorf? Crosslinguistic Differences in Temporal Language and Thought', *Language Learning*, 58(s1):

63–79, https://doi.org/10.1111/j.1467-9922.2008.00462.x, http://www.casasanto.com/papers/Casasanto2008_BigBadWhorf.pdf

Casasanto, Daniel. 2013. 'Development of Metaphorical Thinking: The Role of Language', in *Language and the Creative Mind*, ed. by M Borkent, J. Hinnell et al. (Stanford: CSLI Publications), pp. 3–18, http://casasanto.com/papers/Casasanto_Development_of_Metaphorical_Thinking_2013.pdf

Chekhov, Anton. 1988. *Plays*, trans. by Michael Frayn (London: Methuen).

Chevalier-Karfis, Camille. 2008. 'Famous French Poem "Demain dès l'aube" by Victor Hugo', *French Today*, 2 January, https://www.frenchtoday.com/french-poetry-reading/poem-demain-des-l-aube-hugo

Chomsky, Noam. 1986. *Knowledge of Language: Its Nature, Origin and Use* (New York: Praeger).

Clanchy, Kate (ed.). 2018. *England: Poems from a School* (London: Picador).

The Classic of Mountains and Seas. 1999. Trans. by Anne Birrell (Harmondsworth: Penguin).

Coghlan, Andy. 2012. 'Young Goats Can Develop Distinct Accents', *New Scientist*, 16 February, https://www.newscientist.com/article/dn21481-young-goats-can-develop-distinct-accents

Creative Multilingualism. 2020. https://www.creativeml.ox.ac.uk

Creative Multilingualism. 2020a. LinguaMania: The Podcast, https://podcasts.ox.ac.uk/series/linguamania

Creative Multilingualism. 2020b. 'Punch Records', https://www.creativeml.ox.ac.uk/about/partners/punch-records

Creative Multilingualism. 2020c. 'Resources', https://www.creativeml.ox.ac.uk/resources

Creative Multilingualism (Careers). 2016. 'What do Modern Languages Students Do after Graduating?', https://www.creativeml.ox.ac.uk/blog/working-languages/what-do-modern-languages-students-do-after-graduating

Creative Multilingualism (Careers). 2020. 'How Languages Help in Your Career', https://www.creativeml.ox.ac.uk/careers

Creative Multilingualism (MPP). 2018a. 'MFL teaching activity: Buzzy Bees', 2:18, posted online by Creative Multilingualism, YouTube, 18 September 2018, https://www.youtube.com/watch?v=WVZgJWuQMt0

Creative Multilingualism (MPP). 2018b. 'MFL teaching activity: Illnesses & Injuries', 2:55, posted online by Creative Multilingualism, YouTube, 18 September 2018, https://www.youtube.com/watch?v=VmEBiKdRfEs

Creative Multilingualism (MPP). 2018c. 'MFL teaching activity: Sevens', 1:39, posted online by Creative Multilingualism, YouTube, 18 September 2018, https://www.youtube.com/watch?v=MEfakN_QXC4

Creative Multilingualism (MPP). 2020a. 'Multilingual Drama Teaching Activities', https://www.creativeml.ox.ac.uk/resources/multilingual-drama-teaching-activities

Creative Multilingualism (MPP). 2020b. 'Multilingual Performance Project (MPP)', https://www.creativeml.ox.ac.uk/mpp

Creative Multilingualism (Slanguages: Oxygen). 2018a. 'Oxygen: A Hip-hop Translation', web page with films and other materials relating to the event on 11 October, Creative Multilingualism, https://www.creativeml.ox.ac.uk/oxygen-hip-hop-translation.

Creative Multilingualism (Slanguages: Oxygen). 2018b. '*Oxygen* Translated into Hip-hop Theatre: The Full Performance', 1:03:38, posted online by Creative Multilingualism, YouTube, 10 December 2018, https://www.youtube.com/watch?v=bozjOgLLR-U

Creative Multilingualism (Slanguages: Yòrùbá Sonnets). 2019a. 'Yòrùbá Sonnets', web page with films and other materials relating to the event on 15 February (see Lékan Babalolá et al. 2019b), Creative Multilingualism, https://www.creativeml.ox.ac.uk/yoruba-sonnets

Creative Multilingualism (Slanguages: Yòrùbá Sonnets). 2019b. 'Yòrùbá Sonnets: Audience Feedback Postcards Completed during the Post-Performance Q&A on 15 February 2019' (see Lékan Babalolá et al. 2019b), unpublished. Selection: Creative Multilingualism, 19 February 2019, https://www.creativeml.ox.ac.uk/blog/exploring-multilingualism/yoruba-sonnets-audience-feedback

Creative Multilingualism (Slanguages: Yòrùbá Sonnets). 2019c. 'Yòrùbá Sonnets with Lékan Babalolá: Post-Performance Q&A', film of event (see Lékan Babalolá et al. 2019b), 19:42, posted online by Creative Multilingualism, YouTube, 12 September 2019, https://www.youtube.com/watch?v=9x982hY9I3E

Croft, William, and D. Alan Cruse 2004. *Cognitive Linguistics* (Cambridge: Cambridge University Press), https://doi.org/10.1017/cbo9780511803864

Crystal, David. 1998. *Language Play* (London: Penguin).

Crystal, David. 2008. *A Dictionary of Linguistics and Phonetics*, 6th edn (Malden, MA: Blackwell).

Crystal, David. 2010. *The Cambridge Encyclopedia of Language*, 3rd edn (Cambridge: Cambridge University Press).

Csikszentmihalyi, Mihaly. 1997. *Creativity: The Psychology of Discovery and Invention* (New York: HarperCollins).

Curtis, Julie. 2015. Notes from public discussion at Liubimovka Festival, with Ivan Vyrypaev.

Curtis, Julie. 2018. 'Collaboration and Ownership in Cross-Cultural Creativity', *Creative Multilingualism*, 28 November, https://www.creativeml.ox.ac.uk/blog/exploring-multilingualism/collaboration-and-ownership-cross-cultural-creativity This blog post gives an academic perspective on the process of adapting *Oxygen* for a UK audience.

Cushen, Patrick J., and Jennifer Wiley. 2011. 'Aha! Voilà! Eureka! Bilingualism and Insightful Problem Solving', *Learning and Individual Differences*, 21(4): 458–62, https://doi.org/10.1016/j.lindif.2011.02.007

Dahl, Östen. 2005. 'Tea', in *The World Atlas of Language Structures*, ed. by Martin Haspelmath et al. (Oxford: Oxford University Press), pp. 554–57.

Damrosch, David. 2003. *What Is World Literature?* (Princeton: Princeton University Press).

Darwin, Charles. 1871. *The Descent of Man, and Selection in Relation to Sex* (London: John Murray), https://doi.org/10.5962/bhl.title.2092

Department for Education. 2013. 'Statutory Guidance. National Curriculum in England: Languages Programmes of Study', *GOV.UK*, https://www.gov.uk/government/publications/national-curriculum-in-england-languages-progammes-of-study/national-curriculum-in-england-languages-progammes-of-study

Department for Education. 2015. *Modern Foreign Languages: GCSE Subject Content* (London: DFE), https://assets.publishing.service.gov.uk/government/uploads/system/uploads/attachment_data/file/485567/GCSE_subject_content_modern_foreign_langs.pdf

Desfayes, Michel. 1998. *A Thesaurus of Bird Names: Etymology of European Lexis through Paradigms*, 2 vols (Sion, Switzerland: The Museum of Natural History).

Dewaele, Jean-Marc. 2015. 'On Emotions in Foreign Language Learning and Use', *The Language Teacher*, 39: 13–15.

Dollinger, Stephen J., Philip A. Burke and Nathaniel W. Gump. 2007. 'Creativity and Values', *Creativity Research Journal*, 19(2–3), 91–103, https://doi.org/10.1080/10400410701395028

Dudrah, Rajinder, Philip Bullock, Julie Curtis and Noah Birksted-Breen. 2020. 'Languages in the Creative Economy', Research Strand 4 of Creative Multilingualism, https://www.creativeml.ox.ac.uk/research/creative-economy

Dugdale, Sasha. 2006. 'Oxygenating Theater: A Translator's Note', *Theater*, 36(1), 45–47, https://doi.org/10.1215/01610775-36-1-45

Duncan, Dennis, et al. 2019. *Babel: Adventures in Translation* (Oxford: Bodleian Library).

Duolingo. 2020. https://www.duolingo.com/

Eco, Umberto. 1993. *La ricerca della lingua perfetta nelle cultura europea* (Rome: Laterza).

Eco, Umberto. 1997. *The Search for the Perfect Language*, trans. by James Fentress (London: Fontana).

Edexcel. 2016. *GCSE (9-1) French. Specification* (Harlow: Pearson Education Limited), https://qualifications.pearson.com/en/qualifications/edexcel-gcses/french-2016.html

Edmondson, Willis. 1997. 'The Role of Literature in Foreign Language Learning and Teaching: Some Valid Assumptions and Invalid Arguments', in *Applied Linguistics Across Disciplines*, ed. by Anna Mauranen and Kari Sajavaara (AILA Review No. 12 – 1995/6), pp. 42–55.

Edwards, John. 2012. *Multilingualism: Understanding Linguistic Diversity* (London: Continuum).

Endangered Languages Project. 2020. www.endangeredlanguages.com

English PEN. 2013. *Brave New Voices — Learning Resources and Animations*. https://www.englishpen.org/outreach/young-people/brave-new-voices-translation-animations/

Ethnologue. 2020. https://www.ethnologue.com

Ethno-ornithology World Atlas. 2020. https://ewatlas.net

Evans, Nicholas. 2010. *Dying Words: Endangered Languages and What They Have to Tell Us* (Oxford: Wiley-Blackwell).

Evans, Nicholas, and Nicholas Thieberger. 2013. 'The Web of Words and the Web of Life', 3rd International Conference on Language Documentation and Conservation, 23 February, University of Hawai'i, Hawai'I, https://scholarspace.manoa.hawaii.edu/handle/10125/26184

Farmer, David. 'Drama Resource: Books on Drama for Language Teaching and Learning', *Drama Resource*, https://dramaresource.com/books-on-drama-for-language-teaching-and-learning/

Fauconnier, Gilles, and Mark Turner. 2008. 'Rethinking Metaphor', in *The Cambridge Handbook of Metaphor and Thought*, ed. by Raymond W. Gibbs, Jr. (Cambridge: Cambridge University Press), pp. 53–66, https://doi.org/10.1017/cbo9780511816802.005

Faust, Miriam, Elisheva Ben-Artzi and Nili Vardi. 2012. 'Semantic Processing in Native and Second Language: Evidence from Hemispheric Differences in Fine and Coarse Semantic Coding', *Brain and Language*, 123(3): 228–33, https://doi.org/10.1016/j.bandl.2012.09.007

Featherstone, Vicky. 2015. 'Afterword', in *Royal Court: International*, ed. by Elaine Aston and Mark O'Thomas (Basingstoke: Palgrave MacMillan), pp. 185–86, https://doi.org/10.1057/9781137487728_6

Feld, Steven. 1990. *Sound and Sentiment*, 2nd edn (Durham, NC: Duke University Press).

Financial Times. FT Career Starters. Films.

Finnish Immigration Service Refugee Advice Centre. 2010. *Interpretation in the Asylum Process: Guide for Interpreters* (Helsinki: AT-Julkaisutoimisto Oy), https://migri.fi/documents/5202425/6164491/Interpretation+in+the+asylum+process+-+guide+for+interpreters+%28en%29

Fisher, Linda. (2013). 'Discerning Change in Young Students' Beliefs about Their Language Learning through the Use of Metaphor Elicitation in the Classroom', *Research Papers in Education*, 28(3): 373–92, https://doi.org/10.1080/02671522.2011.648654

Gandhi, Mohandas K. 2007. *An Autobiography or The Story of my Experiments with Truth*, trans. from Gujarati by M. Desai (Harmondsworth: Penguin).

Garamendi, Patricia W. 1996. 'Peace Corps… More Than You Can Imagine', in *At Home in the World: The Peace Corps Story*, ed. by Mark D. Gearan et al. ([n.p.]: Peace Corps), pp. v–vii, https://babel.hathitrust.org/cgi/pt?id=umn.31951d012241914;view=1up;seq=6

Garner, M. 2004. *Language: An Ecological View* (Oxford: Peter Lang).

Gibbs, Raymond W. 1994. *The Poetics of Mind: Figurative Thought, Language and Understanding* (Cambridge: Cambridge University Press).

Gill, Sam, and Irene Sullivan. 1992. *Dictionary of Native American Mythology* (Santa Barbara, CA: ABC-CLIO).

Giora, Rachel, Ofer Fein et al., 'Weapons of Mass Distraction: Optimal Innovation and Pleasure Ratings', *Metaphor and Symbol*, 19(2) (2004): 115–41, https://doi.org/10.1207/s15327868ms1902_2

Glucksberg, Sam. 2003. 'The Psycholinguistics of Metaphor', *Trends in Cognitive Sciences*, 7(2): 92–96, https://doi.org/10.1016/s1364-6613(02)00040-2

Goff, Kathy, and Paul E. Torrance. 2002. *The Abbreviated Torrance Test for Adults* (Bensenville, IL: Scholastic Testing Service).

Gosler, Andrew G. 2017. 'The Human Factor: Ecological Salience in Ornithology and Ethno-Ornithology', *Journal of Ethnobiology*, 37(4): 637–62, https://doi.org/10.2993/0278-0771-37.4.637

Gosler, Andrew G. 2018. 'Knowledge of Nature and the Nature of Knowledge,' Paper presented at the International Society for Ethnobiology Conference, 9 August, Belém, Brazil.

Gosler, Andrew G. 2019. 'What's in a Name: The Legacy and Lexicon of Birds', *British Wildlife*, 30: 391–97.

Gosler, Andrew G., and Caroline M. Jackson-Houlston. 2012. 'A Nightingale by Any Other Name? Relations Between Scientific and Vernacular Bird Naming', *Proceedings – Ecosystem Services: Do We Need Birds?*, Proceedings of the British Ornithologists' Union's 2012 Annual Conference, 3–5 April, University of Leicester, Leicester, https://www.bou.org.uk/bouproc-net/ecosystem-services/gosler&jackson-houlston.pdf

Gosler, Andrew, Karen Park and Felice S. Wyndham. 2020. 'Creating a Meaningful World: Nature in Name, Metaphor and Myth', Research Strand 2 of Creative Multilingualism, https://www.creativeml.ox.ac.uk/research/naming

Graham, Suzanne, and Linda Fisher. 2020a. 'Creative Teaching Resources', Creative Multilingualism, https://www.creativeml.ox.ac.uk/creative-teaching-resources

Graham, Suzanne, and Linda Fisher. 2020b. 'Demain, dès l'aube: PowerPoint and Lesson Plan', in 'French Creative Teaching Resources', Creative Multilingualism, https://www.creativeml.ox.ac.uk/french-creative-teaching-resources

Graham, Suzanne, Linda Fisher, Julia Hofweber and Heike Krüsemann. 2020. 'Linguistic Creativity in Language Learning', Research Strand 7 of Creative Multilingualism, https://www.creativeml.ox.ac.uk/research/

Gramling, David. 2016. *The Invention of Monolingualism* (London: Bloomsbury Academics), https://doi.org/10.5040/9781501318078

Guo, Xiaoting 郭小亭. *Ji Gong Quan Zhuan* (The Adventures of Monk Ji).

Hale, Susan. 1891. *Mexico* (New York: G. P. Putnam's Sons).

Hanauer, David. I. 2001. 'The Task of Poetry Reading and Second Language Learning', *Applied Linguistics*, 22(3): 295–23, https://doi.org/10.1093/applin/22.3.295

Harmon, D. 1996. 'Losing Species, Losing Languages: Connections Between Biological and Linguistic Diversity', *Southwest Journal of Linguistics*, 15(1&2): 89–108.

Haugen, Einar. 1972. *The Ecology of Language* (Stanford: Stanford University Press).

Helgesson, Stefan, and Pieter Vermeulen (eds). 2016. *Institutions of World Literature: Writing, Translation, Markets* (New York and Abingdon: Routledge).

Hiddleston, Jane, and Wen-chin Ouyang (eds). [Forthcoming: 2021.] *Multilingual Literature as World Literature* (London: Bloomsbury).

Hoang, Ha. 2014. 'Metaphor and Second Language Learning: The State of the Field', *TESL-EJ*, 18(2).

Hofweber, Julia, and Suzanne Graham. 2018. 'Linguistic Creativity in Language Learning: Investigating the Impact of Creative Text Materials and Teaching Approaches in the Second Language Classroom', *Scottish Languages Review*, 33: 19–28.

Hufeisen, Britta, and Nicole Marx (eds). 2014. *EuroComGerm – Die sieben Siebe: Germanische Sprachen lesen lernen*, 2nd edn (Frankfurt: Editiones EurocomRom).

Hugo, Victor. 1847. 'Demain, dès l'aube'. With an English translation by Camille Chevalier-Karfis (2008), https://www.frenchtoday.com/french-poetry-reading/poem-demain-des-l-aube-hugo

Hugo, Victor. 1973. *Les contemplations* (Paris: Gallimard).

Hunn, Eugene S. 1999. 'Size as Limiting the Recognition of Biodiversity in Folk Biological Classifications; One of Four Factors Governing the Cultural Recognition of Biological Taxa', in *Folkbiology*, ed. by D. Medin and S. Atran (Cambridge, MA: Harvard University Press), pp. 47–69.

Huth, Alexander G., et al. 2016. 'Natural Speech Reveals the Semantic Maps that Tile Human Cortex', *Nature*, 532: 453–58, https://doi.org/10.1038/nature17637, https://www.ncbi.nlm.nih.gov/pmc/articles/PMC4852309

Ibn al-Nadīm. 1988. *Al-Fihrist* (Cairo: Dār al-Masīra).

Indiana Jones and the Last Crusade. 1989. Dir. by Steven Spielberg (Paramount).

The Instructive and Entertaining Fable of Pilpay, an Ancient Indian Philosopher: Containing a Number of Excellent Rules for the Conduct of all Ages, and in all Stations, under Several Heads. 1987. Trans. by Gilbert Gaulmin (London: Darf).

Intergovernmental Science-Policy Platform on Biodiversity and Ecosystem Services. 2019. *Global Assessment Report on Biodiversity and Ecosystem Services*, https://ipbes.net/global-assessment

International Citizen Service. 2020, https://www.volunteerics.org/

International Ecolinguistics Association. 2020, http://ecolinguistics-association.org

International Phonetic Association. 2020. 'Full IPA Chart', http://www.internationalphoneticassociation.org/content/ipa-chart

International Society of Ethnobiology. 1988. 'Declaration of Belém', http://www.ethnobiology.net/what-we-do/core-programs/global-coalition-2/declaration-of-belem/

Irwin, Robert. 1994. *The Arabian Nights: A Companion* (London: Penguin).

Janson, Tore. 2012. *The History of Languages: An Introduction* (Oxford: Oxford University Press).

Johns, Brendan T., Melody Dye and Michael N. Jones. 2015. 'The Influence of Contextual Diversity on Word Learning', *Psychonomic Bulletin & Review*, 23: 1214–20, https://doi.org/10.3758/s13423-015-0980-7

Johnston, Chris. 2010. *Drama Games for Those Who Like to Say No* (London: Nick Hern Books).

Jones, Rodney H. (ed.). 2016. *The Routledge Handbook of Language and Creativity* (Abingdon: Routledge), https://doi.org/10.4324/9781315694566

Kharkhurin, Anatoliy V. 2009. 'The Role of Bilingualism in Creative Performance on Divergent Thinking and Invented Alien Creatures Tests', *The Journal Of Creative Behavior*, 43: 59-71, https://doi.org/10.1002/j.2162-6057.2009.tb01306.x

Kharkhurin, Anatoliy V. 2012. *Multilingualism and Creativity* (Bristol: Multilingual Matters).

Kim, Myonghee. 2004. 'Literature Discussions in Adult L2 Learning', *Language and Education*, 18: 145–66, https://doi.org/10.1080/09500780408666872

Kislorod. 2009. Dir. by Ivan Vyrypaev (Ded Moroz).

Klein, Wolfgang. 1986. *Second Language Acquisition*, Cambridge Textbooks in Linguistics (Cambridge: Cambridge University Press).

Kohl, Katrin, Marianna Bolognesi and Ana Werkmann Horvat. 2019. 'The Creative Power of Metaphor: Multimedia Output', Creative Multilingualism, https://www.creativeml.ox.ac.uk/creative-power-metaphor-multimedia-output

Kohl, Katrin, Marianna Bolognesi and Ana Werkmann Horvat. 2020. 'The Creative Power of Metaphor', Research Strand 1 of Creative Multilingualism, https://www.creativeml.ox.ac.uk/research/metaphor

Kövecses, Zoltán. 2010. *Metaphor: A Practical Introduction*, 2nd edn (Oxford: Oxford University Press).

Krauss, Michael. 1992. 'The World's Languages in Crisis', *Language*, 68(1): 4–10, https://doi.org/10.1353/lan.1992.0075

Lakoff, George, and Mark Johnson. 2003. *Metaphors We Live By*, 2nd edn (Chicago: University of Chicago Press), https://doi.org/10.7208/chicago/9780226470993.001.0001

Lakoff, George, and Mark Johnson. 2018. *Leben in Metaphern: Konstruktion und Gebrauch von Sprachbildern*, trans. by Astrid Hildenbrand, 9th edn (Heidelberg: Auer).

Lakoff, George, and Mark Turner. 1989. *More than Cool Reason: A Field Guide to Poetic Metaphor* (Chicago: University of Chicago Press), https://doi.org/10.7208/chicago/9780226470986.001.0001

Landry, Richard. G. 1973. 'The Enhancement of Figural Creativity through Second Language Learning at the Elementary School Level', *Foreign Language Annals*, 7: 111–15, https://doi.org/10.1111/j.1944-9720.1973.tb00073.x

Lasagabaster, David. (2000). 'The Effects of Three Bilingual Education Models on Linguistic Creativity', *IRAL-International Review of Applied Linguistics in Language Teaching*, 38(3–4): 213–28, https://doi.org/10.1515/iral.2000.38.3-4.213

Laufer, Batia, and Jan Hulstijn. 2001. 'Incidental Vocabulary Acquisition in a Second Language: The Construct of Task-Induced Involvement', *Applied Linguistics*, 22: 1–26, https://doi.org/10.1093/applin/22.1.1

Leikin, Mark. 2013. 'The Effect of Bilingualism on Creativity: Developmental and Educational Perspectives', *International Journal of Bilingualism*, 17(4): 431–47, https://doi.org/10.1177/1367006912438300

Lennon, Brian. 2010. *In Babel's Shadow* (Minnesota: University of Minnesota Press), https://doi.org/10.5749/minnesota/9780816665013.001.0001

Lewis, Brett, and Michael Avon Oeming. 1998. *Bulletproof Monk* (Portland/Oregon: Image Comics).

Lewis, M. Paul. 2009. *Ethnologue: Languages of the World* (Dallas: SIL International), http://www.ethnologue.com

Linguee. 2020. https://www.linguee.com

Littlemore, Jeannette, and Graham Low. 2006. *Figurative Thinking and Foreign Language Learning* (Basingstoke, UK: Palgrave Macmillan), https://doi.org/10.1057/9780230627567

Littlemore, Jeannette, Paula Pérez Sobrino et al. 2018. 'What Makes a Good Metaphor? A Cross-Cultural Study of Computer-Generated Metaphor Appreciation', *Metaphor and Symbol*, 33(2): 101–22, https://doi.org/10.1080/10926488.2018.1434944

Loh, Jonathan, and David Harmon. 2005. 'A Global Index of Biocultural Diversity', *Ecological Indicators*, 5(3): 231–41, https://doi.org/10.1016/j.ecolind.2005.02.005

Loh, Jonathan, and David Harmon. 2014. *Biocultural Diversity: Threatened Species, Endangered Languages* (Zeist: WWF-Netherlands).

Lubart, Todd I. 1999. 'Creativity Across Cultures', in *Handbook of Creativity*, ed. by Robert J. Sternberg (Cambridge: Cambridge University Press), pp. 339–50, https://doi.org/10.1017/cbo9780511807916.019

Macfarlane, Robert, and Jackie Morris. 2017. *The Lost Words* (London: Hamish Hamilton)

Maffi, Luisa (ed.). 2001. *On Biocultural Diversity: Linking Language, Knowledge and the Environment* (Washington, DC: Smithsonian Institution Press).

Magi: Adventure of Sinbad マギ シンドバッドの冒険. 2016. Dir. by Yoshikazu Miyao (Lay-duce).

Maher, John C. 2017. *Multilingualism: A Very Short Introduction* (Oxford: Oxford University Press), https://doi.org/10.1093/actrade/9780198724995.001.0001

Mahfouz, Naguib. 1979. *Layālī alf layla* (Cairo: Maktabat Miṣr).

Mahfouz, Naguib. 2001. *Arabian Nights and Days*. Trans. by Denys Johnson-Davies (Cairo: American University in Cairo).

Maiden, Martin, Aditi Lahiri and Chiara Cappellaro. 2020. 'Creating Intelligibility across Languages and Communities', Research Strand 3 of Creative Multilingualism, https://www.creativeml.ox.ac.uk/research/intelligibility

Maley, Alan. 1989. 'Down from the Pedestal: Literature as Resource', in *Literature and the Learner: Methodological Approaches*, ed. by Ronald Carter, Richard Walker and Christopher Brumfit (Cambridge: Modern English Publications), pp. 10–23.

Maley, Alan, and Alan Duff. 1990. *Literature* (Oxford: Oxford University Press).

Maley, Alan, and Nik Peachey. 2015. *Creativity in the English Language Classroom* (London: British Council), https://www.teachingenglish.org.uk/sites/teacheng/files/pub_F004_ELT_Creativity_FINAL_v2%20WEB.pdf

Marsh, David, and Richard Hill. 2009. *Study on the Contribution of Multilingualism to Creativity: Final Report*, Public Services Contract no EACEA/2007/3995/2, http://www.dylan-project.org/Dylan_en/news/assets/StudyMultilingualism_report_en.pdf

Martin-Jones, Marylin, Adrian Blackledge and Angela Creese (eds). 2012. *The Routledge Handbook of Multilingualism* (Abingdon: Routledge), https://doi.org/10.4324/9780203154427

McCann, William J., Horst G. Klein and Tilbert D. Stegmann. 2003. *EuroComRom – The Seven Sieves: How to Read All the Romance Languages Right Away*, 2nd edn (Aachen: Shaker).

Mehmedbegovic, Dina, and Thomas H. Bak. 2019. 'Bilingualism, Multilingualism and Plurilingualism: Living in two or more languages', 27 March 2019, *Healthy Linguistic Diet*, http://healthylinguisticdiet.com/bilingualism-multilingualism-and-plurilingualism-living-in-two-or-more-languages/

Mehmedbegovic-Smith, Dina, and Thomas H. Bak. 2020. *Healthy Linguistic Diet*, http://healthylinguisticdiet.com/

Memrise. 2020. https://www.memrise.com

Mendelssohn-Bartholdy, Felix. 2000. *Musik zu Ein Sommernachtstraum von Shakespeare, op. 61* (Wiesbaden: Breitkopf & Härtel).

Mill, John S. 1833. 'What Is Poetry?', https://www.uni-due.de/lyriktheorie/texte/1833_mill1.html.

Moretti, Franco. 2005. *Graphs, Maps, Trees: Abstract Modes for Literary History* (London: Verso).

The Monkey King 西游记之大鬧天宫. 2014. Dir. by Cheang Pou-soi (Filmko Entertainment).

Morrissy-Swan, Tomé. 2018. 'Have Americans re-invented the Yorkshire pudding as the 'Dutch Baby?', *The Telegraph*, 14 May, https://www.

telegraph.co.uk/food-and-drink/news/have-americans-re-invented-yorkshire-pudding-dutch-baby/

Müller, Lisa-Maria, et al. 2018. 'Language Learning Motivation at the Transition from Primary to Secondary School', OASIS Summary of Graham, Suzanne, et al. (2016), *British Educational Research Journal*, https://oasis-database.org/concern/summaries/0g354f20t?locale=en

NASA. 2019. 'July 20, 1969: One Giant Leap for Mankind', July 20, https://www.nasa.gov/mission_pages/apollo/apollo11.html

Nation, Kate. 2017. 'Nurturing a Lexical Legacy: Reading Experience is Critical for the Development of Word Reading Skill', *Science of Learning*, 2(1): 3, https://doi.org/10.1038/s41539-017-0004-7

Nettle, Daniel, and Suzanne Romaine. 2000. *Vanishing Voices: The Extinction of the World's Languages* (Oxford: Oxford University Press).

OED. 2020. 'Updates to the OED', https://public.oed.com/updates/

OED. 2020. www.oed.com

OED. 2019a. 'mama put, *n.*', *OED*, https://www.oed.com/view/Entry/82854804?redirectedFrom=mama+put#eid

OED. 2019b. 'omnishambles, *n.*', *OED*, https://www.oed.com/view/Entry/83178718?redirectedFrom=omnishambles#eid

OED. 2019c. 'peoplekind, *n.*', *OED*, https://www.oed.com/view/Entry/78879462?redirectedFrom=peoplekind#eid

OED. 2019d. 'whatevs, *int.* and *pron.*', *OED*, https://www.oed.com/view/Entry/79334939?redirectedFrom=whatevs#eid

Ouyang, Wen-chin. 2005. 'Whose Story Is It? Sindbad the Sailor in Literature and Film', in *New Perspectives on [the] Arabian Nights: Ideological Variations and Narrative Horizons*, ed. by Wen-chin Ouyang and Geert Jan van Gelder (London and New York: Routledge), pp. 1–16.

Ouyang, Wen-chin, Jane Hiddleston, Laura Lonsdale and Nora Parr. 2020. 'Creativity and World Literatures: Languages in Dialogue', Research Strand 5 of Creative Multilingualism, https://www.creativeml.ox.ac.uk/research/world-literatures

Owen, Stephen, and Robert Woore. 2019. 'Teaching Reading to Beginner Learners of French in Secondary School', OASIS Summary of Woore, Robert., et al. 2018, https://oasis-database.org/concern/summaries/nc580m68d?locale=en

Paran, Amos. 2008. 'The Role of Literature in Instructed Foreign Language Learning and Teaching: An Evidence-Based Survey', *Language Teaching*, 41: 465–96, https://doi.org/10.1017/s026144480800520x

Park, Sowon S. (ed.). 2016. *The Chinese Scriptworld and World Literature*, a special issue of the *Journal of World Literature*, 1.

Peris, Ernesto, Esteve Clua et al. 2005. *EuroComRom – Los siete tamices: Un fácil aprendizaje de la lectura en todas las lenguas románicas* (Aachen: Shaker).

Peterson, David J. 2015. *The Art of Language Invention: From Horse-Lords to Dark Elves, the Words Behind World-Building* (New York: Penguin).

Philombé, René. 1977. *Petites gouttes de chant pour créer l'homme: Poèmes* (Yaoundé-Messa: Éditions Semences africaines).

Pinker, Steven. 1994. *The Language Instinct: The New Science of Language and Mind* (London: Penguin).

Pipek, Pavel, et al. 2018. 'Dialects of an Invasive Songbird Are Preserved in Its Invaded but Not Native Source Range', *Ecography*, 41: 245–54, https://doi.org/10.1111/ecog.02779

Plato. 1926. *Cratylus*, in *Cratylus. Parmenides. Greater Hippias. Lesser Hippias*, trans. by Harold North Fowler, Loeb Classical Library 167 (Cambridge, MA: Harvard University Press), pp. 1–193.

Poe, Edgar Allen. 1845. 'The Thousand-and-Second Tale of Scheherazade', in *Godey's Lady's Book*, February 1845.

Pollack, John. 2012. *The Pun Also Rises: How the Humble Pun Revolutionized Language, Changed History, and Made Wordplay More Than Some Antics* (New York: Avery).

Prismatic Jane Eyre: An Experiment in the Study of Translations, https://prismaticjaneeyre.org/

Project MEITS, Heather Martin and Wendy Ayres-Bennett (eds). 2019. *How Languages Changed My Life* ([n.p.]: Archway).

Project Trust. 2020. https://projecttrust.org.uk/

Pruce, Daniel. 2017. 'Learning Languages', *Foreign Office Blogs*, 1 June, https://blogs.fco.gov.uk/danielpruce/2017/06/01/learning-languages/

Punch Records. 2020. https://www.wearepunch.co.uk/

Reynolds, Matthew. 2016. *Translation: A Very Short Introduction* (Oxford: Oxford University Press), https://doi.org/10.1093/actrade/9780198712114.001.0001

Reynolds, Matthew (ed.). 2020. *Prismatic Translation* (Cambridge: Legenda).

Reynolds, Matthew, Sowon S. Park, Giovanni Pietro Vitali and Eleni Philippou. 2020. 'Creating New Meanings : Prismatic Translation', Research Strand 6 of Creative Multilingualism, https://www.creativeml.ox.ac.uk/research/prismatic-translation

Robinson, Andrew. 2009. *Writing and Script: A Very Short Introduction* (Oxford: Oxford University Press), https://doi.org/10.1093/actrade/9780199567782.001.0001

Ronen, Shahar, et al. 2014. 'Links that Speak: The Global Language Network and Its Association with Global Fame', *PNAS*, 111: E5615–22, https://doi.org/10.1073/pnas.1410931111

Rowling, J. K. 1997–2007. *Harry Potter and the Philosopher's Stone* (1997), *Harry Potter and the Chamber of Secrets* (1998), *Harry Potter and the Prisoner of Azkaban* (1999), *Harry Potter and the Goblet of Fire* (2000), *Harry Potter and the Order of the Phoenix* (2003), *Harry Potter and the Half-Blood Prince* (2005), *Harry Potter and the Deathly Hallows* (2007) (London: Bloomsbury).

Runco, Mark A. 2007. *Creativity. Theories and Themes: Research, Development and Practice* (Amsterdam: Elsevier).

Sacks, Oliver. 2012 (1989). *Seeing Voices: A Journey into the World of the Deaf* (London: Picador).

Saussure, Fernand de. 1983. *Course in General Linguistics*, ed. by Charles Bally and Albert Sechehaye, trans. and annotated by Roy Harris (London: Duckworth).

Scholastic Testing Service, Inc. 2020. *The Torrance® Tests of Creative Thinking and Gifted Education Products at STS*, https://www.ststesting.com/gift/

Scott, Virginia. M., and Julie A. Huntington. 2002. 'Reading Culture: Using Literature to Develop C2 Competence', *Foreign Language Annals*, 35: 622–31, https://doi.org/10.1111/j.1944-9720.2002.tb01900.x

Shakespeare, William. 2013. *The Tempest*, ed. by David Lindley (Cambridge: Cambridge University Press), https://doi.org/10.1017/cbo9781139109369

Silverfish Films. 2019. 'Do We Think Differently in Different Languages?', 4:10, *BBC Ideas*, 24 October, https://www.bbc.com/ideas/videos/do-we-think-differently-in-different-languages/p07ry35k

Sinbad. 2015–16. Dir. by Shinpei Miyashita (Nippon Animation).

Sinbad: Legend of the Seven Seas. 2003. Dir. by Patrick Gilmore and Tim Johnson (DreamWorks).

Sinbad the Sailor. 1947. Dir. by Richard Wallace (RKO Radio Pictures).

Singh, Ranjay, Jules Pretty and Sarah Pilgrim. 2010. 'Traditional Knowledge and Biocultural Diversity: Learning from Tribal Communities for Sustainable Development in Northeast India', *Journal of Environmental Planning and Management*, 53(4): 511–33, https://doi.org/10.1080/09640561003722343

Singleton, David, and Larissa Aronin (eds.). 2018. *Twelve Lectures on Multilingualism* (Bristol: Multilingual Matters), https://doi.org/10.21832/9781788922074

Slanguages. 2020. A project under the aegis of 'Languages in the Creative Economy', Research Strand 4 of Creative Multilingualism, https://www.creativeml.ox.ac.uk/projects/slanguages

Stacey, Kiran, and Helen Warrell. 2013. 'David Cameron Urges UK Schools to Teach Mandarin', *Financial Times*, 4 December, https://www.ft.com/content/056eb1da-5ccd-11e3-81bd-00144feabdc0

Stepp, J. R., F. S. Wyndham and R. K. Zarger (eds). 2002. *Ethnobiology & Biocultural Diversity* (Athens: University of Georgia Press).

Stibbe, Arran. 2015. *Ecolinguistics: Language, Ecology and the Stories We Live By* (Abingdon: Routledge).

Stormzy. 2017. 'Blinded by Your Grace Pt. 2', *Gang Signs and Prayer* (Merky Records).

Stormzy. 2018. 'Stormzy - Blinded by Your Grace Pt. 2 & Big For Your Boots [Live at the Brits '18]', 4:51, posted online by Stormzy, YouTube, 22 February 2018, https://www.youtube.com/watch?v=ReY4yVkoDc4

Sutherland, William J. 2003. 'Parallel Extinction Risk and Global Distribution of Languages and Species', *Nature*, 423(6937): 276–79, https://doi.org/10.1038/nature01607

Swain, Merrill. 1985. 'Communicative Competence: Some Roles of Comprehensible Input and Comprehensible Output in its Development', in *Input in Second Language Acquisition*, ed. by Susan M. Gass and Carolyn G. Madden (Rowley, MA: Newbury House), pp. 235–53.

Swift, Jonathan. 1726. *Gulliver's Travels* (London: Benj. Motte).

Tauli-Corpuz, Victoria. 2016. 'Statement of Ms. Victoria Tauli-Corpuz, Special Rapporteur on the Rights of Indigenous Peoples, at the 71st session of the General Assembly', 17 October, New York, https://www.ohchr.org/EN/NewsEvents/Pages/DisplayNews.aspx?NewsID=20748&LangID=E

Tchaikovsky, Petr. 1892. *Hamlet (de W. Shakespeare). Ouverture, mélodrames, fanfares, marches et entr'actes pour petit orchestre, op. 67* (Moscow: Jurgenson).

Terralingua. 2017. 'What Is Biocultural Diversity?', https://terralingua.org

Thériault, Gilles-Claude. 2013. 'HUGO, Victor - Demain dès l'aube (version 2).', 4:12, posted online by Gilles-Claude Thériault, YouTube, 11 September 2013, https://www.youtube.com/watch?v=lvuy4wCSHUA

Thierry, Guillaume. 2016. 'Neurolinguistic Relativity: How Language Flexes Human Perception and Cognition', *Language Learning*, 66(3): 690–713, https://doi.org/10.1111/lang.12186

Thomason, Sarah Grey. 2001. *Language Contact: An Introduction* (Edinburgh: Edinburgh University Press).

Thornton, Thomas F. (ed.). 2012. *Haa Leelk'w Has Aani Saax'u / Our Grandparents' Names on the Land* (Seattle: University of Washington Press).

Tinsley, Teresa, and Kathryn Board. 2017. *Languages for the Future. The Foreign Languages the United Kingdom Needs to Become a Truly Global Nation* (London:

British Council), https://www.britishcouncil.org/research-policy-insight/policy-reports/languages-future-2017

A Touch of Zen. 1971. Dir. by King Hu (Union).

Turner, Patricia, and Charles Russell-Coulter. 2001. *Dictionary of Ancient Deities* (Oxford: Oxford University Press).

Vyrypaev, Ivan. 2002. *Kislorod*, performed by Teatr.doc, Moscow, October.

Vyrypaev, Ivan. 2004. *Oxygen*, trans. by Sasha Dugdale, staged as an internal rehearsed reading (date not recorded), Royal Court Theatre, London.

Vyrypaev, Ivan. 2006. '*Oxygen*', trans. by Sasha Dugdale, https://doi.org/10.1215/01610775-36-1-49

Vyrypaev, Ivan. 2009/10. *Oxygen*, trans. by Sasha Dugdale, dir. by Deborah Shaw, Royal Shakespeare Company/LIFT, Institute of Contemporary Arts, Stratford-upon Avon (17 September 2009); London (15–18 July 2010).

Vyrypaev, Ivan. 2017. 'Open Letter in Support of Kirill Serebrennikov', *Snob.ru*, 24 August, https://snob.ru/profile/26058/blog/128291

Vyrypaev, Ivan, 2018. *Oxygen*, trans. by Sasha Dugdale, adapted and performed by Lady Sanity and Stanza Divan, dir. by Noah Birksted-Breen, produced by Sputnik Theatre Company, Birmingham City University and Creative Multilingualism, 11 October.

Warner, Marina. 2011. *Stranger Magic: Charmed States & the Arabian Nights* (London: Chatto & Windus).

Weinreich, Max. 1963. *Languages in Contact: Findings and Problems* (The Hague: Mouton).

Werkmann Horvat, Ana, Marianna Bolognesi and Katrin Kohl. (a) 'Processing of Literal and Metaphorical Meanings in Polysemous Verbs: An Experiment and its Methodological Implications', in revision for *Journal of Pragmatics*.

Werkmann Horvat, Ana, Marianna Bolognesi and Katrin Kohl. (b). 'Demolishing Walls and Myths: On the Status of Conventional Metaphorical Meaning in the L2 Lexicon,' in preparation.

Werner, Edward T. Chalmers. 1922. *Myths and Legends of China* (New York: Harrap).

Weygandt, Susanna. 2018. 'Revisiting *Skaz* in Ivan Vyrypaev's Cinema and Theatre: Rhythm and Sounds of Postdramatic Rap', *Studies in Russian and Soviet Cinema*, 12(3): 195–214, https://doi.org/10.1080/17503132.2018.1511260

Wilkins, John. 1668. *An Essay Towards a Real Character and a Philosophical Language* (London: S. Gellibrand), https://books.google.co.uk/books?id=BCCtZjBtiEYC

Wu, Ch'eng-en. 1961. *Monkey*. Trans. by Arthur Waley (London and New York: Penguin).

Wu, Ch'eng-en. 1977–83. *The Journey to the West*. Trans. by Anthony Yu (Chicago and London: Chicago University Press).

WWF. 2020. 'Protected Areas and Indigenous Territories', http://wwf.panda.org/knowledge_hub/where_we_work/amazon/vision_amazon/living_amazon_initiative222/protected_areas_and_indigenous_territories/

Wyndham, Felice S. 2009. 'Spheres of Relations, Lines of Interaction: Subtle Ecologies of the Rarámuri Landscape in Northern Mexico', *Journal of Ethnobiology*, 29(2): 271–95, https://doi.org/10.2993/0278-0771-29.2.271

Wyndham, Felice S. 2010. 'Environments of Learning: Rarámuri Children's Plant Knowledge & Experience of Schooling, Family, and Landscapes in the Sierra Tarahumara, Mexico', *Human Ecology*, 38(1): 87–99, https://doi.org/10.1007/s10745-009-9287-5

Wyndham, Felice S., Ada M. Grabowska-Zhang, Andrew G. Gosler, Karen E. Park, John Fanshawe, David Nathan, Heidi Fletcher and Josep del Hoyo. 2016. 'The Ethno-ornithology World Archive (EWA): An Open Science Archive for Biocultural Conservation', *Revista Chilena de Ornitología*, 22: 141–46.

Wyndham, Felice S., and Karen Park. 2018. '"Listen Carefully to the Voices of the Birds": A Comparative Review of Birds as Signs', *Journal of Ethnobiology*, 38(4): 533–49, https://doi.org/10.2993/0278-0771-38.4.533

[Zamenhof, L.L.] Dr. Esperanto. 1889. *An Attempt Towards an International Language*, trans. by Henry Phillips, Jr. (New York: Holt).

Zhang, Shudong. 2005. 中华印刷通史 (*A General History of Chinese Printing*) (Taipei: XingCai Literary Foundation).

List of Illustrations

Cover

Cedoux Kadima, *Mappa Mundi* (2017), mixed media on canvas. Commissioned by Creative Multilingualism for its *LinguaMania* event at the Ashmolean Museum, Oxford, on 27 January 2017. Visitors were asked to inscribe what they would bring back from the ends of the earth.

Introduction

Fig. 1	Mohandas K. Gandhi in South Africa (1906). Wikimedia Commons, Public Domain, https://commons.wikimedia.org/wiki/File:Gandhi_London_1906.jpg#/media/File:Gandhi_London_1906.jpg	7
Fig. 2	Sheela Mahadevan with her grandparents Ganga Narayanan and Guruvayur Krishna Narayanan. Reproduced with their kind permission. Photograph by Subramaniam Mahadevan (2020).	9
Fig. 3	London Bus 29. Photograph by mattbuck (2012). Wikimedia Commons, CC BY-SA 3.0, https://en.wikipedia.org/wiki/London_Buses_route_29#/media/File:Camden_Road_railway_station_MMB_05.jpg	12
Fig. 4	Ramen with soft boiled egg, shrimp and snow peas. Photograph by Michele Blackwell (2019) on Unsplash, https://unsplash.com/photos/rAyCBQTH7ws	15

Chapter 1

Fig. 1	Even well-worn metaphors are not 'dead'. They can gain new force when they are highlighted as meaningful, for example by elaboration. *Peanuts* © 1976 Peanuts Worldwide LLC. Dist. by Andrews McMeel Syndication. Reprinted with permission. All rights reserved.	26
Fig. 2	This cartoon about examinations of doctoral theses exemplifies the conceptual metaphor that 'ARGUMENT IS WAR'. 'Thesis Defense' (2014), xkcd.com, CC BY-NC 2.5, https://imgs.xkcd.com/comics/thesis_defense.png	32
Fig. 3	'That's one small step for a man, one giant leap for mankind' (Neil Armstrong). This is a photograph by Neil Armstrong of his fellow astronaut Buzz Aldrin on the Moon (1969). NASA. Wikimedia Commons, Public Domain, https://commons.wikimedia.org/wiki/File:Aldrin_Apollo_11_original.jpg#/media/File:Aldrin_Apollo_11_original.jpg	38
Fig. 4	The flyer announcing performances of *Yòrùbá Sonnets* in 2019 at Wolfson College, Oxford, and other venues visually and textually signals an exuberant fusion of ethnic heritage, cultures, traditions, languages and artistic forms. Babalolá et al. 2019c. Reproduced by kind permission of Lékan Babalolá.	40

Chapter 2

Fig. 1	Francis (?) Darwin (c. 1858). Drawing on the back of the original manuscript for Charles Darwin's *On the Origin of Species* (1859) by one of Darwin's children. Reproduced by kind permission of William Darwin.	49
Fig. 2	Akkadian cuneiform on the wings of a stone bas-relief eagle-headed genie from Nimrud, Assyria. This giant figure was meant to magically protect a doorway. Held at the Ashmolean Museum, Oxford. Reproduced by kind permission of the Ashmolean Museum, Oxford (exhibit); photograph by Felice S. Wyndham (2014).	54
Fig. 3	Children's mural depicting a kingfisher, leaves and river names, West Oxford Community Centre. Photograph by kind permission of Felice S. Wyndham (2019).	57

List of Illustrations   293

Fig. 4   Abel Rodríguez, *Ciclo anual del bosque de la vega* (2009–2010).   62
Details of ecological relations with land animals and fish, drawn from memory by Abel Rodríguez, Nonuya Indigenous man from the Middle Caquetá River. He is a great authority on the world of plants and forests, and is considered a leading light for the exchange of knowledge with the academy and the art world, based on his interaction of more than three decades with researchers in the tropical forest. Reproduced by kind permission of Abel Rodríguez.

Fig. 5   Logo of the 2019 symposium *Intersections of Language and Nature*, organized by Karen Park, Felice S. Wyndham, John Fanshawe and Andrew Gosler. It brought together scholars from Indigenous communities, conservation practice, the arts and academia to address the parallel and intersecting threats facing linguistic and biological diversity (www.iln2019.com). Reproduced by kind permission from Karen Park.   63

Chapter 3

Fig. 1   Félix Gallet, 'Arbre généalogique des langues mortes et vivantes [...]' ('Genealogical tree of dead and living languages [...]') (Paris, c. 1800). Bibliothèque nationale de France. Public Domain, https://gallica.bnf.fr/ark:/12148/bpt6k8546015   72

Chapter 4

Fig. 1   Left to right: Simon Redgrave from Punch Records and artists Ky'Orion and RTKal, speaking after a performance at the first Creative Multilingualism conference, Taylor Institution, University of Oxford, 28 January 2017. Reproduced by kind permission of Kyle Greaves aka Ky'Orion, Joshua Holness aka RTKal and Simon Redgrave. Photograph by John Cairns (2017), CC BY-NC.   88

294   *Creative Multilingualism*

Fig. 2   Left to right: Lady Sanity, Rajinder Dudrah, Stanza Divan   88
and Noah Birksted-Breen at a Q & A following the Research
and Development performance of *Oxygen* at Birmingham
City University, 11 October 2018. Reproduced by kind
permission of Noah Birksted-Breen, Rajinder Dudrah, Liam
Lazare-Parris aka Stanza Divan and Sherelle Robbins aka
Lady Sanity. Photograph by Katy Terry (2018), CC BY-NC.

Fig. 3   RTKal performing at the first Creative Multilingualism   104
conference, Taylor Institution, University of Oxford, 28
January 2017. Reproduced by kind permission of Joshua
Holness aka RTKal. Photograph by John Cairns (2017), CC
BY-NC.

Chapter 5

Fig. 1   Wen-chin Ouyang. Reproduced with her kind permission.   110
Photograph by Dai Yazhen (2018).

Fig. 2   Yamlīkha, who tells the young Hāsib a story in 'The Tale of   114
Hāsib Karīm al-Dīn' from *The Arabian Nights*, is a serpent
queen, a common motif in world literature. Nuwa, the
Chinese goddess of creation depicted here, is imagined
as a serpent queen. Illustration from Edward T. Chalmers
Werner. 1922. *Myths and Legends of China* (New York:
Harrap). Wikimedia Commons, Public Domain, https://
commons.wikimedia.org/wiki/File:Nuwa2.jpg#/media/
File:Nuwa2.jpg

Fig. 3   Sun Wukong, the hero of *The Journey to the West*, transforms   117
his hair into miniature monkey kings. Screenshot from *The
Monkey King* 西游記之大鬧天宮. 2014. Directed by Cheang
Pou-soi.

Fig. 4   'Nine Tails Fox', from the Chinese *Classic of Mountains*   121
and Seas (山海經), which has existed since the fourth
century. Image by Hu Wenhuan 胡文煥 (1596–1650) in
山海經圖 (sixteenth century). Wikimedia Commons,
Public Domain, https://commons.wikimedia.org/wiki/
File:%E5%8D%97%E5%B1%B1%E7%B6%93-%E4%B9%9
D%E5%B0%BE%E7%8B%90.svg

Fig. 5	Douglas Fairbanks Jr. in *Sinbad the Sailor* (1947). Directed by Richard Wallace. Visualization of Sinbad in this film is arguably a creative fusion of Arabic storytelling, European translation, orientalist fantasy and Hollywood filmmaking.	123

Chapter 6

Fig. 1	This map shows the global distribution of translations of *Jane Eyre*, from the first one in 1848 to the present day, in *Prismatic Jane Eyre: An Experiment in the Study of Translations*, https://prismaticjaneeyre.org/maps/. Reproduced by kind permission of Matthew Reynolds and Giovanni Pietro Vitali.	135
Fig. 2	Eleni Philippou. Reproduced with her kind permission. Photograph by Keith Barnes (2019).	138
Fig. 3	'Semantic Selectivity', Alexander G. Huth et al. (2016). This figure presents a 'semantic atlas' of the human brain. Using fMRI, the authors mapped which brain areas respond to the meanings of each word, discovering that these maps are highly similar across individuals speaking the same language. © Alexander Huth / The Regents of the University of California.	142
Fig. 4	Mukahang Limbu. Reproduced with his kind permission. Photograph by Helen Bowell (2018).	144

Chapter 7

Fig. 1	Photograph by Mykl Roventine (2009), Wikimedia Commons, CC BY 2.0, https://commons.wikimedia.org/w/index.php?curid=8277883	154
Fig. 2	Photograph by owner of Pet Rock Net (2003), Wikimedia Commons, CC BY-SA 3.0, https://commons.wikimedia.org/w/index.php?curid=7549364#/media/File:Pet_rock.jpg	154
Fig. 3	Photograph by Sherwin Ilagan Solina (2011), Wikimedia Commons, Public Domain, https://commons.wikimedia.org/w/index.php?curid=17836500	154
Fig. 4	Photograph by Camlacaze (2013), CC BY-SA 4.0, https://commons.wikimedia.org/w/index.php?curid=42135378	155

Chapter 8

Fig. 1	Family tree diagram depicting relationships between Indo-European languages — assuming a common ancestor that remains elusive (2020). Reproduced by kind permission of Chiara Cappellaro.	179
Fig. 2	Multilingual Performance Project workshop, 2019. Photograph by Ben Gregory-Ring (2019).	189

Chapter 9

Fig. 1	George Hodgson. Reproduced with his kind permission. Photograph by Maimouna Dembele (2018).	210
Fig. 2	Jessica Benhamou. Reproduced with her kind permission. Photograph by Brittany Ashworth, CC BY.	214
Fig. 3	Which Sectors do Modern Languages Graduates Work in? Data collected by the University of Oxford Careers Service. Diagram by Katy Terry (2020).	219

Chapter 10

Fig. 1	Sign languages build on visible cues such as facial expression and gesture. Unlike British Sign Language (BSL), 'Urban Sign Language' (USL) has no official status. It reflects shared usage in parts of the Birmingham deaf community. Posters created for the *Slanguages* exhibition 2017, Wolfson College, Oxford, reproduced by kind permission of Rinkoo Barpaga (Artist), Nick Drew (Design), Rajinder Dudrah (Birmingham City University) and Simon Redgrave (Punch Records).	232
Fig. 2	Esperanto vocabulary is mainly derived from Romance languages. Nouns have no grammatical gender. Can you spot the markers for nouns, noun plurals and adjectives? Some common words in Esperanto. Picture compilation by Sharlene Matharu (2020).	237

Why Learn a Language?

Fig. 1　Communication network. Image by Gordon Johnson, from Pixabay, https://pixabay.com/vectors/social-media-connections-networking-3846597/　253

Acknowledgements

Fig. 1　Mannequins Edna and Eddie helped Creative Multilingualism to make language visible at public engagement events. Here is team member Edna eliciting body part metaphors at Curiosity Carnival in Oxford's Natural History Museum, on 29 September 2017. Photograph by Ian Wallman (2017).　310

Notes on the Authors and Contributors

The collaborative research programme **Creative Multilingualism** (2016 to 2020) was funded by the Arts and Humanities Research Council (AHRC) in the context of its ambitious Open World Research Initiative. Its seven research strands involved a large number of researchers from many disciplines, whose profiles and publications are available here: https://www.creativeml.ox.ac.uk/. This volume reflects our collaborative research and it has also benefited from the expertise of contributors beyond the research team.

Jonathan Black
Contributor

Jonathan joined Oxford University as Director of the Careers Service in 2008 after a career that included blue-chip management consultancy, international academic publishing and co-founding a medical publishing start-up. He conducts coaching sessions, workshops and innovative programmes that provide hands-on career experience, and runs research programmes on what is required to secure a graduate-level job. In 2017 he published *How to Find the Career You've Always Wanted* and he writes the fortnightly 'Dear Jonathan' careers column for the *Financial Times*.

Noah Birksted-Breen
Postdoctoral Researcher, Strand 4: Creative Economy

Noah is a theatre-maker and scholar, specializing in new writing in the UK and Russia. He founded Sputnik Theatre Company — the only British company dedicated solely to bringing new Russian plays to UK stages. For Sputnik, he has directed and translated new Russian plays for Soho Theatre, BBC Radio 3's Drama of the Week, Southwark Playhouse and Theatre Royal Plymouth (http://sputniktheatre.co.uk). He completed his PhD at Queen Mary University of London in 2017 on 'Alternative Voices in an Acquiescent Society: Translating Russian New Drama for UK stages (2000–2014)'.

Marianna Bolognesi
Postdoctoral Researcher, Strand 1: Metaphor

Marianna is Senior Assistant Professor in Linguistics at the University of Bologna, Italy. Following two years as European Union Marie Curie postdoctoral researcher at the Metaphor Lab, University of Amsterdam, she joined Creative Multilingualism from 2017 to 2019, working on the interplay between metaphor, linguistic diversity and human creativity. Her current research focuses on the relationship between language and thought, and on the semantic representation of word meaning in the mind and its expression in pictorial and verbal modes of communication.

Philip Ross Bullock
Senior Researcher, Strand 4: Creative Economy

Philip is Professor of Russian Literature and Music at the University of Oxford, and Fellow and Tutor in Russian at Wadham College, Oxford. He has published widely on various aspects of Russian culture from the eighteenth century to the present and has a particular interest in the reception of Russian culture abroad. His most recent book is *Pyotr Tchaikovsky* (2016).

Chiara Cappellaro
Postdoctoral Researcher, Strand 3: Intelligibility

Chiara is a researcher in the Faculty of Linguistics, Philology and Phonetics at the University of Oxford. Her interests and expertise lie in morphology, sociolinguistics, historical linguistics and Italian and comparative Romance linguistics. Contributing to Creative

Multilingualism has allowed her to broaden her interests to areas such as receptive multilingualism and intelligibility across cognate varieties.

Kate Clanchy
Contributor

Kate is a teacher and writer. In 2018, she published *England: Poems from a School*, a collection of her migrant students' poems, and was awarded an MBE for Services to Literature. Her most recent book, *Some Kids I Taught and What They Taught Me* (2019), was described by Sir Philip Pullman as the 'best book about writing and teaching and children I have ever read'.

Julie Curtis
Senior Researcher, Strand 4: Creative Economy

Julie is Professor of Russian Literature and Fellow of Wolfson College, University of Oxford. Her recent books are *Mikhail Bulgakov* (2017) and *A Reader's Companion to Mikhail Bulgakov's 'The Master and Margarita'* (2019); and she has edited a volume of scholarly essays and interviews with theatre-makers entitled *New Drama in Russian: Performance, Politics and Protest in Russia, Ukraine and Belarus* (2020).

Rajinder Dudrah
Co-Investigator and Lead, Strand 4: Creative Economy

Rajinder is Professor of Cultural Studies and Creative Industries at Birmingham City University. He has taught, researched and published widely across film, media and cultural studies, and is the founding Co-Editor of the scholarly journal *South Asian Popular Culture*. Rajinder is also Co-Investigator for the AHRC-funded 'Diaspora Screen Media Network', and two of his recent books include: *The Evolution of Song and Dance in Hindi Cinema* (co-edited with Ajay Gehlawat, 2019) and *Bollywood Travels: Culture, Diaspora and Border Crossings in Popular Hindi Cinema* (2012).

John Fanshawe
Partner, Strand 2: Naming

John is a Senior Strategy Adviser at BirdLife International. Before taking up that role in 2005, he was Head of Policy and Advocacy at BirdLife in 1998–2003, and Head of Development Programmes in 1993–1995. As a Senior Strategy Advisor, he is coordinating a programme on birds, culture and conservation, including a series of collaborations with authors, artists and musicians. See also http://egi.zoo.ox.ac.uk/members/dr-john-fanshawe/

Linda Fisher
Co-Investigator, Strand 7: Language Learning

Linda is Reader in Languages Education at the Faculty of Education, University of Cambridge. She teaches and researches in multilingualism, multilingual identity, language teacher education and creativity in language learning. A key research interest is how people's beliefs about their capacity for language learning influence their motivation and progression, and the role of metaphor in this process.

Andrew Gosler
Co-Investigator and Lead, Strand 2: Naming

Andrew is based at the University of Oxford, where he holds a position between the Department of Zoology and School of Anthropology as Associate Professor in Applied Ethnobiology and Conservation. He was Principal Investigator on an AHRC-funded project to develop the Ethno-ornithology World Atlas in 2013. An experienced teacher of field ornithology, his recent research focuses on the growing disconnection of people from nature and their declining knowledge of natural history. See also http://egi.zoo.ox.ac.uk/members/dr-andrew-gosler/

Suzanne Graham
Co-Investigator and Lead, Strand 7: Language Learning

Suzanne is Professor of Language and Education at the Institute of Education, University of Reading. She teaches and researches creativity in language learning, second language listening and reading comprehension, and motivation for and beliefs about language learning. Her recent research, funded by the Nuffield Foundation, has explored the role of teacher-related factors in how learners' motivation for, and attainment in, language learning develops as they move from primary to secondary school. See http://www.reading.ac.uk/education/about/staff/s-j-graham.aspx

Jane Hiddleston
Co-Investigator, Strand 5: World Literatures

Jane is Professor of Literatures in French at the University of Oxford, and Official Fellow in French at Exeter College, Oxford. She has published widely on francophone literature and postcolonial theory, including most recently *Decolonising the Intellectual: Politics, Culture, and Humanism at the End of the French Empire* (2014), and *Writing After Postcolonialism: Francophone North African Literature in Transition* (2017). She is currently working with Wen-chin Ouyang on three edited volumes on world literature and multilingualism.

Julia Hofweber
Postdoctoral Researcher, Strand 7: Language Learning

Julia is a postdoctoral researcher at University College London, formerly at the University of Reading. Her research interests are wide, but she is primarily interested in the cognitive processes involved in language acquisition and bilingualism. In her PhD, she investigated the relationship between code-switching and mental flexibility in bilinguals. In her research for Creative Multilingualism, she explored educational practices that have the potential to enhance linguistic creativity in the second language.

Katrin Kohl
Principal Investigator, and Lead for Strand 1: Metaphor

Katrin is Professor of German at the University of Oxford. Her research interests in German literature focus on poetry and poetics, including the work of F. G. Klopstock, R. M. Rilke and the holocaust survivor H. G. Adler. Further fields of research are rhetoric and the theory and practice of metaphor, and she is currently writing a monograph on 'The Creative Power of Metaphor'. Leading Creative Multilingualism has immeasurably broadened her linguistic and disciplinary perspectives.

Heike Krüsemann
Postdoctoral Researcher, Strand 7: Language Learning

Heike is a researcher in Language and Education. Her research interests include learner motivation, linguistic creativity and the relationship between language and identity. She writes on language(s) and culture, and in 2018 completed her PhD on 'Language Learning Motivation and the Representation of German, Germans and Germany in UK Schools and the Press'.

Aditi Lahiri
Co-Investigator, Strand 3: Intelligibility

Aditi is Professor of Linguistics at the University of Oxford and Vice-President (Humanities) of the British Academy. Her research focuses on understanding how languages change and how that is related to the way in which the human brain processes and stores words, despite the incredible variability in every-day language production, native as well as non-native. She uses a mixture of techniques ranging from the philological study of old manuscripts to experiments measuring people's brainwaves (EEG recordings) to see how they respond to a variety of different speech sounds or words.

Laura Lonsdale
Associated Researcher, Strand 5: World Literatures

Laura is Associate Professor of Spanish at the University of Oxford. Her research explores literary multilingualism in the Spanish-speaking world, and her monograph *Multilingualism and Modernity: Barbarisms in Spanish and American Literature* was published in 2018. She is also Co-Editor of *The Routledge Companion to Iberian Studies* (2017), which promotes a comparative approach to the multilingual cultures of the Iberian Peninsula.

Martin Maiden
Co-Investigator and Lead, Strand 3: Intelligibility

Martin is a Romance linguist and Statutory Professor of the Romance Languages at the University of Oxford, and a Fellow of Trinity College, Oxford. He is Director of the Oxford Research Centre for Romance Linguistics, a Fellow of the British Academy and a Member of Academia Europaea. He has particular research interests in the historical development of Italian and Romanian (with other Romance languages of south-eastern Europe). His most recent book is *The Romance Verb: Morphomic Structure and Diachrony* (2018).

Wen-chin Ouyang
Co-Investigator and Lead, Strand 5: World Literatures

Wen-chin is Professor of Arabic and Comparative Literature at SOAS University of London and a Fellow of the British Academy. She is looking at the Silk Roads as a model for new comparative literature and world literature that will enable South–South comparisons, such as Arabic and Chinese, and make visible the global circulation of ideas, poetics, literary genres and world views along multiple contact hubs.

Karen Park
Co-Investigator, Strand 2: Naming

Karen is Assistant Professor of Linguistics at the University of Pittsburgh. Her research interests include language change, documentation and maintenance, generative syntax, Austronesian languages, ethno-ornithology, and biocultural diversity and conservation. She was the Principal Organizer of the 2019 Intersections of Language and Nature Symposium (www.iln2019.com) at the University of Pittsburgh, which encouraged collaboration between language documentation and conservation.

Sowon S. Park
Co-Investigator, Strand 6: Prismatic Translation

Sowon is Assistant Professor of English and Affiliate Faculty of Cognitive Science Emphasis at UC Santa Barbara. She is Principal Investigator of a Crossroads-funded project that brings together research on unconscious memory in Neuroscience, Artificial Intelligence and Literary Studies (http://um.english.ucsb.edu/). She edited the special issue of the *Journal of World Literature*, 1(2), on 'Chinese Scriptworld and World Literature' (2016) and is Co-Editor of the Global Asias Series published by Oxford University Press.

Nora E. Parr
Postdoctoral Researcher, Strand 5: World Literatures

Nora is a Humboldt Foundation Fellow at the Freie Universität Berlin. She was formerly based at SOAS, and has been a research fellow with the Global Challenges Research Fund (GCRF) project Rights for Time/Time for Rights. Her work on contemporary Arabic and Palestinian Literature centres on re-defining critical terms through cross-context analysis, and has focused in particular on the terms 'nation' and 'trauma'. She was Visiting Researcher at the Council for British Research in the Levant (Jordan and Palestine), and serves as Middle East Subject Editor at the Literary Encyclopedia.

Eleni Philippou
Postdoctoral Researcher, Strand 6: Prismatic Translation

Eleni is a Postdoctoral Research Fellow at St Anne's College, Oxford. Her book *Speaking Politically: Adorno and Postcolonial Fiction* (2020) explores the implications of Adorno's critical theory for literary studies. Her key research interests are postcolonial and world literature, contemporary literature and critical theory. In recent years, her research has moved strongly towards comparative literature, and translation theory and practice. She is also an active poet, with a number of her poems published in both British and international anthologies and journals.

Matthew Reynolds
Co-Investigator and Lead, Strand 6: Prismatic Translation

Matthew is Professor of English and Comparative Criticism at the University of Oxford, where he chairs the Oxford Comparative Criticism and Translation research centre (OCCT). Among his books are *Prismatic Translation* (2019), *Translation: A Very Short Introduction* (2016), *Likenesses: Translation, Illustration, Interpretation* (2013) and the novels *The World Was All Before Them* (2013) and *Designs for a Happy Home* (2009).

Daniel Tyler-McTighe
Director, Multilingual Performance Project

Daniel is a Research Fellow in Performing Arts at Royal Birmingham Conservatoire and Adjunct Professor at Millikin University. He is a theatre-maker who has staged productions at international theatre festivals in Shanghai, Almagro and Madrid and throughout England. He has created theatre with, by and for young people and community groups at the national theatres of Korea and Spain, Warsaw Palace of Culture and several UK theatres. His practice-as-research PhD from Loughborough University was titled 'Contemporary Shakespeares: Adapting, Theatre-Making and Ghosting'.

Ana Werkmann Horvat
Postdoctoral Researcher, trand 1: Metaphor

Ana is a postdoctoral researcher at the Institute of Croatian Language and Linguistics in Zagreb, Croatia. Following completion of her doctoral thesis on 'Layers of Modality' at the University of Oxford, her research as part of the Creative Multilingualism team was concerned with language processing and figurative language. Her recent research focuses on how figurative language is understood by monolingual and multilingual native speakers and language learners.

Felice S. Wyndham
Postdoctoral Researcher, Strand 2: Naming

Felice's research interest is ecological knowledge conservation in the service of Indigenous peoples' and local communities' resource and land rights. Her recent writings are on narratives of deep historical ecologies in the Americas. As Principal Investigator of a 2017–2019 British Academy-funded project, she developed participatory ethno-ecology work with Ayoreo, Yshir and other communities in Paraguay and Mexico. For more on her work see www.narratinglandscapes.net

Acknowledgements

On behalf of the research team, the Editors would like to thank Open Book Publishers for enabling us to publish our work in an open access format, and in particular Alessandra Tosi, Adèle Kreager, Anna Gatti and Luca Baffa for their expertise and advice during the planning, peer review and production process.

We owe thanks to Jane Hiddleston for coming up with the concept of Creative Multilingualism. It has stimulated four years of excitingly interdisciplinary research and is at the heart of this collaborative volume.

We are immensely grateful to our wonderful Programme Manager Bhee Bellew and equally wonderful Web and Social Media Manager Katy Terry for their creative ideas and unstinting support throughout our project. They have been central to the fabric and work of our team, and this volume could not have been produced without them. Natasha Ryan, the Outreach and Schools Liaison Officer of Oxford's Faculty of Medieval and Modern Languages, and many other individuals in the Faculty and the Humanities Division have also assisted our work with invaluable advice and support.

The universities in our consortium and our partners from beyond academia have contributed vitally to our research, our public engagement work and our policy initiatives, as have the members of our focus groups and especially our Advisory Board under the chairmanship of Professor Colin Riordan, Vice-Chancellor of Cardiff University.

Above all, we should like to thank the Arts and Humanities Research Council for its vision in funding the Open World Research Initiative (OWRI). This has enabled us to develop an ambitious research programme which has inspired us to conduct research in new ways, enriching our understanding of linguistic diversity and its significance for humanity. It has allowed us to collaborate with each other and co-create projects with our partners in a process of inspiring dialogue, opening up new questions and broadening the dissemination of our ideas. OWRI has provided a framework for joining forces with the three other teams led from the universities of Cambridge, King's College London and Manchester respectively, while also giving us the opportunity to fund many other colleagues from the United Kingdom and other parts of the world. Their involvement has immeasurably enhanced our investigation of the nexus between language diversity and creativity.

Finally, our thanks go to the many hundreds of people who have helped us to celebrate languages and make Creative Multilingualism a manifesto for change — speaking passionately at our conferences, co-curating multilingual exhibitions, analysing prismatic translations of *Jane Eyre*, bringing our research to life in videos and podcasts, joining in the fun at LinguaMania, participating in our experiments, studies and creative writing workshops, and acting, conducting, singing, rapping and drumming in our multilingual performances.

Fig. 1 Mannequins Edna and Eddie helped Creative Multilingualism to make language visible at public engagement events. Here is team member Edna eliciting body part metaphors at Curiosity Carnival in Oxford's Natural History Museum, on 29 September 2017. Photograph by Ian Wallman (2017).

Index

Abbreviated Torrance Test for Adults (ATTA) 155–156, 165, 172
Académie Française 243
adaptation 27, 82, 89, 99–100, 107, 109, 119, 121–122, 228, 238
Æthelweard 56
Africa 4, 10, 40, 77, 111, 124, 137, 160, 210, 230
Afrikaans 13, 73
AI. *See* artificial intelligence (AI)
Akbar, Emperor 120
Aladdin 120, 122
Aldrin, Buzz 38
A Level (UK) 185
Alf layla wa-layla. *See Arabian Nights, The*
Ali Baba 120, 122
alienation 70
Al-Māwardī 116
alphabets 19, 81, 139, 140, 142, 196. *See also* script
Altshuler, Michael 26
Alzheimer's disease. *See* dementia
Anglophone 3, 8, 137, 207, 211, 243
animal communication 226–228, 250
anime 122–123
anthropology 18, 45, 47–63, 231
Appalachia 61
Arabian Nights: Sinbad's Adventures (film) 122
Arabian Nights, The 114, 117, 119–122, 130
Arabic 7, 12, 19, 29, 77–79, 81, 109–110, 116–117, 119–121, 123–126, 130, 139, 145, 182, 250
Arab-Israeli conflicts 90
Aristotle 37
Armstrong, Neil 38

artificial intelligence (AI) 5, 37
ATTA (Abbreviated Torrance Test for Adults). *See* Abbreviated Torrance Test for Adults (ATTA)
Atwood, Margaret 57
Australia 29
authentic text 165
Aymara 29
Azerbaijani 139, 141
Aztecs 55

Babalolá, Lékan 39
Balinese 117
Barnes, Julian 112, 114–115, 118
  England, England 112, 114, 118
Barpaga, Rinkoo 232–234
Barth, John 122
  Last Voyage of Somebody the Sailor, The 122
Bassa 226
Baudelaire, Charles 39
  'Élévation' 39
Beckett, Samuel 97
  Ghost Trio 97
Beethoven, Ludwig van 97
  Ghost Trio 97
behaviourism 224
Bell, Currer 136
Bengali 70, 73, 77, 82, 145, 182, 208–210
Benhamou, Jessica 214
bilingualism 2, 4–5, 21, 29, 110, 133, 153, 156, 170, 178, 205, 208, 210, 213
biocultural diversity 47–63, 67
biodiversity ix, 47–63, 125, 231, 249
biology 18, 49, 53, 58, 69
BirdLife International 61

birds 27, 47, 50, 53, 54, 56, 156, 172, 173, 190, 191, 227. *See also* naming: of birds
  yellowhammers 228
Birds, The (project) 190–191
Birksted-Breen, Noah 88
Birmingham 19, 87–88, 102–104, 188, 190, 193–194, 231, 233–234
Birmingham Repertory Theatre 188, 190, 193–194
body language 191, 204, 250
  in the workplace 204
body parts 74, 186, 192, 197
Borges, Jorge Luis 236
Boroditsky, Lera 28
  'How Languages Construct Time' 28
borrowing. *See* linguistic borrowing
brain hemisphere 36, 139
Brave New Voices (project) 182
Brazil 40, 59
British Academy 217
  Born Global: Implications for Higher Education 217
British Council 158, 210
Brontë, Charlotte 19, 131, 135–136
  Jane Eyre 19, 131, 134–137, 148
Brown, Theodore L. 27
Buddhism 115–117
Bulgarian 73, 77–79, 81
Bulletproof Monk (film) 117–118

C4 102
Calderón, Pedro 188
calque, calquing. *See* loan translation
Cambridge Handbook of Creativity, The 13
Cambridge Handbook of Metaphor and Thought, The 31
Cameron, David 10
Cangjie 55
career 20, 203–222, 231, 234
cartoons 26, 32, 122, 240
Casasanto, Daniel 30
Catalan 74–75, 81

CEFR. *See* Common European Framework of Reference for Languages (CEFR)
Chaucer 56
Chekhov, Anton 96–97
  Cherry Orchard, The 97
  Uncle Vanya 96
Ch'eng-en Wu 115
  Journey to the West 115, 117
China 10, 55, 111, 113, 115–116, 120, 230
Chinese 10, 19, 52, 55, 79, 109–110, 112–121, 131, 136, 142, 207, 227, 230, 250
Chomsky, Noam 224–225
  I-language and E-language 224
Christianity 115
Classic of Mountains and Seas 121
classroom language learning. *See* language learning: classroom language learning
cognition 26–29, 37, 47, 140, 157, 208, 223, 225–226
cognitive flexibility 160, 170
cognitive science 37, 226–227
colonialism 9–10, 17, 59, 111, 230, 235, 242
colour 226–227
comedy 19, 145, 195
comics 115–118, 122–123
Commedia. *See* Dante: *Divine Comedy*
Common European Framework of Reference for Languages (CEFR) 165
community languages 105, 207
conlangs. *See* constructed languages
conservation 47–58, 60–63, 67
constructed languages 223, 236, 238
  High Valyrian 238
  Quenya 238
  Sindarin 238
convergence. *See* language convergence
corpus 37, 43, 207
Côte d'Ivoire 160
creative arts 3, 87–105
Creative Commons licence 4

creative economy 87–105
creative personality 157
creativity. *Passim*
  general creativity 152–161, 165–166
  linguistic creativity. *Passim*
Crystal, David 22, 177, 225, 230, 238–241
  Language Play 238
culture. *Passim*
  cultural change 58
  cultural diversity 8, 48–49, 68, 181, 226, 264 *and passim*
  cultural identity 11, 55, 226, 237 *and passim*
curiosity 151, 157–158, 164–165, 174, 209
curriculum 163, 182
Czech 77

Daily Mail 103
dance 40, 91, 134, 231, 251
dancehall. *See* music: dancehall
Dani 226
Danish 73, 75
Dante 132, 134–135
  Divine Comedy 132–133, 135
Daoism 115–117
Darwin, Charles 48–49, 62
  Descent of Man, The 48
Dastān of Amīr Ḥamza. See Ḥamzanāma
Declaration of Belém 59
Defiance (series) 238
dementia 178, 209, 253
Devanagari 139
Devilman 102
Devine, George 98
Dewaele, Jean-Marc 159
dialect 5–6, 79, 81, 103, 133, 141, 178, 207, 227–230, 246
dictionary 33, 56, 132–133, 190, 205–207, 213, 218, 242–243
Digital Arts and Humanities Commons (DAHC) 143
digraphic languages 139
discourse analysis 58

diversity. *See* biocultural diversity; *See* biodiversity; *See* culture: cultural diversity; *See* language: diversity
Dizzee Rascal 102
Dollinger, Stephen 157
Dothraki 20, 235, 238, 246
drama 17, 19, 87–105, 108, 144, 158, 181, 188–190, 192–197, 200, 213
Dudrah, Rajinder 88
Dugdale, Sasha 92, 100
Dungeons & Dragons 5
Duolingo 212, 236, 238
Dutch 14, 73, 75, 80–81, 186
Dutch East India Company 111

East India Company 111
ecolinguistics 58
Edmondson, Willis 161
education 2, 3, 7, 8, 36, 71, 219, 234. *See also* language learning
emojis 6, 190
emotions 1, 11, 29, 157–159, 164–166, 173–174, 180, 191, 239
empathy 160, 166, 175, 219
England 5, 54, 69–70, 111–114, 118, 144, 151, 153, 158–159, 163, 188, 208
English 2–3, 7–12, 14–15, 17, 26, 28–29, 31–33, 35, 39–40, 42–43, 52–54, 56, 69–71, 73, 75–77, 79, 81–82, 92–93, 100, 109–114, 116–120, 122–123, 126, 132–134, 136–137, 139–140, 143–146, 151, 162, 177–178, 180, 182, 186–187, 189, 206–209, 211, 213, 216, 227, 229–230, 240, 242–243, 245, 250
  as lingua franca 8, 10
  'plain English' 206–207
  Queen's English 12
  Scouse 5
Englishness 112
environment 5–6, 8, 16, 29, 36, 42, 47–63, 92, 120, 123, 157–158, 178, 217, 226–227, 231, 250
eponyms 53
Esperanto 20, 236–237
Ethiopia 111
ethnobiology 59

Ethno-ornithology World Atlas (EWA) 18, 63, 67
etymology 34, 71–75, 206, 238, 250
Evans, Nicholas 58
evolution 48, 52, 56, 67, 246

Fairbanks Jr., Douglas 123
false friends 32, 250
Faroese 73
Farsi 119, 145
Fauconnier, Gilles 31
Featherstone, Vicky 98
Feld, Steven 50
feng shui 112–113
film 9, 17, 90, 92, 96, 99, 107, 116, 118, 122–123, 136, 200, 213–215, 222, 251
First International Congress of Ethnobiology 59
flexible thinking 158, 164, 166, 174
folklore 121
folk song. *See* music: folk song
food 8, 14–15, 57, 111, 116, 166–167, 185, 198, 213, 222, 242
foreign language classroom anxiety (FLCA) 159
foreign language enjoyment (FLE) 159
foreignness 69–83, 101, 112
French 9–10, 12, 14, 17, 33, 52, 69, 73–77, 80–82, 110, 120–121, 124, 126, 132–133, 152–153, 160, 162, 165–166, 171, 174–175, 180–182, 185, 192, 195, 206–210, 214, 243, 250
Frisian 73
Friulian 69, 74
funk. *See* music: funk

Game of Thrones 235, 238, 246
games 5, 115, 117, 190, 192–196, 200, 238, 241
Gandhi, Mohandas K. 7, 92
 An Autobiography or The Story of My Experiments with Truth 7
garage. *See* music: garage
Garbay, Bruno 175
GCSE (UK) 163, 181, 208–209
Georgian 117

German 9–10, 14, 26, 32–33, 69, 71, 73, 75–81, 110, 126, 133, 136, 138, 144, 152–153, 165–167, 178, 186–187, 192, 206–209, 229, 240, 243, 250
 Bavarian 5
Germany 5, 118
gesture 16, 40, 97, 188, 189, 204, 233, 234. *See also* body language; *See also* sign language
Getty Research Institute 143
Ghetts 102
Gill, Sam 55
globalization 15, 129–130, 204, 208, 235
Google 224
Google Translate 145, 215
grammar 58, 133, 153, 163–164, 211–213, 218, 236, 239, 241
 universal grammar 224
graphic novel 122
Greaves, Kyle. *See* Ky'Orion
Greek 42, 77, 81, 120, 132, 137–138, 152, 227, 250
Green, Debbie Tucker 92
Grenfell Tower 100, 103
grime. *See* music: grime
Gujarati 7, 73
Guo, Xiaoting 116
 Ji Gong Quan Zhuan 115

Hale, Susan 55
Ḥamzanāma 116, 119–120
Harry Potter. *See* Rowling, J. K.: *Harry Potter*
Haugen, Einar 55
'Healthy Linguistic Diet' 178, 208
Hebrew 29, 77, 121, 152
heritage 6, 11, 29, 38, 40, 61, 69, 125, 160, 204, 209, 252
High Valyrian. *See* constructed languages: High Valyrian
Hildegard of Bingen 235
 'Lingua Ignota' 235
Hindi 7, 9, 70, 73, 77, 117, 141, 144, 208, 250
Hinduism 115
Hinglish 17, 208

hip-hop. *See* music: hip-hop
Ho, Chi Minh 140
   Declaration of Independence 140
Hodgson, George 210
Holness, Joshua. *See* RTKal
Hugo, Victor 174–175
   'Demain, dès l'aube' 174
humanities 1, 38, 42–43
humour 134, 156, 173, 223–224, 238, 241
Huntington, Julie A. 160–161
Hurricane Irma 174

Ibn al-Muqaffaʿ 116
   Kalīla wa-Dimna 116, 119–120
Ibn al-Nadīm 120
   al-Fihrist 120
Icelandic 70, 73, 75
iconicity 53
idiolect 230
idioms 133, 135, 206, 211
imagination 29, 158–160, 164, 166, 174–175, 215, 219, 225, 237, 242
immigration 134, 218, 231
imperialism 98, 111–113, 121
India 4, 9, 70, 111, 115, 120, 208, 230
Indiana Jones and the Last Crusade (film) 118
Indigenous languages 47–63
Indigenous peoples 49, 60–62, 231, 240
Industrial Revolution 230
Intergovernmental Science-Policy Platform on Biodiversity and Ecosystem Services (IPBES) 61
International Concrete Poetry movement 142
International Phonetic Alphabet (IPA) 82
Internet 10, 27, 67, 92, 133, 204, 213, 224, 230, 238
interpretation 56, 58, 89, 92–93, 96–98, 133–134, 141, 207, 218, 222, 226, 243, 251
Ishiguro, Kazuo 141
   Never Let Me Go 141

Italian 15, 69–70, 73–77, 80–81, 120, 136, 182, 186, 250
Italy 69

Japanese 15, 77–79, 120, 122–123, 140, 144, 152, 182, 186, 195, 207–208, 227, 240, 250
Ji Gong (character) 115, 116. *See also* Guo, Xiaoting: *Ji Gong Quan Zhuan*
Jme 102
Johnson, Mark 31, 37, 42. *See also Metaphors We Live By*
jungle. *See* music: jungle

Kalīla wa-Dimna. *See* Ibn al-Muqaffaʿ: *Kalīla wa-Dimna*
Kannada 9, 139
Kano 102
Kim, Myonghee 163
King, Stephen 99
   Body, The 99
kinship 33–34
Kislorod (film) 90, 96
Kitāb Naṣīḥat al-mulūk 116
Korean 120, 139–140, 144, 208
Krauss, Michael 60
Kuuk Thaayorre 29
Ky'Orion 87–88, 103

Ladin 74
Lady Leshurr 102
Lady Sanity 87–88, 98, 100–101
Lakoff, George 31, 37, 42. *See also Metaphors We Live By*
language
   barrier 19, 70, 144
   contact 56, 85, 180
   convergence 77, 85
   difference. *Passim*
   diversity ix, 1–4, 8, 18–19, 25, 30–31, 33, 46–50, 62, 67–68, 84, 87, 107, 124, 151, 177, 180–182, 203, 223, 225–227, 231, 235–236, 243, 249–250, *and passim*
   ecology 54–56

extinction 59–60, 67, 228, 231
play 20, 177, 223, 239–240, 245
predictability across languages 75
revitalization 62
language borrowing 250
language families 77, 212
  Germanic languages 73, 75, 83
  hidden resemblances between unrelated languages 76–77
  Indo-Aryan languages 73
  Indo-European languages 73–74, 77, 179–180, 236
  Romance languages 73–76, 83, 186, 237
  Slavonic languages 73
  visualized through tree-diagrams 73, 179
language learning ix, 2, 8, 17, 19, 36, 83, 87, 151–188, 203–224, 246, 249
  benefits of 151, 181, 205, 209
  classroom language learning 151, 156
  'immersion' 180
  in the workplace 205
Language Lives 6–9, 12, 14, 109, 119, 137, 144, 151, 208–209, 214
language loss. *See* language: extinction
languages. *See* Afrikaans; Arabic; Balinese; Bassa; Bengali; Bulgarian; Catalan; Chinese; constructed languages; Czech; Dani; Danish; Dutch; English; Esperanto; Faroese; Farsi; French; Frisian; Friulian; Georgian; German; Greek; Gujarati; Hebrew; Hindi; Icelandic; Italian; Japanese; Korean; Latin; Malayalam; Maltese; Mandarin; Norwegian; Persian; Polish; Portuguese; Punjabi; Romanian; Russian; Sanskrit; Sardinian; Scots Gaelic; sign language; Spanish; Swahili; Swedish; Taiwanese; Tamil; Turkish; Urdu; Vietnamese; Welsh; Yoruba; Welsh
language teaching 22, 46, 151–176, 181, 185, 189, 192, 196, 205, 218
  creative approach 151–167

functional approach 164–167
Latin 10, 26, 28–29, 32, 74, 81, 152, 206, 208–209, 227, 235, 242, 250
Lazare-Parris, Liam. *See* Stanza Divan
Leikin, Mark 153
Lethal Bizzle 102
Levant Company 111
Lewis, Brett 117
lexical diversity 124, 157
Limbu, Mukahang 144
lingua franca 3, 8, 10–11, 110, 210, 230, 235
Linguee 207
linguistic borrowing 16, 77, 80, 186, 227, 236, 250
linguistic creativity. *Passim*
linguistic diversity. *See* language: diversity
linguistic ecology. *See* language: ecology
linguistics 18, 30–31, 37–38, 42, 45, 47, 49, 52, 58, 60, 68, 225, *and passim*
linguistic sign 51–53
  arbitrary nature of 51, 53
literature
  Arabic 110, 116, 125
  Caribbean 124
  European 139
  Francophone 124
  in language learning 160–164
  national 129
  non-European 140
  postcolonial 124
  post-Soviet 97
  world 19, 109–126, 129, 143
loan translation 80, 126
loanword. *See* linguistic borrowing
London 12, 102, 181
Lost Words, The 56, 67
Luxmoore, Kate 39

Macfarlane, Robert 56
Magi: Adventure of Sinbad (film) 122
Mahfouz, Naguib 122
  Layālī alf layla 122
Malayalam 9, 139

Maltese 81
mammals 49, 227–228
Mandarin 10, 28, 109–110, 144, 208
Martin, Chris 152
Martin, George R. R. 238
  Song of Ice and Fire, A 238
May, Theresa 81, 103
Memrise 213
Mendelssohn, Felix 96
mentalese 228
metaphor 18–19, 25–43, 45–47, 56, 145, 162, 170, 191
Metaphors We Live By 31, 42
Mexico 55
migration 17, 103, 125, 165, 229
Mill, John Stuart 159
  'What is Poetry?' 159
mime 40, 188
Mississippi 61
Monkey King. *See* Sun Wukong
Monkey King, The (film) 117
monolingualism 4–5, 8, 70–71, 100, 128, 146, 153, 177–178, 205, 207–208, 230
Morris, Jackie 56
Moscow 19, 87, 89–90, 92
multilingualism. *Passim*
Multilingual Performance Project (MPP) 19, 181, 188–198, 200
music 41, 91–93, 96–98, 101–103, 105, 122, 134, 151, 175, 190, 214, 250–251
  dancehall 102
  folk song 40
  funk 40
  garage 102
  grime 19, 87, 89, 102–103, 105
  hip-hop 19, 87, 89, 93, 98, 100, 102–103, 105, 108
  jungle 102
  rap 19, 87, 89, 92–93, 96, 102–103
myth 16, 18, 55, 61, 116, 141, 191, 235, 252

Nakba 125–126
naming 18, 47–63, 67–68, 226
  of birds 53–54, 56
nation 60, 113, 124, 141, 143, 230, 236

nationalism 8, 11, 59, 60, 69, 133, 139, 141, 143. *See also* literature: national
National Trust 57
natural sciences 1–2
nature 47–48, 50, 55–63
Navajo 55
neologism 17, 27, 35, 53, 132, 147, 162, 205, 242–243
Nepal 144, 208
Nettle, Daniel 60
neural networks 208
neuroscience 37, 42, 141–143, 178, 226
New York Times 14
Nonuya 62
Norwegian 73, 75

Occitan 74
Oeming, Michael Avon 117
onomatopoeia 53
openness 157–158, 160, 164, 166, 174, 209
opera 252
ornithology 18, 47
Ouyang, Wen-chin 110
Oxford 87
Oxford English Dictionary 206, 242–243
Oxford Junior Dictionary 56–57, 67
Oxford Spires Academy 132, 143–144, 147

Panchatantra. *See* Ibn al-Muqaffaᶜ: *Kalīla wa-Dimna*
paralinguistics 204
Paran, Amos 161
performance 13–14, 19, 39–41, 87–105, 107, 188–192, 195, 216, 250
Persian 7, 81, 110, 116–117, 119–120, 135, 206
Peterson, David J. 235, 238
  Art of Language Invention, The 238
Philippou, Eleni 138
Philombé, René 162
  'L'homme qui te ressemble' 162
'Philosophical Language' 236. *See also* constructed languages
philosophy 29–30, 42, 45, 60, 101, 142, 159, 225, 236, 246

phonetics 16, 139–140, 142
phonocentrism 142
Pilpay. See Ibn al-Muqaffaᶜ: *Kalīla wa-Dimna*
Pinker, Steven 228, 246
  Language Instinct, The 228, 246
Pinter, Harold 99
Plato 29, 51
  Cratylus 51
play. *See* language: play
plurilingualism 4–5
Poe, Edgar Allen 122
  'Thousand-and-Second Tale of Scheherazade, The' 122
poetry 26, 36–37, 39, 41, 45, 50, 91, 109, 131–134, 137, 139, 143, 145–146, 148, 158–162, 171, 174–176, 178, 180–185, 238–239, 241, 252
Polish 12, 70, 73, 138, 141, 145, 182, 210, 236
politeness 119
politics 15, 92, 204, 213
Pollack, John 241
  Pun Also Rises, The 241
Portman, Natalie 152
portmanteau 53
Portuguese 70, 73–75, 77, 81–82, 136, 145, 152, 182, 250
predictability. *See* language: predictability across languages
Presnyakov Brothers 99
proto-Germanic 73
proto-Indo-European' 73
psycholinguistics 31, 42, 226
psychology 28, 37, 42, 45, 93
Punch Records 88, 104, 233–234
Punjabi 70, 73, 210
punning 20, 240–241

Quenya. *See* constructed languages: Quenya

Racine, Jean 188
rap. *See* music: rap
Redgrave, Simon 88
register 5–6, 109, 112, 133, 178, 234

Robbins, Sherelle. *See* Lady Sanity
Rodríguez, Abel 62
Romaine, Suzanne 60
Roman Empire 10, 74, 235
Romanian 70, 73–75, 77–81, 182
Romansh 74
Rowling, J. K. 111, 152
  Harry Potter 111, 114, 121, 152
Royal Court Theatre 90, 92, 98
Royal Society of Literature 145
Royalty 87, 103
RTKal 87–88, 103–104
Runco, Mark 157
Russia 73, 89–93, 100–101, 105–106, 146
Russian 19, 73, 77–81, 87, 89–93, 96, 98–101, 106–107, 222, 250
Russianness 100
Russian Revolution (1917) 90

Sanskrit 7, 9, 120
Sardinian 74
Saussure, Ferdinand de 51–52, 68
  Cours de linguistique générale 51
Scots Gaelic 70
Scott, Virginia M. 160–161
script 19, 29, 81–82, 131, 139–143, 147, 194, 212, 238
  Arabic 19, 29
  Chinese 19, 139, 142
  Chữ Nôm 139–140
  cuneiform 54
  Cyrillic 139
  Hebrew 29
  Latin 29, 139
  Runic 139
self-transcendence 157
semiotics 68
September 11 attacks 90
Seven Sieves 83
Shakespeare, William 40, 56, 90, 96, 112, 188, 240
  Hamlet 96
  Midsummer Night's Dream, A 96
  Tempest, The 96
Sigarev, Vasilii 99

Plasticine 99
sign language 16, 189–191, 234, 246, 250
  British Sign Language 204, 233–234
  Chinese Sign Language 204
  Urban Sign Language 233–234
Silk Road 113, 115, 120
Sinbad (film trilogy) 122
Sinbad the Sailor 122, 130
Sinbad the Sailor (film) 122–123
Sinbad: Legends of the Seven Seas (film) 122
Sindarin. *See* constructed languages: Sindarin
Skepta 102
slang 207, 234, 242
Slanguages 231, 233–234
Slash 102
Slovenian 69
social sciences 1–2, 42
Socrates 51
South Africa 7, 13, 137
Soviet Union 91
space-time 25, 42
Spanish 73–81, 126, 152, 181–182, 185–186, 192, 195, 207, 240, 250
speech community 4, 11, 16–17, 58, 229, 241–242
sport 213
Sputnik Theatre 100
standardization 11, 16, 133, 139, 141, 207, 229, 231, 234
Stanza Divan 87–88, 98, 100–101
Star Wars 242
Stormzy 102–103
  Gangs, Signs & Prayer 102
storytelling 50, 116–117, 120, 122–123
Streets, The 102
Sudan 111
Sufism 115, 117
Sullivan, Irene 55
Sun Wukong 115, 117, 121
sustainability 1, 3, 58, 60, 62
Swahili 120, 145, 250
Swain, Merrill 163

swear words 209
Swedish 73, 75, 77–80, 182
Swift, Jonathan 237
  Gulliver's Travels 237
symbolism 53, 174–175
synchronic 33

Tadjo, Véronique 160
  'Raconte-moi' 160
Taiwanese 110
Taiwo, Olu 39–41
Tale of Genji, The 140
Tamil 9
Tang dynasty 115
Tauli-Corpuz, Victoria 62
Teatr.doc 90
technology 2, 5, 27–28, 37, 122, 142–143, 156, 172–173, 223, 230–231
Telegu 9
Terralingua 48
theatre. *See* drama
Thériault, Gilles-Claude 175
Thieberger, Nicholas 58
Thierry, Guillaume 30
Tolkien, J. R. R. 237–238
  Lord of the Rings, The 238
toponyms 53
Touch of Zen, A (film) 118
Tower of Babel 235
Trainspotting 99
transferable skills 203, 212, 214, 216–217, 240
translanguaging 124
translation ix, 3–4, 8, 15, 19, 32, 58, 80, 89, 92–93, 96, 99–102, 104, 109, 113, 120, 122–123, 129, 131–148, 180, 182, 200, 206–207, 213, 215, 217–218, 234, 246, 251
  machine translation 217
  prismatic translation 92, 131–148
translingualism 182
transmogrification 121
trauma 125–126
Trilla 102
Trinidad 40

Turkish 12, 117, 120, 140, 250
Turner, Mark 31

Ulster Scots 70
United Nations 61, 134, 218
universal grammar. *See* grammar: universal grammar
unpredictability 158–159, 165–166
Urdu 117, 144–145, 182, 206, 208, 250

Vas'kovskaya, Irina 99
Vietnamese 139–141
Virgil 26
 Georgics 26
vocabulary 5, 16, 36, 46, 53, 58–59, 83, 152–153, 157, 161–166, 171, 196–197, 211, 213, 218, 226, 229, 236–237, 239–240
 vocabulary development 162
Vyrypaev, Ivan 19, 87, 89–94, 96–98, 100
 Oxygen 19, 87–98, 100–101, 104–105, 107–108

Warlpiri language 226

Welsh 10, 70, 77, 210, 227
Weygandt, Susanna 96
Wiley 102
Wilkins, John 236
Wilson-Haughton, Reece. *See* Royalty
world literature. *See* literature: world
World Wide Fund for Nature (WWF) 61
writing system. *See* script
Wuxia 118

Xuanzang 115

Yamlīkha 114
Yavapai 55
Yoruba 39–41
Yòrùbá Sonnets 39–40
Yosemite 61
young learners 71, 151–167, 187

Zamenhof, Ludwik Lejzer 236
Zuckerberg, Mark 152

About the publishing team

Alessandra Tosi was the managing editor for this book.

Adèle Kreager performed the copy-editing, proofreading and indexing.

Anna Gatti designed the cover using InDesign. The cover was produced in InDesign using Fontin (titles) and Calibri (text body) fonts.

Luca Baffa typeset the book in InDesign. The text font is Tex Gyre Pagella; the heading font is Californian FB. Luca created all of the editions — paperback, hardback, EPUB, MOBI, PDF, HTML, and XML — the conversion is performed with open source software freely available on our GitHub page (https://github.com/OpenBookPublishers).

This book need not end here...

Share

All our books — including the one you have just read — are free to access online so that students, researchers and members of the public who can't afford a printed edition will have access to the same ideas. This title will be accessed online by hundreds of readers each month across the globe: why not share the link so that someone you know is one of them?

This book and additional content is available at:

https://doi.org/10.11647/OBP.0206

Customise

Personalise your copy of this book or design new books using OBP and third-party material. Take chapters or whole books from our published list and make a special edition, a new anthology or an illuminating coursepack. Each customised edition will be produced as a paperback and a downloadable PDF.

Find out more at:

https://www.openbookpublishers.com/section/59/1

Like Open Book Publishers

Follow @OpenBookPublish

Read more at the Open Book Publishers BLOG

You may also be interested in:

Whose Book is it Anyway?
A View From Elsewhere on Publishing, Copyright and Creativity
by Janis Jefferies and Sarah Kember (eds.)

https://doi.org/10.11647/OBP.0159

The Politics of Language Contact in the Himalaya
by Selma K. Sonntag and Mark Turin (eds.)

https://doi.org/10.11647/OBP.0169

Hyperion, or the Hermit in Greece
Howard Gaskill

https://doi.org/10.11647/OBP.0160

www.ingramcontent.com/pod-product-compliance
Lightning Source LLC
Chambersburg PA
CBHW040323300426
44112CB00021B/2861